T0287999

Letters from Alabama

Philip Henry Gosse.
(Courtesy of the National Portrait Gallery—London)

Letters from Alabama
Chiefly Relating to Natural History

PHILIP HENRY GOSSE

EDITED BY GARY R. MULLEN AND TAYLOR D. LITTLETON

The University of Alabama Press • Tuscaloosa

Original edition published 1859
Revised and annotated edition published 1983
University of Alabama Press edition published 1993
University of Alabama Press second edition published 2013

Typeface: Garamond Pro

Cover illustration: Original watercolor by P. H. Gosse. Southern pearly-eye, *Lethe portlandia* (Fabricius) (top two) and two forms of Common wood-nymph, *Cercyonis pegala* (Fabricius) (bottom four); on Coral bean, *Erythrina herbacea* Linnaeus, from *Entomologia Alabamensis*. Copyright © The British Library Board, Loan MS 108 (10), f.21.

Cover design: Michele Myatt Quinn

∞

The paper on which this book is printed meets the minimum requirements of American National Standard for Information Sciences—Permanence of Paper for Printed Library Materials, ANSI Z39.48 1984.

Library of Congress Cataloging-in-Publication Data

Gosse, Philip Henry, 1810–1888.
Letters from Alabama : chiefly relating to natural history / Philip Henry Gosse ; edited by Gary R. Mullen and Taylor D. Littleton. — University of Alabama Press 2nd ed.
p. cm. — (Library of Alabama classics)
Original ed. published 1859.
Includes index.
ISBN 978-0-8173-1789-8 (trade cloth : alk. paper) — ISBN 978-0-8173-5735-1 (quality paper : alk. paper) — ISBN 978-0-8173-8647-4 (e book)
1. Natural history—Alabama. 2. Alabama—Description and travel. I. Mullen, Gary R. (Gary Richard) II. Littleton, Taylor. III. Title. IV. Series: Library of Alabama classics.
QH105.A2G6 2012
508.761—dc23
2012020089

Contents

List of Illustrations

Mantis 212
Shipping Cotton on the Alabama River 232

Tables

Acknowledgments

We wish to thank the following individuals for their taxonomic assistance in determining the identity and current scientific names of the plants and animal species that Gosse mentions in *Letters from Alabama* (appendix): Botanists: Curtis Hansen, curator, John Freeman Herbarium, Auburn University; and Caroline Dean, Opelika, Alabama. Entomologists: Richard Brown, Director, Mississippi Entomological Museum; Terry Schiefer and JoVonn Hill, Mississippi State University; Lance Durden, Georgia Southern University; David Wagner, University of Connecticut; and Charles Ray and Wayne Clark, Auburn University. Herpetologist: Craig Guyer, Auburn University. Ornithologist: Geoffrey Hill, Auburn University. Mammalogist: Troy Best, Auburn University. Marine ichthyologists: Richard Wallace, Auburn University (retired), Fairhope, Alabama; and experienced fisherman Leo A. (Tony) Smith, Auburn University (retired), St. George Island, Florida. We also recognize the taxonomic work done by Daniel Jones and Ken Marion, University of Alabama at Birmingham, for the 1983 edition of *Letters from Alabama* (Birmingham: Overbrook Press).

We are also grateful to The University of Alabama Press for permission to include material in the introduction that previously appeared in *Philip Henry Gosse: Science and Art in "Letters from Alabama" and "Entomologia Alabamensis"* (2010). Special thanks to Elizabeth Motherwell, acquisitions editor for the natural sciences, The University of Alabama Press, for her encouragement and support in preparing this new edition of Gosse's *Letters from Alabama* as a volume in the Library of Alabama Classics.

Letters from Alabama

Introduction

Letters from Alabama provides an engaging personal account of the early antebellum plantation period in the Black Belt region of central Alabama by the young Englishman Philip Henry Gosse (1810–1888). It was 1838, just nine years after Alabama achieved statehood. Steamboats had opened up travel and commerce on the Alabama River as far north as the developing port cities of Selma and Montgomery. The state capital had been moved from Cahawba to Tuscaloosa, the Second Creek War had ended just two years earlier, the Creek Indian Removal west to the Indian Territory had concluded the previous year, and Andrew Jackson had just completed his second term as US president. The Alabama frontier was beginning to enjoy newly acquired amenities and prosperity made possible by the production of cotton on the rich prairie soils of Alabama's Black Belt, linked by a major waterway to the bustling port of Mobile, 120 miles to the south. It was in this setting that Gosse arrived in Mobile on May 14, 1838, aboard a small schooner on which he had booked passage from Philadelphia more than a month earlier. He had celebrated his twenty-eighth birthday as the sole passenger on board.

Gosse was born in Worcester, England, but grew up in the port city of Poole, Dorsetshire, on the southwestern coast. As a young boy, he became intrigued with natural history while exploring the abundant marine life along the seashore and in the tidal pools bordering the harbor. His formal education was limited to five years at a day school, from age eight to thirteen, and less than two years thereafter at a boarding school where he was introduced to classical literature and the rudiments of Latin and Greek. His father, Thomas Gosse (1765–1844), was himself educated in the classics and supported his family as an itinerant painter of miniature portraits. It was from his father that Philip Henry developed his love of books and, equally important, that he learned the basic techniques of painting in miniature. By his teenage years he had become an avid reader, especially on subjects of natural history and travels to exotic places. He redrew and colored pictures of the fascinating animals that illustrated those accounts.

At the age of fifteen, Gosse dropped out of school to take a job as a clerk at Garland & Sons, a counting house in Poole that was engaged in the thriving North Atlantic trade in cod and seal pelts between Poole and Newfoundland. Two years later, Gosse was offered the opportunity to go to Newfoundland under a six-year contract as an indentured clerk in the firm's shipping office at Carbonear. He accepted, despite heartfelt misgivings about leaving his family and home at such a young age. It was while in Newfoundland that Gosse developed a fascination for insects and began painting them in miniature, and he remained in Carbonear two more years after fulfilling his indenture. In 1835, in part due to the religious and political unrest in Newfoundland at the time, he decided to move to what was then Lower Canada (present-day Quebec). There he purchased two hundred acres of agricultural land in Compton Township, located south of Sherbrooke, about twenty miles north of the Vermont (US) border. He spent the next three years struggling to turn a profit as a farmer while supplementing his meager income during the winter months as a teacher at nearby government schools.

Discouraged, homesick, and financially strapped, even after selling his farm in the spring of 1838, Gosse wrestled with two options: returning to England or traveling to the Carolinas and the American Deep South, where he had been told that schoolmasters were in high demand. He finally made the decision to travel overland from Compton to Philadelphia, hoping to find employment with one of the American naturalists at the Academy of Natural Sciences. If he were to be unsuccessful, he had resolved to return to England and establish a school of his own or, alternatively, to continue his journey south. To Gosse's disappointment he found no one in Philadelphia with sufficient funds to hire him. While there, however, at the Academy of Natural Sciences, he met Timothy Conrad (1803–1877), an authority on molluscan fossils. Conrad had spent two years in the 1820s in Monroe County, Alabama, collecting fossil shells from the rich Eocene deposits in the bluffs overlooking the Alabama River at Claiborne. Aware that acquaintances of his in the Claiborne area were looking for a schoolmaster, Conrad provided Gosse with a letter of introduction to a local planter, possibly a family member or friend of Charles Tait (1768–1835), Alabama's first federal district court judge. Conrad had stayed at the Tait home in Claiborne during his earlier visits to Alabama to collect fossils. With letter in hand, Gosse departed

Philadelphia on April 18, 1838, aboard the schooner *White Oak,* whose destination was Mobile.

Upon his arrival at Mobile four and a half weeks later, Gosse spent the night in the city before embarking the next day on the high-pressure packet steamboat *Farmer* for the trip up the Alabama River to Claiborne. On board he met another passenger, the distinguished jurist Reuben Saffold (1788–1847), chief justice of the Alabama Supreme Court in 1835–1836. Judge Saffold was en route to Cahawba, where he maintained his law office, and to his plantation in southeastern Dallas County near the community of Pleasant Hill. Planters there were in the process of constructing a schoolhouse and were looking to hire a schoolmaster. On meeting Gosse and learning that he had previous teaching experience and was looking for employment, Saffold persuaded Gosse not to disembark at Claiborne but to continue upriver to King's Landing, located on a wide bend of the Alabama River just below Cahawba. This was the nearest river access to Pleasant Hill, ten miles to the east by way of a well-traveled stagecoach and postal road. During the ensuing months Gosse visited Judge Saffold and his family on several occasions at their log plantation home, Belvoir. The high-style Greek Revival antebellum mansion that now stands on the site was built by the Saffolds several years after Gosse's departure. Belvoir was added to the Alabama Register of Historic Places in 1990. Variously referred to over the years as the Saffold House, Mason House, and McQueen House, it is now owned by Arthur and Bess Collias of Canton, Massachusetts, who have invested many years in Belvoir's restoration.

Gosse spent most of his time in Alabama, from mid-May to the end of December 1838, as a boarder at the Buddy Bohannon Plantation (Gosse spelled it Bohanan), located northwest of the Saffold House and Pleasant Hill. Rising early each day, he walked two miles to the rough-hewn log schoolhouse, situated in a small clearing and partially surrounded by Mush Creek and "on every side . . . shut in by a dense wall of towering forest trees."[1] It was during those early morning walks and his returns in late afternoon that he derived his greatest pleasures—collecting insects, plants, and other organisms; observing their habitats and behavior; and carefully recording his observations in his scientific journal. In doing so Gosse captures for us vivid images of the surrounding "primeval forests" in all their "inexpressible grandeur" (117); the beautiful tall-grass prairies of the Black Belt region, including Prairie Knoll, just a short distance from the Bohannon site, one of his favorite locations for collecting insects and wildflowers; and the extensive agricultural fields dominated by cotton. Together with his diary accounts of everyday plantation life, social interactions, local customs, visits to Cahawba and Selma, and frontier life in Dallas County, Gosse's journal formed the basis of *Letters from Alabama*. He devoted special attention to the ecological diversity of the region and the study of insects, as he notes in his preface: "The direction of my thoughts was principally towards Natural History; and Entomology was the particular branch which at that period I most studied. Hence a large (perhaps an undue) portion of the remarks concerns Insects" (v–vi). Unfortunately, Gosse's journal and diary seem to have disappeared sometime after 1890, and their fate or whereabouts remains unknown.

To appreciate the nature and extent of Gosse's contributions to our knowledge of Alabama's natural history in the early nineteenth century, one need only look at the number of plant and animals species that he collected and observed, as charmingly recorded in *Letters from Alabama*. They total 408 species, including some 189 species of plants, 94 species of insects, 14 species of marine fishes, 59 species of birds, 21 species of mammals, and 15 species of reptiles and amphibians. The tables in the appendix provide listings of the individual taxa, with the original common and scientific names that Gosse used, together with the common and scientific names by which the respective organisms are known today. Firsthand accounts of an additional 16 animal taxa are included in Gosse's narrative. Most of these are marine invertebrates (e.g., corals, mollusks) and terrestrial invertebrates (e.g., ticks, pseudoscorpions, spiders)

Of particular interest, Gosse barely comments in *Letters from Alabama* about the time and effort that he devoted to illustrating the plants and animals he collected and observed while in Dallas County. This work is evident in the twenty-nine engravings that complement the text, seven of which (all insects) bear his initials *PHG*. The engravings were produced from the original watercolors that Gosse meticulously painted in his room at the Bohannon place. In describing his daily schedule and the oppressive summer heat and humidity, he writes at the end of his letter of July 5: "The morning hours . . . are the only part of the day that can habitually be rendered effective to science . . . My usual plan is, to take a long walk through the forest in the morning before the sun is very high;

and in the heat of the day, if business permits, arrange my captures, write, or paint insects and flowers" (193). Although he makes no mention of it, Gosse produced forty-nine pages of exquisitely detailed watercolors of insects, wildflowers, and other plants during his Alabama visit. They are beautifully preserved in his original sketchbook that he titled *Entomologia Alabamensis*. After remaining in the Gosse family for 154 years, the sketchbook was placed on loan to the British Library by Gosse's great-granddaughter Jennifer Gosse in 1992. It is now a permanent part of the manuscripts collection of the British Library. All forty-nine insect watercolors are reproduced in Mullen and Littleton, *Philip Henry Gosse: Science and Art in "Letters from Alabama" and "Entomologia Alabamensis."*

By early October, Gosse was having serious reservations about remaining in Alabama, disturbed particularly by the "disquieting elements … [of] the institution of slavery."[2] He had been subjected to threats of bodily harm when he questioned the status quo and treatment of slaves. Reluctant to express his opinions and fearing retaliation, he ceased recording his personal thoughts and mentioning social issues in his diary. And after discovering that someone had entered his room, rifled through his possessions, and opened and read his personal correspondence, he suffered both anxiety and melancholy. As his son, Edmund, later wrote: "It sickened him, and it had much to do with his abrupt departure."[3] In mid-December Gosse attended a meeting of the Methodist Society at Selma, following which he felt called to become a Wesleyan minister and to stay in Alabama to preach and visit. Shortly thereafter, however, he reassessed his situation and decided to return immediately to England. On December 31, Gosse boarded the ship *Issac Newton* in Mobile for his return voyage to Poole, never to return to Alabama or the American continent.

Gosse originally submitted his manuscript about his Alabama experiences to the Society for Promoting Christian Knowledge (SPCK) in London in 1854. To his disappointment, the SPCK's Committee of General Literature and Education did not approve acceptance, concluding that "it was considered to be not expedient to publish this work in its present entire form."[4] Instead, he was referred to the editor of *The Home Friend,* a popular British magazine at that time produced in London. *The Home Friend* published Gosse's piece anonymously as a serial in 1855, without illustrations, under the title "'Letters from Alabama.'" Gosse subsequently published a revised version in book form, identifying himself as the author and adding the engraved illustrations. *Letters from Alabama (U.S.), Chiefly Relating to Natural History*, published by Morgan and Chase, London, in 1859, appears in full in this volume.

Inspired by religious fervor as a direct result of his American experience, Gosse was to devote a significant part of his remaining life to preaching, ministering, and writing on religious topics. However, he is best remembered for his extraordinary accomplishments and contributions to science and natural history. He authored more than 40 books and 270 scientific papers and religious tracts. In addition to writing some of the first textbooks for teaching zoology and natural history, including *An Introduction to Zoology* (1844) and a series titled Natural History (1848–1854), he produced a two-volume illustrated work on *The Birds of Jamaica* (1847, 1848–49) and the first illustrated field guide for observing and identifying marine organisms along the British coast. Among his most popular books were *A Naturalist's Sojourn in Jamaica* (1851), *A Handbook to the Marine Aquarium* (1855), *Evenings at the Microscope* (1859), and *The Romance of Natural History* (1860). He is credited among the first to devise a formula for artificial sea water, leading to the development of the first saltwater aquariums. He designed the first public aquarium, which opened in London in 1858; corresponded with Charles Darwin; and was elected a Fellow of the Royal Society, London, in 1856. After a long and remarkably productive life, Philip Henry Gosse died at the age of seventy-eight, in St. Marychurch, Devon, on August 23, 1888.

GRM

"There is perhaps no river so winding as the Alabama" was one of the first observations recorded by Philip Henry Gosse in the spring of 1838 as he began the journals he would carefully transcribe for the next eight months of his residence in the little community of Pleasant Hill (33). When he boarded the small steamer in Mobile Bay, he could not have known that his journey upriver would carry him into perhaps the most formative period of his life. The unexpected offer onboard ship of a position as schoolmaster became an opportunity to commit himself further—as a professional author—to a scientific and artistic career investigating the scenes of natural history.

Prior to his arrival at King's Landing, he had already, in what would in 1840 become his first publication, *The Canadian Naturalist*, given us a literary sense of finding himself in the wondrous world of nature:

> Perhaps one of the chief pleasures of natural history, especially entomology, is the perpetual novelty and variety we find in it . . . the endless diversity of habits, locality, structure, form, colour, to be found in insects is such a source of pleasure as effectively prevents us from feeling weariness or melancholy . . . It seems almost a contradiction in terms for a naturalist to be low in spirits.[5]

He made a commitment, as he continued, to investigate "the mysteries of nature . . . hidden from the unobservant . . . but continually disclosed to him who walks through the world with an open eye." There is an artless self-confidence and eagerness for the quest that would permeate all of Gosse's writing, and here, during his tenure in Alabama, he would find time to continue what he always called his "woodland rambles," recording through the "open eye" those journal entries he would subsequently organize and publish as *Letters from Alabama*.

That full publication would not occur until some twenty years after the journal record itself had been completed. By then, in 1859, Gosse had secured a certain reputation of scientific distinction through his writings on marine organisms and had been elected as Fellow of the Royal Society. Thus *Letters from Alabama* is retrospective in character and may be seen as a kind of personal odyssey begun by Gosse at the age of twenty-eight during a lonely and uncertain period in his long career. "I was quite alone," he wrote on first arriving, "knowing neither the place nor the inhabitants" (35); and though within three months he could say that he had begun "at length to be known by his proper name, instead of 'the stranger,'" there are only a few scattered references to others in the small settlement and no evidence of any familiar companions (228). He did, however, through his private rambles, come to know the "place" intimately. His investigative distance from the community is illustrated briefly in his September account of a rare evening excursion with Jones, the plantation overseer, "through a neighboring swamp. His object was to get a little sport, in the way of hunting raccoons, opossums, wild cats or any other game that might occur; mine, rather to see the interior of the lone forest, with its strange sights and sounds, beneath the gloom of night" (256). On publication of *Letters from Alabama*, Gosse made clear that "the direction of my thoughts" was toward natural history and entomology especially (v). His vision of this subject is expansive, offering the reader an almost complete exposure to the environs of Pleasant Hill—only a few miles downriver from Selma, which had been established eighteen years before Gosse's arrival—its climate, geography, characteristic plants and timber, history and tall tales, bird migrations, and the trivia of human and seasonal adaptations. The work seems to address a dual audience: the English reader unfamiliar with the novelty of this remote and "hilly region of Alabama"—which parenthetically on the title page he identifies as being in the "U.S."—whose natural history had become an integral part of his life, and zoologists whose knowledge of American entomology could be strengthened by his recordings. He places his observations and interpretations within an epistolary format—nineteen "letters" as he called them, dated at irregular intervals amidst a structural calendar of the circling seasons, May to December. The epistolary arrangement itself may be indebted to, among other sources, Gosse's easy and oft-quoted familiarity with the masterpiece of his great eighteenth-century predecessor Gilbert White, whose well-known *The Natural History of Selborne* (1789) contains a series of letters written to fellow naturalists.[6] White found the revelations of natural history within the confines of his own parish and garden, just as Gosse was discovering his in the neighborhood of Pleasant Hill.

Gosse's letters are addressed to an unknown reader and seem designed to bridge the cultural distance between frontier Alabama and Victorian England. Almost all of them maintain a fine ironic space between the immediacy of the open-eye field observations and Gosse's retention of an identity as the English visitor who has accommodated himself—often in a half-humorous or sympathetic manner—to the small details of the life around him. For example, in the letter of June 1, he creates a fictional trans-Atlantic recipient: "suppose you just transport yourself (in imagination) to Alabama" and conducts him through a leisurely day, beginning with such breakfast oddities as "hominy" and "waffles," to a stroll to and from the schoolhouse where the song of the mockingbird (the "leader of the American orchestra") is interwoven with a comprehensive litany of entomological and botanical sights along the way, and concluding with the companion being invited "to take a little supper," not what "we are accustomed to call tea but for Americans the last meal of only three in the day" (68).

This engaging and familiar manner is sustained throughout the letters in a heightened and evocative descriptive style that at times is both tranquil and reflective, as in a December 1 passage, where the accuracy of the journal notations are enhanced by Gosse's memories. Gosse's remembrance of Canada is called up as he sees a migratory snowbird, which had been such a common sight in Canada, hopping about and sitting on every fence:

> How slight a thing will touch the chords of sympathy! The smallest object, the faintest note, will sometimes awaken association with some distant scene or by-gone time, and conjure up in a moment, all unexpected, a magic circle, which unlocks all the secret springs of the soul, and excites emotions and affections that had slept for months or perhaps years! . . . The first time I saw it in these distant southern regions, it seemed like an old friend come to tell me of old familiar faces and to converse with me of old familiar scenes.[7]

This symbolic reclamation—here, of Canada in a memoir written about Alabama—is suggested often in the hundreds of episodes appearing on almost every page of *Letters from Alabama*: the descriptive sounds of the turtle dove, for example, are "something inexpressibly touching, soothing our spirits and calming us into unison with the peaceful quiet of nature" (59). Such a serene phrase may have been composed years after the 1838 residence or on a given evening after supper and the daily walk from the schoolhouse. But it is the "unison," the web of associations discovered within the human and natural world, that gives *Letters from Alabama* its dominant character.

That dominant character finds its expression in the literary style inherent in each of the letters. Don't "expect from me anything like a continuous narrative," he explains in the letter of July 1, protesting that his recordings are only "peeps through Nature's keyhole at her recondite mysteries" (134). Yet what a reader regularly encounters is an interwoven sequence of observations that are in their careful eclecticism indeed a "continuous narrative," combining brief images of the frontier locale with superb descriptions of the plant and animal life seen on a given woodland ramble, all united through the genial roving presence of Gosse himself, expressing his undoubted wonder at that "perpetual novelty and variety" of natural history he had first voiced in *The Canadian Naturalist*.[8]

In no letter is this style better illustrated than in that of June 16, with its engaging density and leisurely pace as Gosse returns "from a pleasant ride to Cahawba . . . formerly the seat of government of the state, but now," he found, "much decayed and has a very desolate appearance." The ride there and back had, as always, been "solitary indeed but not the less pleasant for that," because human society, he reflects, can often be uncongenial and boring, "but nature is always congenial, and always conversible" (100). Here, on the banks of what he calls the "romantic river," of this new southern state to which his long journey had brought him, Gosse coins the odd word that seems to define not only the artistic shape of this mid-summer letter but that of the whole work itself. Nature offers to those who will listen a conversation, to which Gosse has responded, and he will now present to the reader a record ("rough notes" he called them in his first letter) of how that conversation can enhance the spirit, preventing us, as he had written years earlier, "from feeling weariness or melancholy."[9]

And thus, he recites the litany of colors, sounds, and miniature narratives that contribute to the letter becoming a text complete in itself:

> On suddenly turning round a point of the forest, . . . I surprised a Blue Heron . . . intently gazing into the water, as if cut in stone. . . . Herons are shy, retiring birds, delighting in the gloomy solitude of marshes, or unfrequented lakes, or where the large rivers flow through the untouched forest. Their form is gracefully slender, and the color . . . of the present species is a lavender-blue, the head and neck purplish. A pretty moth which I had not seen before was rather numerous: the wings are horizontal, white, fantastically marked into numerous divisions by bands of dark-brown . . . (101–2)

And on the return from Cahawba, Gosse's "curiosity was much excited" as he investigated the source of a "most deafening shrieking, extremely shrill and loud . . . produced by a small dusky species of frog. . . . Wishing much to witness the act of uttering the sound, . . . I waited patiently, quiet and motionless a long time." The culprit emerging from the marshy pool allowed Gosse to see and describe in some 150 words the bodily rhythm as another "piercing shriek . . . somewhat like that of a penny trumpet" was sounded (104).

In its style and content the letter seems a microcosm of the whole, and like a few of the other letters, its evocations of the natural world are enhanced pictorially by etchings of two woodland scenes: "The woods are frequently enlivened by the antics of playful Squirrels of large size . . . several species, of which the most common is the Fox-squirrel"; and the "Ruby-throat Humming-bird," which delights to visit that "most magnificent plant, the Trumpet-flower . . . whose deep capacious tubes are just the thing for him . . . sometimes half-a-dozen at once round a single bush . . . now rushing off in a straight line like a shooting star, now returning as swiftly, while their brilliant plumage gleams in the sun like gold and precious stones" (114).

This verbal and visual texture in part defines the "unnamed" readership to whom the letters are addressed. Not only will they, Gosse assumes, be genuinely interested in the entomology and various small wonders so faithfully recorded in the 1838 journals, but now, in 1859, as he artistically shapes the final text, he can confidently expand the educational conversation by assuming the reader will be interested in scientific additions and literary references to such diverse writers as Spenser, Virgil, and William Cullen Bryant. Some of this information Gosse would not likely have had ready at hand during the late Alabama afternoons or evenings when, as he states in the letter of July 5, he found the time and energy to "write, or paint insects and flowers" (193). In the June 16 letter, for example, in Gosse's description of the quail's Bob-White sound—"one of the most prominent and most frequent of the sounds which strike a stranger here" (105)—he records an extensive verbatim anecdote about the species from the work of Alexander Wilson, Audubon's predecessor in the study of American ornithology; and Gosse's discussion of the Fox-squirrel includes a poetic passage from William Cowper's *The Task* which "exquisitely portrays" the tree-top behaviors of "our little English species" (125).

As Gosse looked back, quite likely with some affection, at most of his Alabama experience, he also added information about local customs, including such trans-Atlantic facts as that "stewed, or made into a pie, squirrel is excellent eating" (128); and a new vocabulary in which he had been instructed: "Let me tell you one or two idioms, in which the Alabamians rejoice. . . . *whip* is to *overcome* or *beat* ('He *whipped* me at leaping'); *tote* is to *carry* ('I *toted* the bucket'); *make tracks* is to *go away; good* has the sense of *well* ('He writes *good*'); *right* for *very* ('It is a *right* pretty book') (128). "But," he writes, "what has all this to do with natural history?—not much, in good truth" (109–10). These sometimes whimsical additions are doubtless portions of the final text that, as Gosse states in his 1859 preface, "have been revised," and they help convey a certain agreeable authenticity to an eight-month life in "a part of the United States," "visited by comparatively few Europeans" (v).

One of Gosse's conceptions of natural history explicit in the final text was not revised from its inception in his 1838 field notes. While here and elsewhere in his writings Gosse's meticulous scientific descriptions were perhaps unmatched among his nineteenth-century peers, in persuasion he was what in our contemporary vocabulary would be called a "creationist," finding the origin and meaning of behaviors in the natural world in the providential power of the God of Genesis. "We observe facts," he had written in *The Canadian Naturalist*, "but when we presume to inquire why these things are so, we are baffled and repulsed . . . the primary cause must be referred to the Father who, we may be assured, appoints the seasons, and watches over the welfare of the meanest objects of his creation."[10] This almost contradictory union of vigorous investigation of nature's secrets and an unyielding Christian determinism made Gosse unable to accommodate the new biology of the Victorian revolution. Yet he knew most of the scientific community of his time, corresponding, for example, with Darwin himself on various botanical and zoological matters. Gosse's career, to be sure, may reflect a certain historical relevance in that, his eventual scientific distinctions notwithstanding, he was one of thousands whose theological principles resisted the concept of evolutionary change. Still, within the texts of the two works written during his American experience, no zealous intrusions compromise the clarity of his unpretentious inquiries. And his magnificent watercolor legacy of scientific art, the *Entomologia Alabamensis,* painted as a kind of visual parallel text to *Letters from Alabama*, helps to validate—to use one of his favorite locutions—his not unworthy place in the cultural lifetime of his century.

The range of Gosse's emotions in his appraisals of what he saw as the Alabama character is expressed in the several small accounts of his experiences with the inhabitants of Pleasant Hill. His schoolroom, "a funny little place" with its split-pine-board desks, is filled with urchins slow to conjugate verbs and who know little of what in "crowded cities is thought worth knowing," but these "tumultuous boys," he writes, read a language in "the sounds and sights of the wilderness" (108–9). He recounts several scenes in which they instruct him about local insects, until then foreign to his experience: the cicada, which he had always wanted to examine, and the "chameleon," or green anole, whose color-changing prowess he had thought "a mere fable" (74). This affection and respect moves to sympathy for those planter families caught in the inevitable summer droughts (letter of June 10) to amusement in his mock-heroic description of a night's horseback ritual of possum hunting (letter of August 15).

He had already, as many nineteenth-century visitors would do, noted the restlessness of the American character, its inability to sustain itself among the thousand amenities that the English "delight to accumulate around us, and which are so many links to enchain us to a given spot" (156–57). And in the letters of July 15 and September 1, he astutely described those contradictory qualities that future writers of southern fiction and history would also confirm. "The manners of these Southerners differ a good deal from those of their more calculating compatriots, the Yankees of the north and east." But the former's admirable qualities of generous hospitality and frank cordiality must be placed against his "darkest side": a hostility to alleged intrusion into considered assumptions and beliefs, and a fierce independence that often transcends the law and sustains beneath the surface of community a quarrelsome and reckless violence in human relationships (250–51).

In one of his earliest letters, that of May 20, Gosse describes his initial walk from the river to his place of employment as lush with flowery vistas, there is an abundance of bird and animal life, and he notes the "charm of absolute novelty that attended everything here." He regretted that he had not come earlier in the spring when "the gate of Eden is, as it were, re-opened." But he also saw then, for the first time, "negro slaves performing the labors of agriculture," and he was immediately revolted by their inhuman treatment (40). Within the fiction of the letters chronology, Gosse instinctively understood, by September, that the Edenic Alabama whose grandeur and beauty had meant so much to his educational odyssey had been irretrievably corrupted by slavery, "a huge deadly serpent" (253). Thus his unflagging honesty about the cultural boundaries of natural history obligated him, further in the letter of September 1, to abandon his usual persona of detached observer and directly express his feelings. The letter itself is only five pages long, in a text of over three hundred pages, and is a deliberate insertion, having nothing to do with the entomology of the preceding or following letters, or with his thematic calendar of seasons.

Gosse had firsthand knowledge of the cruelty intrinsic to the slavery system, as he witnessed some of the lashings of both men and women in his own residential community, and he knew of the other horrors: repressive labor, the desperation of hunger, the use of night patrols and bloodhounds to capture runaways—all recorded in the September 1 letter. Given his time and place, Gosse's voice seems both authentic and perceptive: "the institution is doomed . . ." and when its certain end comes "perhaps swiftly . . . it can hardly be other than a terrible convulsion" (254–55). Gosse's oracular predictions, written well before the American Civil War, also included a belief that dangerous social and political disarray would occur once thousands of slaves "uneducated . . . and smarting under a sense of accumulated wrongs" were emancipated (254–55). These attitudes and his hatred of the system helped to motivate his departure from Alabama, although his loneliness, lack of intellectual companionship, and perhaps longing for a domestic life were also relevant.

Comparisons between Gosse, both in his art and writing, and John James Audubon are almost irresistible. The one would never meet the other, but Gosse knew Audubon's work. Both wrote about what they had already drawn and painted, their ecological descriptions being as precise as their illustrations of birds and insects. And Gosse's portraits in *Entomologia Alabamensis*—life-size accurate reproductions exquisitely drawn and with their brilliant colors—may be properly compared with those in *Birds of America* (1838), one of the greatest works of nature art in American history. And, even as Gosse was assembling his own journals and artwork toward the end of 1838, it is a minor but arresting coincidence that the final volume of Audubon's masterpiece was being printed.[11] Moreover, in 1838 Charles Darwin was also correlating his vast notebooks speculating on the nature of heredity, environment, and the emergence of new species for publication in 1839 as *A Journal of Researches into the Geology and Natural History of the Various Countries Visited by HMS* Beagle.[12] And perhaps it is within this wider cultural context that the significance of Gosse's Alabama experience may be found.

Despite his doctrinaire views, Gosse shares with Audubon and, indeed, with William Bartram, the pioneering traveler who preceded them both in exploring and describing the Alabama River landscape, a verbal sense of the naturalist's sacred duty. In Gosse's metaphor, all three of them walked through the world with an open eye, confirming in an exalted language an ideal conception of America's relationship with nature. The messages sent forward by these writers and artists assert that relationship as an interrelated web of the human and natural condition, one gently demanding wonder and reverence. To William Bartram, this world is "a glorious apartment of the boundless palace of the sovereign Creator . . . a glorious display of the Almighty hand."[13] Audubon writes in his study of American birds, "admiring the manifestations of the glorious perfections of their Omnipotent Creator . . . have I sought to search out the things which have been hidden since the creation of this wondrous world, or seen only by the naked Indian."[14] And Gosse, in the letter of July 1, musing as always on the "omnipotent Creator," who allowed, for example, a concentration amidst a "blossomed field" of millions of insects, each pursuing a separate pathway of existence, writes, "I have often thought that no one can appreciate the grandeur, the sublimity of this sentiment . . . like the devout naturalist" (149–50).

Here we may perhaps sense at least a minor cultural moment. For even as Gosse could perceive in the entomology of an Alabama field the "grandeur" of the providential hand, another devout naturalist, Charles Darwin, writing in that same publication season of 1859, was describing in the closing sentences of his masterpiece a profound pattern "produced by laws acting around us" that would alter forever our understanding of natural history. This pattern is such that "from so simple a beginning endless forms most beautiful and most wonderful have been, and are being created." And to Darwin: "There is grandeur in this view of life."[15]

Whatever small relevance Gosse's early work may have for the Victorian narrative or for the Alabama story, the form and content of *Letters from Alabama*— written in a relatively confined, but no less unique, American space of time and geography—allow us to place Gosse within the great tradition of nature writing. Such writing, however personalized its artistic style, almost always sends us messages—like letters—affirming the place in nature's web of such details as the environmental adaptations of mud turtles, the "night music" of katydids, or the habits of swallowtail butterflies. These are among the letters we most like to receive, a sharing between writer and reader of timeless things we readers did not understand that we needed to know. Keeping us aware of our critical—even sacred—connection to the strange majesty of this invisible pattern is the special province of the naturalist, a province quietly defined in the work of Philip Henry Gosse. He was a temporary visitor in our distant Alabama past, but his letters speak to us still in their spirit of generosity: like the account of May 20, 1838, of his first "woodland ramble," as he climbed the steep hill from the winding river, "If it afford you half as much pleasure to read it as it afforded me to walk it, I shall feel well repaid" (41).

TDL

Notes

1. Philip Henry Gosse, *Letters from Alabama* (London: Morgan and Chase, 1859), 44. All citations in the text are from this edition.

2. Edmund Gosse, *The Life of Philip Henry Gosse, F.R.S.* (London: Kegan, Paul, Trench, Trübner and Co., 1890), 142.

3. Ibid., 143.

4. R. B. Freeman and Douglas Wertheimer, *P. H. Gosse: A Bibliography* (Kent: Wm Dawson & Sons Ltd, 1980), 66.

5. Philip Henry Gosse, *The Canadian Naturalist* (London: John Van Voorst, 1840), 226.

6. Gilbert White, *The Natural History of Selborne* (London: Cassell & Company, 1789).

7. Philip Henry Gosse, *Letters from Alabama*, 294.

8. Philip Henry Gosse, *The Canadian Naturalist*, 226.

9. Ibid.

10. Ibid., 187–88.

11. John James Audubon, *The Birds of America* (London: Published by the Author, 1827–1838).

12. Charles Darwin, *A Journal of Researches into the Geology and Natural History of the Various Countries Visited by HMS* Beagle (London: Henry Colburn, 1839).

13. William Bartram, *The Travels of William Bartram*, ed. Mark Van Doren (New York: Dover Publications, 1955), 15.

14. John James Audubon, "The Raven," *Selected Journals and Other Writings*, ed. Ben Forkner (New York: Penguin Books, 1997), 566.

15. Charles Darwin, *On the Origin of Species*, 1859 (New York, Avenel-Penguin Books, 1976), 459–60. Gosse signed his preface as "Torquay, July 1859"; Darwin's book was published on November 24.

LETTERS FROM ALABAMA,

(U.S.)

CHIEFLY RELATING TO

NATURAL HISTORY.

BY

PHILIP HENRY GOSSE, F.R.S.

LONDON: MORGAN AND CHASE,

TICHBORNE COURT, 280, HIGH HOLBORN.

1859.

Title Page of the original edition of *Letters from Alabama* (1859, London: Morgan and Chase). Courtesy of the Hoole Special Collections of the University of Alabama Libraries

Table of Contents

Preface

The following pages contain records of impressions made upon my mind during a residence of seven or eight months in the hilly region of the State of Alabama. It is a part of the United States visited by comparatively few Europeans; and those who have ever seen it have almost exclusively confined their acquaintance with it to the brief glances obtained from the interior of a stage coach, or the deck of a river steamer. The aspect of nature, in particular, presented much that was novel and beautiful to me, and induced me to believe that what had pleased me in the observation might please others in the recital.

The direction of my thoughts was principally towards Natural History; and Entomology was the particular branch which at that period I most studied. Hence a large (perhaps an undue) portion of the remarks concerns Insects; and this may perhaps be the rather tolerated, because less is known in Europe of American Entomology, than of other branches of Zoology, which are popularly studied.

These letters have already appeared in the form of contributions to a magazine entitled "The Home Friend." They have been revised, and are now reproduced, in the hope that they may prove a not wholly valueless contribution to Natural History.

P. H. G.
TORQUAY,
July, 1859

Letter I

Your desire to have some information of the country in which the good providence of God has for the present allotted my residence, shall be gratified so far as my opportunities of observation will admit. I shall communicate it more readily, because from the very hasty and imperfect notion I have yet formed, I think it probable that scenes, circumstances, and manners, differ widely from those to which you and I have been accustomed.

As a preliminary, however, it may not be altogether uninteresting to give a slight sketch of the voyage from Philadelphia. A sea-voyage, under the best circumstances, can scarcely be other than tedious. Even when performed in a stately and commodious vessel, with a skilful, gentlemanly, and obliging commander, a disciplined crew, and agreeable fellow-passengers, the wearied eye wanders from sea to sky, and from sky to sea, in a vain search for some object to break the dreary uniformity: to-day is like yesterday, and to-morrow will be as to-day. If the poor occupationless passenger endeavour to beguile his tedium, and indulge his literary propensities, by "keeping a log," so few are the facts that occur, that he is often reduced to debate with himself the propriety of recording such "remarkable events" as that "the cook dropped a pewter spoon overboard," or that "the pig came upon the quarter-deck;" and happy indeed is he when he has an opportunity of announcing, in the words of the north-country mate, "Little wind and less weather; caught a dolphin, and—lost him!" If, therefore, you find in my letter a tendency to treat of "small deer," I trust you will make charitable allowances, and admit the truth of the Irish proverb, which sets forth the difficulty of extracting blood from a turnip.

It would be needless to waste many words about Philadelphia. My impressions of it were agreeable; there are not many splendid or imposing edifices, but the general character is that of a genteel and respectable middle-class. If there is little to astonish or dazzle, there is perhaps less to displease: an air of chaste and sobered elegance pervades the whole. The streets are straight, wide, and clean, and are rendered peculiarly pleasant by rows of trees on each side, among which the stately plane or buttonwood is conspicuous. The people who walk in them

The Schuylkill

are remarkably few in number for a large city, and their deportment is generally quiet and orderly. One cannot help feeling that William Penn has left the character of his sect strongly, indelibly, impressed on the city which he founded.

The broad and beautiful river on which it stands —the silvery Delaware, with its gently sloping banks, green and fertile—is a very great ornament and no less an advantage to the city; for though it can scarcely be called a commercial town, a goodly array of shipping finds its way thither, and a rather dense forest of masts shoots up from the fair bosom of the Delaware.

The men of science I found, as usual, kind and obliging; the venerable Professor Nuttall was prosecuting his labours among the dried plants in the herbarium of the Academy of Natural Sciences, and the urbane Peale was as busy in the fine Museum which forms one of the chief attractions of the city. My most prominent idea was that of Wilson the ornithologist. Here was his residence; here he kept school; here I looked upon the birds which he shot and skinned with his own hands; here are the scenes so often mentioned in his delightful volumes; the meadows below Philadelphia, the marshy flats of the Schuylkill, the rushy half-submerged islets of the Delaware, Thompson's Point, the quondam residence of the night-heron or qua-bird, and the notorious Pea Patch, the resort of myriads of crows. The recognition of these places gave a charm and an interest to the scenes, which they would not otherwise have possessed, for to me there is always a peculiar pleasure in visiting those spots which have been hallowed (so to speak) by the eminent of bygone days. One old man I met with who had been personally acquainted with the ornithologist; though the latter had been a constant visitor at his house, he could not remember many anecdotes of him, but one thing he narrated was sufficiently characteristic. "Wilson and I," said he, "were always disputing about the sparrows; he would have it that the sparrows here were different from those of the old country; I knew well enough they were just the same, but I could not persuade him of it." It is scarcely necessary to say that the American sparrows are quite distinct from the European species.

With a fine breeze right aft, and bright weather, the little schooner, "White Oak," left the quay of Philadelphia on the 18th of April, and sailed rapidly down the mirror-like river. The numerous flats and sand-bars, however, impeded, and sometimes arrested, our progress, and we had to make a temporary stay at a mean little fishing village, that bears the pompous title of Delaware City, situated on the canal which connects the Delaware with the Chesapeake. In the canal a man was taking herring with a dip-net, which he readily sold on the bank at fifty cents per hundred. At length we entered on the widening bay of Delaware. It was so cold that ice a quarter of an inch thick was formed on deck, and this on the 20th of April, in the latitude of Lisbon.

The number of white-sailed craft spotting the river made a lively scene; and the banks being very low and flat caused the land to have a singular appearance, being visible only at a very short distance, and beginning to come into view in small isolated patches, which if one jumped on the taffrail were seen to be connected, and the trees often appearing at first as if growing out of the water. Numerous large fires had been lighted on the shores for the purpose of consuming the old dead grass of the marshes, to afford room for the growth of a new crop, and the smoke and flame being visible both before and after the land was apparent, it seemed as if some "smart" Yankee had realized the achievement of setting the Delaware on fire. But all indications of land soon faded from view, the twinkling lights on Cape May and Henlopen glimmered for a moment through the deepening shadows of night, and long before morning we were on the heaving bosom of the grim Atlantic.

A miserable episode in life is the commencement of a voyage, under such circumstances as those which greeted my returning consciousness on the next morning. The wind was as dead on end as possible, blowing a strong gale, and so cold that it pierced through bone and marrow; a heavy swell with a breaking sea was running, that continually washed the decks from stem to stem; the little schooner pitching, and tossing, and diving, as if every dip would be her last. In vain did I seek refuge from the weather by going below; the filthy hole called a cabin, hardly large enough to turn in, and not nearly high enough to stand upright in, was redolent of tar, grease, fusty cloths, mouldy biscuits, and a score of other unendurable odours combined, which those only can imagine who, like me, have been the tenants of a little trading craft. The single berth or sleeping place on each side, in dimensions and appearance resembled a dog-kennel more than anything else, the state of the blankets in which, thanks to the grave-like darkness of the hole, was but partially revealed, to sight at least. The agony of seasickness, aggravated beyond measure by the closeness and fetor of the confined air below, drives me on deck again, where, shivering as in an ague fit, I endeavour to screen myself by crouching beneath the bulwarks (scarcely knee-high) from the sea, spray, and rain, which the gale is driving across the decks. We sometimes are made to feel how great an intensity of wretchedness can be condensed into a brief space, without any infliction more severe than a combination of what may be rightly termed trivial sufferings.

Those who know the sea only in connexion with the spacious deck and gorgeously-furnished saloon of a packet steamer, can form but a poor notion of the accommodation of a little coasting schooner. Imagine a closet, of no geometrical shape, some seven feet by six, and about a yard and a half high, with huge beams at intervals, against which, until taught to stoop by painful experience, you thump your forehead every time you attempt to cross. In the centre a deal table is screwed to the floor, leaving just space enough to squeeze one's body round on each side. A sort of chest running along one side, called a locker, serves the double purpose of a seat, and a box for holding musty sails, flags, balls of spun-yarn, and sundry other articles, the savour of whose presence becomes but too manifest, whenever the little cover of the single square hole is removed, to rummage the contents. On the opposite side to this are two cupboards, also bearing the same name of lockers, though generally innocent of anything like a lock, the doors of which, continually getting unfastened, slam to and fro in the rolling and lurching of the vessel with convulsive violence, revealing, as they open, a jug or two, and some glass tumblers, inserted in round holes cut in the shelves, and perhaps a tea-pot and some cups and saucers similarly secured; but all in the most disgusting state of dirtiness. The remainder of this side is occupied by the door, giving entrance from the foot of the companion-ladder, on the one hand, and on the other by the skipper's "stateroom."

The remaining two sides are formed into cells just large enough (and but barely) to allow an adult person to lay himself along, as if in a coffin. Some eight inches of board are the sleeper's protection from rolling out into the cabin, while his limbs chafe against the side of the vessel at every lurch. Careful must he be that he start not up suddenly in the night; for, if he do, a stunning blow on the forehead will remind him that the ceiling is not more than fifteen inches from his face as he lies. Such are the sleeping-berths, one on each side—the cell below each being stowed with all sorts of rubbish, into which the miserable slave of a cabin-boy is continually diving, by night and day, to find nobody knows what, to the infinite molestation of the sleepless passenger above.

The same smutty Ganymede ever and anon disappears beneath the cabin-table, presently emerging with a tub of potatoes, a tallow-candle, or something of more dubious character. Stimulated by curiosity, I peeped under the table one day, and saw a ring fixed in the floor, which I pulled, and up came a piece of the plank, uncovering the "lazarette," a dark and musty pit, into which one glance was sufficient for that and all future occasions.

Pleasant society will make amends for many inconveniences, but in my case the skipper was a churlish, vulgar, illiterate fellow, and his crew of the very same stamp as himself. The fact of my being a "Britisher" was quite enough to warrant an incessant display of petty annoyance, which just kept short of actual insult. The conversation was of the lowest sort; and it was not the smallest infliction, that every night I was compelled to hear, as I lay in my wretched berth, the interchange of obscene narratives between the skipper and his mate, before I could close my eyes in sleep. Dirt, dirt, was the rule everywhere; dirt in the cabin, dirt in the caboose, dirt in the water-cask; dirt doubly begrimed on the table-cloth, on the cups and glasses, the dishes and plates that served the food;

while the boy who filled the double office of cook and waiter, was the very impersonation of dirt. The only resource was to eat with as little thought as possible, to see as little as possible, and to be upon deck as much of the time as possible; and this last habit was facilitated by the glorious weather which speedily set in after we were well off the land.

All minor discomforts were forgotten, or at least felt to be compensated, when I saw that mysterious current, commonly known by the name of the Gulf-stream, or by sailors, more elliptically, "the Gulf;" a strong and ever-running river, if I may so term it, in the sea, whose banks are almost as well defined as if they were formed of solid earth, instead of the same fickle fluid as the torrent itself. It first becomes appreciable on the western coast of Florida, gently flowing southward, till it reaches the Tortugas, when it bends its course suddenly eastward, and runs along the Florida Reef, increasing in force, till it rushes with amazing velocity through the confined limits of the Strait of Florida, and pours a vast volume of tepid water into the cold bosom of the Atlantic. Here, unrestrained, it widens its bounds, and slackens its speed, though such is the impetus with which it has been impelled, that it is distinctly perceptible on the banks of Newfoundland, and may be traced by its effects even to the shores of Western Europe.

Our contact with this wonderful stream was indicated by the increased temperature of the water, as well as by the long strings or ridges of the yellow Gulf-weed, which are commonly to be observed stretching across its course. Sometimes it occurs in immense fields, as it did to Columbus, when the ocean appeared like a vast meadow, and the course of his vessels was impeded by the floating "grass." When I saw these strings and patches I was well pleased, for I knew I should not lack entertainment as long as this singular plant continued abundant. Its own structure is most interesting and surprising; for though it may be conjectured to have had an original root, a "local habitation," at some remote age, no connexion with the shores or bottom of the sea subsists now, for it evidently shoots and increases as it floats, free on the surface of the waves. It consists of a multitude of well-formed leaves, with a rib running down the centre, and notched edges, set alternately on angular stems, which bear a great number of little globular, berry-like air-vessels, about as large as currants, the office of which is to float the plant.

But to a voyager glad of any source of amusement, the Sargasso-weed is most welcome, because of the shelter which it affords for hosts of small marine ani-

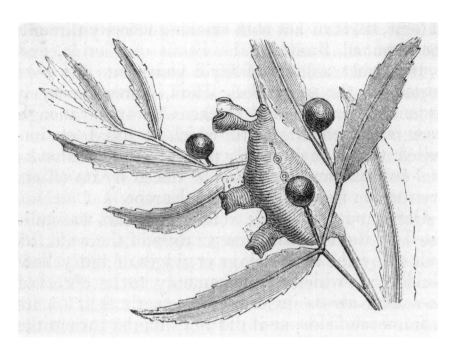

The Scyllaea

mals. Fishes of various kinds crowd around and beneath it, for the sake of preying on the invertebrate creatures that browse on its leaves, or play among its branches. That curious sea-slug, the *Scyllaea,* one of the naked-gilled mollusca, crawls with its narrow grooved foot about the stems, and surprises one with its uncouth, almost shapeless form, and leather-like consistence. But the most vivacious, and therefore the most amusing of the denizens of this floating forest that I found, were the different sorts of crabs and shrimps that abounded in it. Their numbers, their variety, the brilliant hues of many, the peculiarities of structure that fitted them for an ocean-life, the instincts which impelled the strong to prey on the weaker, and the latter to escape, with the watchfulness, cunning, agility, and artful devices continually brought into exercise by both parties in this predatory warfare, afforded an instructive entertainment for many an hour.

It would make this letter far too long, if I were to describe in detail all that was interesting to me as a naturalist. The ocean, like the land, is peculiarly prolific in the manifestations of life, beneath the genial influence of the vernal sun; and in the latitudes which I was now traversing, the forms of animal existence assume astonishing variety and brilliancy. That splendid creature, the coryphene, or dolphin of mariners, was a frequent visitant to our little craft; the spotted rudder-fish, and the purple-banded pilot, were often seen beneath the stern: that strange fish, the remora, would occasionally fasten itself by the curious mechanism of its coronal shield to the vessel's quarter or to the side of some lurking shark, thus taking a ride, like those dishonest boys who jump up behind a passing coach, without expense. Shoals of playful porpoises would gambol round us, and presently troop off in haste, as suddenly as they came, and the direful shark was rarely absent, the constant object of hope and fear to sailors,—hope, that they may catch the shark; fear lest, by any mischance, the shark may catch them. Nor is this fear quite groundless, as an unexpected plunge overboard may at any time occur. One of our crew, attempting to strike a dolphin with the harpoon, had posted himself on the taffrail; but in his eagerness, reaching too far, followed his weapon overboard with a splash. I was surprised to see how little impression he made in the water, though falling from such a height; he did not even go beneath the surface, but fell just as a cork would fall into water. His shipmates gave him the end of a rope and hauled him up, amidst some jokes upon his zeal for fishing; though he looked rather serious about it.

A flying-fish would now and then start from a heaving wave, and skim the surface like a bird upon the wing; and many "feathered fowl" were ready to repay the complimentary visit, by diving into the domain-proper of the fish. The petrels, familiar and confiding, trode the yielding billows, or hovered around our vessel as night came on, to the uneasiness of the seamen, who deemed them the presiding spirits of the coming tempest, though, I am sure, most libellously. These little birds are quite silent by day, except that they sometimes utter a faint chirp; but at night they often make an unpleasant screaming. They are the smallest of web-footed birds, being scarcely so large as a swallow, to which, in their manner of flight, they bear a considerable resemblance.

These little observations, trivial as they were, served to beguile the weariness of the "calm latitudes;" and after we had exercised patience awhile, we were favoured with a fair easterly breeze, which soon freshened, and proved the regular trade-wind. You are aware that on both sides of the equator, within the tropics, the wind constantly blows from the eastward with great regularity; a circumstance which, if Columbus had been acquainted with it, might have materially shortened his voyage, and saved him much anxiety of mind and many a sleepless night.

Borne on the wings of this welcome gale, we soon caught sight of Abaco, one of the Bahamas, which we rapidly passed at about two miles' distance. I looked on this spot with very peculiar feelings; the sight of land after a voyage is always grateful, but these southern islands, with their rich and splendid productions, had ever been clothed in my imagination with a halo that made them fairyland. Then, too, the poetic associations of their history: this was the first group that gladdened the heart of the chivalric WORLD-FINDER,—the first-fruits of that vast continent, which the genius and daring of one master-mind opened to admiring Europe. Here he found the meed of his toils, the recompense of his sufferings; here his mighty spirit triumphed, exulted, in the realization of his fondest dreams, and in that hour he lived a life; and here I looked on the very scene of his glory. I had lived to behold the Bahamas; it was an era in my existence! My eyes were strained to their utmost, that I might lose no constituent of the landscape, and yet "they were not satisfied with seeing." I looked eagerly to see any feature of a tropical landscape, and I was gratified by the sight of some of the palms, a low species, with large, broad leaves, probably one of the fan-palms, as well as some members of the plantain tribe *(Musa)*. The south end of the island is high and precipitous; and there is a very singular rock, which has a large vaulted perforation, like the arch of a bridge; this is called the Hole in the Wall, and as it is a very remarkable place, vessels generally endeavour to "make" it, in entering this part of the Gulf of Mexico. While in sight of this land, two beautiful sloops of war passed us, beating out of the Channel, both of which displayed at the gaff end my own country's flag, that "meteor flag," which has

———"braved a thousand years,
The battle and the breeze."

I gazed on it with pride and pleasure, not having seen it before for nearly three years. A little land-bird flew from one to the other, and then towards us, seemingly seeking a resting-place, but without alighting. I took it to be one of the *Sylviae*. Them and the Hole in the Wall we soon left far behind, as we ran before the freshening "trade," and passing island after island, soon came in sight of the countless little kays, or islets, on the Florida reef. The water on this reef

The Hole in the Wall

is very shoal, which is strongly indicated by its colour; instead of the deep blue tint which marks the ocean, the water here is of a bright pea-green, caused by the nearness of the yellow sands at the bottom; and the shallower the water, the paler is the tint. To me it is very pleasing to peer down into the depths below, especially in the clear water of these southern seas, and look at the many-coloured bottom,—sometimes a bright pearly sand, spotted with shells and corals, then a large patch of brown rock, whose gaping clefts and fissures are but half hidden by the waving tangles of purple weed, where multitudes of shapeless creatures revel and riot undisturbed.

While swiftly gliding over these shoals, we observed many large green turtles (*Chelonia mydas*) swimming on the surface. Some of them appeared to be six feet in length; but they were too wary to allow us to approach nearer than a few yards, diving as we came up to them. But far more numerous were those singularly beautiful *Medusae,* called by seamen the Portuguese men-of-war *(Physalia pelagica)*. Almost all one day we were sailing through a fleet of these little mimic ships, which studded the smooth sea as far as the eye could reach: they were of all sizes, from an inch in length to a foot, or more. I have often seen individuals, in crossing the Atlantic at different times, but never anything approaching such numbers as were here assembled. The animal consists of an oblong transparent membranous bladder, pinched up at the upper part into a kind of rumpled edge; this edge is delicate pink, the bottom is fine blue, and both these colours are gradually blended into the clear membrane, the middle of which is colourless. From one end of the bottom proceeds a large bunch of tentacula, like strings; the middle ones, two or three feet long, hanging down in the water; these are of a brilliant purple hue: these support it in the water, and enable it to regain its upright position when overturned by the sea. The brilliance of the colours varies much, some being only of a pure white. They differ much also in beauty of form: in some the *sail* is merely a narrow ridge or border, in others it rises into a wide and semicircular membrane. The hanging tentacula have, in a very strong degree, the power of stinging the hand of any one who touches them, the effects of which are seriously violent. I think this little fairy creature is one of the most beautiful of the many beautiful things which old Neptune has in his cabinet of curiosities. When floating on the broad wave, its resemblance to a ship in full sail is very striking, and one wonders to see so frail a bark breasting the grim billows, as it would seem that every breaking sea must overwhelm it and dash it to pieces. Yet there it floats most gallantly, and continues to float in spite of wind and wave, now on the lofty crest, now in the deep hollow. Often when passing just under the lee of a vessel, the sudden lull made by the interposition of so great a body between it and the wind, will cause it momentarily to lie flat on the water, instantly resuming its upright position. This "dousing its sails," our sailors delight to consider as an act of homage done to the British flag. I do not believe that it has the power of emptying itself of air and consequently of sinking at pleasure. I have seen them thrown up on a beach, dead as I suppose, and in that state the membrane was not at all collapsed, but as inflated as when floating.

Hitherto, we had kept the trade-wind, and had consequently made rapid progress. We were already within sight of the last kay, or islet, of that long range called the Reef, when the sky began to blacken, and the clouds to gather to the westward, and the wind suddenly flew round to that quarter, and blew with great violence; so we dropped anchor at once, just under some green little islands marked in the charts as Cayo Boca and Cayo Marquess. While lying here, in two fath-

Cayo Boca

oms water, in torrents of rain, the crew were busy fishing, in which they had much success. Some of the fishes they obtained were of great beauty, which I will endeavour to describe. The most numerous kind was a thick-set fish of considerable size, called a groper, covered with olive-coloured irregular spots; the inside of the mouth and throat was of a brilliant vermilion. Another kind, which they called, though by a misnomer, a yellow-tail, had its body marked with longitudinal bands of delicate pink and yellow alternately; the fins were bright yellow, and the tail fine pale crimson. There was another somewhat like this, but much larger, that they denominated a marketfish, of a ruddy silvery tint, with very large scales, the fins and tail bright crimson. Then there was a hog-fish, of singular beauty, shaped somewhat like a perch, with silvery grey scales, the head marked all over with fantastic streaks of brilliant violet blue, like the stripes on a zebra's head. In these tropical seas, even the very fishes, which in our climate are almost universally marked by an unvarying dulness of tint, partake of the same rich and gorgeous colouring, with which nature has delighted to bedeck the insects and birds of these paradisaical groves. These, however, were of the genera *Sparus* and *Labrus;* the sea-breams and wrasses, tribes which might be called the parrots and finches of the finny race, for their gorgeous colours. Still, even here there is deformity; these beauties had the advantage of a foil in the visage of the cat-fish, (*Silurus catus,* LINN.) a monster of remarkably hideous aspect; and in some young sharks, which could not resist the temptation of a baited hook.

For myself, I cannot say I very deeply regretted the delay of our progress, caused by the unpropitious wind; for I entertained hopes, if the rain should abate, to have the gratification of ransacking these little isles, which lay so green and so tantalizing, at about a quarter of a mile distant, just near enough to awaken without gratifying curiosity. But the next morning the sun shone gloriously, and the wind continuing *in statu quo,* even our unimaginative, matter-of-fact captain, proposed to row ashore, and take a peep at Cayo Boca; and I warmly seconded his proposition.

We rowed for a long beach of white sand, and immediately on landing, I ran with eagerness into the bushes armed with my insect-net. I expected to behold a gorgeous display of bright-winged tropical insects, and to make a rich harvest, to provide for which I had loaded myself with boxes. To my disappointment, however, insects were by no means abundant; probably owing to the peculiar nature of the vegetation, which consisted almost wholly of bushes having thick saline leaves, of which there might be a dozen varieties, and a few sedges. The soil was nothing but sand, composed of minute fragments of shells and corals; on close examination, I could not discover a particle of anything else: a great part of the island was overflowed by the sea. I saw *Vanessa orithya* and a little brown *Hesperia*—these were the only butterflies: a few insignificant moths, a small brown *Libellula,* an *Agrion* with blue wings, a large and handsome yellow wasp, a large green locust, an ichneumon, and some *Muscae,* made up the *totale* of the insect population that I met with. I did not see a single coleopterous insect of any species. There were many kinds of birds; among which I recognised the red-winged starling *(Sturnus predatorius),* the same in voice and manners as in Canada, and the king-bird *(Musicapa tyrannus).* The captain said he saw blue and white cranes, (perhaps *Ardea candidissima* and *A. caerulea*), and the willet *(Scolopax semipalmata).* I thought once or twice that I heard the humming-bird, which was not improbable, though I did not see it.

On the beach were many kinds of shells, such as *Pyrula, Leistus, Avicula, Tel-*

lina, Venus, &c., but none of much pretension to beauty of form or colour. A species of *Trochus* was most numerous, very many of which were inhabited by hermit crabs *(Pagurus),* which were thrusting their red claws and antennae out, and crawling about as briskly as bees.

The economy of these creatures is very singular. Unlike the rest of the crab family, the body is soft and unprotected, the head and claws alone being armed with a crustaceous shell; hence our hermit is compelled to have recourse to his wits to supply the deficiency of nature. He resorts to this curious expedient: he seeks along the shore to find an univalve shell, the inhabitant of which is dead, of sufficient capacity to hold his vulnerable body in its recesses, and to afford room to draw his head and claws within the edge upon occasion. It is said he is not easily satisfied; that he turns over, and tries and examines a good many before he can suit himself; and that it is highly amusing, as I am sure it must be, to watch his manoeuvres on such occasions. As he has no power of enlarging his usurped tenement, as its original inhabitant had, it becomes in the course of time too strait for him; he finds himself pinched for room, and looks about as before for one more suitable. He is too wide awake, however, to desert the old one, until he finds a better; he therefore drags it about with him, now slipping out of it to try another then rejecting this and resuming the former, till he perceives a more promising one. At length he finds one of sufficient capacity,—if a little too capacious all the better, it will give him room to grow. He has a strong fleshy finger or hook at his tail, by which he firmly fixes himself in the spire of the shell; and when he draws in his fore parts, he wraps his claws one on the other, and both on his head, in such a manner as to display nothing more than a smooth, hard, shelly surface filling the cavity. He shows fight however sometimes, and can pinch pretty hard.

I observed on the beach some crabs *(Grapsus pictus),* which ran with amazing swiftness. Several kinds of madrepores, corals, and corallines, were thrown up by the tide, and two species of sponge,—one a very large round specimen, a foot in diameter, resembling the common officinal kind, the other crisper and more corally in texture. I spent an hour very pleasantly in these investigations, and was then reluctantly compelled by the captain's anxiety to accompany him on board, soon after which, as the wind had veered a little, we got under way. A white butterfly *(Pontia)* followed us on board, but I could not catch it.

We soon rounded the Tortugas, some half a dozen flat bars of sand, scarcely rising above the surface of the water, one of which has a good lighthouse, and were now fairly in the Gulf of Mexico. Still, however, many tedious days elapsed before our voyage ended, during which little occurred worth noting. Some little feathered visitants came on board to welcome us to their shores, one of which was, I believe, the hermit thrush *(Turdus solitarius),* and another, the American redstart *(Muscicapa ruticilla),* a male of one year old. The latter is a pretty bird; the colours of its plumage, black and bright orange, agreeably contrast with each other. It would fly from side to side and from rope to rope, as if unwilling to leave the vessel; but occasionally it flew off to a long distance, almost out of sight, then would turn round and fly straight back again. After much chasing I caught it in my hand, and while I held it, it manifested great impatience of confinement, squeaking and biting fiercely and violently at my fingers. Of course I let the little creature go, much to the satisfaction of the sailors, who would not give me any assistance in catching it. Sailors in general are very unwilling to molest land-birds that fly on board ships at sea, believing it to be productive of "ill luck." This is not an unpleasing superstition. We had here an instance of the voracity of a shark. A large and beautiful fish shaped like a mackerel, but three feet in length, of a silvery blue tint with opaline changes, called a king-fish, was upon our hook, but while one of the men was drawing it in, a shark seized it, and left deep marks of his serried fangs; it was sadly lacerated all over the body.

Our voyage, even in this domain of the sun, was not wholly made up of cloudless days and spicy breezes. Besides the usual proportion of black squalls and close-reef gales, we encountered one of those terrific storms that are not uncommon in the south. It came on with characteristic rapidity: it had been blowing strong in the afternoon from the S.E.; soon after sunset it lightened freely in the N.W., and the captain considering this as an indication of an approaching gale, every sail was instantly furled except one little rag of a storm-sail. The lightning speedily increased, and before we had our canvas secured, such a storm came on as I had never before witnessed. It was not so much the force of the wind, though it blew heavily, and the shrill gusts shrieked through the naked spars and cordage; but the lightning was terrible. At very short intervals the whole space between heaven and sea was filled with vivid flame, making every rope and spar as plain and distinct as in broadest sunshine, and leaving the eyes obscured in pitchy darkness for four or five seconds after every flash; darkness the most intense and absolute, not that of the night, which was not very dark, but the effect of the blinding glare upon the eye. The thunder was not remarkably heavy, though there were *some* loud explosions. In the height of the gale, the curious electrical appearances called mariner's lights were to be seen on the mast-heads and upper spars, seven or eight at a time. From the deck they looked like dim stars, so much so, that I thought the sky was really becoming clear, and that the stars were appearing in openings between the clouds. The storm lasted an hour or two, and then moderated into a smart breeze, having quickly shifted round to the quarter anticipated.

But soon after this, one fine morning after a good night's run, we saw a long low tongue of land, with some scattered pine-trees on its ridge, and a white light-house at its termination. This was announced to be Mobile Point; two pilot boats were cruising about, from which we took a man and at once passed over the bar. This can only be passed at certain states of the tide, and is always dangerous; the breakers were running on it when we passed. There are several small islands about,—mere low, flat sand-banks, over which the tide runs, but on one of them there is another lighthouse erected. As we passed within a few hundred yards of the point, many specimens of a pretty moth flew on board; they were *Geometrae*, with angular wings, of a rich velvety cream colour, without spots. A very fine individual of the black swallowtail butterfly *(Papilio Asterius)* likewise fluttered about the vessel. Flocks of pelicans *(Pelecanus fuscus)* were flying about, and shoals of dolphins *(Delphinus delphis)* were wallowing and frisking in the water close to the shore. The pilot left us here, and the low point speedily sunk beneath the horizon, as we rapidly ran before a fair breeze up the beautiful bay, which is about thirty miles long. Mobile does not come into view until we are close upon it, being hidden behind a wooded cape or projection, on which is a third lighthouse. But my thoughts of this city, and subsequent adventures, I shall defer to my next, and for the present say, Adieu.

Letter II

Dallas, May 20th, 18—

There is no solitude like that which is felt by him who for the first time walks the streets of a busy city in which he is a total stranger. Crowds of human beings pass by, each possessed of the thoughts, feelings, and affections of a man; yet not one stretches out the hand of friendship, not one bestows a nod of acquaintance, not one gives so much as a glance of recognition. In the gloom of the forest, in the silence of the wilderness, far from human abodes, my heart leaps for joy; there I am not lonely, though alone; there hundreds of objects meet my gaze, with which I have long been accustomed to hold sweet communion.

> "Thanks to the human heart by which we live,
>   Thanks to its tenderness, its joys, and fears;
> To me the meanest flower that blows can give
>   Thoughts that do often lie too deep for tears."

Such thoughts as these obtruded on my mind, as, having landed from the vessel just as day was departing, a time that predisposes to depression, I walked unheeded and unknown through the city of Mobile. These thoughts, however, soon passed off, and gave way to curiosity and surprise. I was struck by an unusual character, a certain something of a foreign appearance, which was forcibly evident, but which I cannot describe, in the streets a little removed from the more commercial part of the city. Perhaps it was owing to the absence of foot-pavements, and to the occurrence of large patches of what looked at a little distance like grass, but consisted only of short weeds very thinly scattered; to the strange trees and plants which shaded the sides, such as the pride of China *(Melia azedarach)*, the honey locust *(Gleditschia triacanthos)*, the fan-palm *(Chamaerops palmetto)*, Adam's needle *(Yucca aloifolia)*, &c.; to the almost universality of open verandas, beneath which the inhabitants were sitting to enjoy the cool breath of evening; or to all these combined, and other causes which escaped my detection.

I was surprised to observe dead horses and cows suffered to lie exposed on the shore, scarce out of the town, a neglect which I should suppose by no means likely in this hot climate to contribute to the health of the inhabitants. The exhalations arising from the extensive muddy flats, which are left uncovered at low water, must likewise be very prejudicial, and probably materially tend to give this town the unhealthy reputation which it possesses. Placed at the mouth of two large rivers, which may be said to drain the whole of the State, and protected by a deep and capacious bay, Mobile may be considered as well situated for commerce; and a flourishing trade exists in cotton, the staple of the State, with Liverpool, London, Havre, and the ports of the northern United States. The shallowness of the water in the bay is, however, a drawback, as vessels above a hundred tons burden cannot come to the town, but are compelled to lie at fifteen or twenty miles' distance, causing great delay in unloading and shipping goods.

Having left all nature still unemerged from the torpor of winter when I departed, and having since spent a tedious period of many weeks on the ocean without any intermission, except that of the brief but pleasant hour spent on Cayo Boca, you will easily understand the enthusiasm with which I embraced the first opening of sunlight the next morning, to hasten into the dense forests which closely environ the town. Everything here was new, scarcely a tree occurred that I was familiar with, and few I can now recollect sufficiently to identify. The magnolias, superb and magnificent as they are, were conspicuous and numerous; the large, glossy, laurel-like leaves gave them a rich and noble appearance, though I saw none of them adorned with the beautiful blossoms for which they are so famous. It may be that I was too late, that the season of flowering was over; for, as I passed up the river, many trees on the banks were richly ornamented with blossoms, especially as I approached the hill country. Large and gorgeously coloured insects hovered over the flowers, or fluttered from bush to bush, in such profusion that I was almost bewildered. I was but scantily furnished with collecting-boxes, and one was no sooner occupied than it had to be emptied, and the former captive rejected for a more tempting prize, until at length I resolved to cease capturing, and content myself with admiring. A handsome locust was numerous in the larva state, of a glossy black, striped longitudinally with showy scarlet. I took a pretty little skipper butterfly which is not figured in Boisduval's splendid "Iconographie;" it is much like *Hesperia malvae,* but still more resembles *H. Proto* of Godart, or *H. Orcus* of Cramer. I observed, in the little pools of dark water by the road-sides and in the woods, numbers of creatures that would dart from the edge into deep water the instant a footstep approached, so quickly that it was almost impossible to catch a glance at their

The Prickly Pear

form. I at length discovered that they were cray-fish *(Astacus americanus),* closely resembling those of our own rivers.

In the waste places around the city, and especially near the shore, the prickly pear *(Opuntia)* grows in large impenetrable thickets. Every one knows the flat, oval, fleshy joints of which this plant is composed, each growing out of the edge of another, and each studded with tufts of bristling spines. Flowers and fruits were both numerous; the latter unripe, indeed, yet sufficiently attractive, from their plump contour and purple hue, to tempt me to essay the taste of one. In a moment I regretted my rashness, for my tongue and lips were filled with fine barbed spines, which continually worked farther in, and gave great pain. One by one, however, I contrived to tear them out, or break them off, but not till I had thoroughly learned the need of caution in eating prickly pears.

As I had no acquaintance in Mobile, I took the first opportunity of proceeding to the mountainous part of the State, to which I had introductions. The same day, therefore, I took passage on board one of the fine high-pressure steamers that throng the Mobile wharves, to go up the Alabama river.

It was evening when we left the city; from which the course of the river winds for many miles through a flat marshy country, and is bordered on each side by a broad belt of reeds, which grow thick and strong out of the very water. By day I suppose this appearance would be unpleasing; but the gloom of night, limiting the view to a few yards around us, and making visible the beautiful fireflies which danced and crawled about the reeds in myriads, or made interrupted lines of radiance as they flew like shooting stars through the air, made the scene one of romantic and high gratification. By and by, we come into more uneven ground, where the high banks reflect a black shadow on the smooth water, seeming to contract the broad river to a brook; the calm, mirror-like surface, unruffled by a zephyr, gives back the light of each individual star; and now and then, as we round some point, a bright red glare, with its watery reflection, suddenly and unexpectedly bursts upon our gaze from the beacon-fire of some woodyard, casting a broad illumination on the opposite bank, which has a startling and poetic effect; while the hoarse and hollow booming of the steam, occurring at regularly measured intervals, seems not out of keeping with the general solemnity of the scene. The busy hum and bustle of the vessel gradually subsided into quietness; but long after all the rest of the passengers had retired to rest, to whom I suppose the scene presented not the charm of novelty, I continued on deck with unabated delight; and when I retired, it was not to sleep, for I could not avoid sitting up in bed, and gazing, through the open window of my berth, on the placid beauty of the night.

At early day, too, I found it delightful to stand alone on the upper deck, and watch the opening morning. It was yet dawn; stillness and quiet prevailed, the decks were yet untrodden, the noise of the day was yet hushed, the bats and the whip-poor-wills were still sweeping over the stream in tortuous flight, both engaged in the same vocation, the pursuit of crepuscular insects. The breadth of wing and rushing flight of the latter deceived me for some time into the notion that they were large swallows; the bat, though of swift wing, had no chance whatever in a race with them. As the eastern sky began to glow and brighten into fiery red, they gradually disappeared, the bats being the first to retire. Soon the sun, with dilated face, peeped over the horizon in cloudless majesty, and flushed with golden light the hills and cultivated fields that surrounded us; but as yet the air was delightfully cool and refreshing, and perfumed with the breath of flowers, which after a while was dissipated by the increasing heat. The river was smooth, and shone like silver, until its surface was broken and swollen by the rushing steamer: before us we had a polished surface, reflecting a cloudless sky; behind us we left a rolling sea, enshrouded beneath a long sable cloud of dense smoke.

Nor was the day without pleasure, though we passed no towns, and very few settlements, at least during the daylight: occasionally we stopped to replenish our stock of wood, which is cut, split, and corded, at certain stations by negroes residing at them; these stations are called wood-yards. The moment the steamer stops, the crew begin to bring the wood on board on their shoulders, and it is astonishing to observe how quickly the great piles are transferred, and we are again on our roaring and rushing course. Here and there we open on some large cleared estate, and fields planted with corn or cotton, as yet scarcely appearing above ground, and perhaps a single negro-hut; but the planters' houses and the general buildings of the farm do not appear, they being situated at a considerable distance from the margin. Every spring the river overflows its banks, and inundates the surrounding country to a wide extent. Of this I saw sufficient traces, though the water had now returned to its wonted channel: high up, on the trees which overhung the water, the branches were incumbered with rubbish that had been left there by the spring flood, and which showed the great extent to which the river had been swollen. In one tree was the carcase of a cow that had probably been drowned in the freshets, and having become entangled among the forked boughs, had been deposited in the odd situation in which I saw it. In general the banks are clothed with tall forests to the water's edge; trees arrayed in all shades of green, of various height and form, some covered with glorious flowers, suddenly appeared and as swiftly vanished, a constantly shifting panorama. Many trees had their tangled roots all exposed by the washing away of the soil from beneath them, others were prostrate in the stream from the op-

Wood-yard on the Alabama

eration of the same cause; sometimes a pretty wooded island appeared, cleaving the stream with its shore of bright yellow sand; now the river expanded into a silvery lake, then narrowed to a gorge, between beetling precipices of limestone rising perpendicularly to the height of several hundred feet.

I was surprised to observe so exceedingly little of animal life: scarcely a single insect (except the fireflies) was to be seen during the whole voyage up, and very few birds. The depth of the forest is not favourable to the development of animal existence; the edges of the woods, or open plains, where light is abundant, where flowers bloom, and herbs seed, are the resorts of birds and insects; and on this account, these charming visitants are found to swarm when man has made a clearing, even in the spot where before scarcely an individual could have been found. A few I saw: the blue heron *(Ardea caerulea),* with double neck and stretched-out legs, slowly flapped his great wings, in his heavy flagging flight from shore to shore; the belted kingfisher *(Alcedo alcyon)* shot along with a harsh rattling laugh, or sitting on some low projecting branch, suddenly plunged headlong into the water beneath, and instantly emerged with his prey; the wood-duck *(Anas sponsa)* flew shyly along the margin, close to the water, beneath the overhanging bushes; now and then we overtook a water-tortoise *(Emys)* swimming at the surface, his body submerged, poking up his head at intervals with a timid curiosity, to see what all the noise was about.

There is perhaps no river so winding as the Alabama. The boat's head is turned towards every point of the compass, and that often within the space of a few minutes: sometimes we may make a run of fifty miles, and be then within three miles of where we were at first. Indeed, at the place where I am now residing, which is about six miles in a direct line from the river, I have been assured that the booming of a steamer's engine will sometimes be heard in the morning, and continue to be audible at intervals for a great part of the day; the vessel having been, perhaps, at no time more than twenty miles distant, in a course of many hours.

It is pleasant to meet another boat in the river, especially in a part of the low country where the course is very tortuous: to catch the faint black line of smoke upon the sky, across the fields and marshes; after an interval to see it again, and faintly hear the roaring of the steam; then again to lose both sight and sound, and again and again to perceive both, gradually becoming more and more plainly perceptible; till at length she bursts into open view round some wooded point, rushes by in her majesty with her freight of human life, and, scarcely giving time to read her name broadly painted on her wheel-boxes, is instantly hidden beneath the black cloud of her own smoke.

Owing to the great number of turns which the river makes, it was not until the second morning that we arrived at King's Landing, having been two nights and one day performing a distance which, in a direct line, is not more than a hundred and twenty miles. Every extensive planter whose estate borders on the river, has what is called a *landing;* that is, a large building to contain bales of cotton; and if the bank be precipitous, as it is in this instance, flights of wide steps leading to the summit, and a slide formed of planks reaching from the warehouse above to the water beneath. When cotton is to be shipped, the steamer is moored beneath the slide, the bale is rolled to the top, and down it shoots with an impetus that would send it across the deck far into the river, were not its impulse deadened by bales already on the deck; and even thus, when a row of bales receives the communicated force, I have seen the outmost one shot into the water, on the same principle that a billiard-ball in motion will impinge upon one at rest, and send it spinning along while itself ceases to move. Here, then, was

I landed an hour before dawn; my trunks placed on the lowest step; and away went the vessel to her destination further up the river.

I was quite alone, knowing neither the place nor the inhabitants; but I was told that I should find a path on the top of the cliff, which would lead me to the manager's house, and that the estate of a gentleman with whom I had some acquaintance lay about ten miles distant. I have said that I was alone, and it was quite dark; but I groped my way for about a quarter of a mile through the lofty forest, and came upon a clearing like a farm-yard, in which were several houses close together. I made my way to the door of one (while a rascally cur kept up a most pertinacious barking), and knocked and shouted loudly to no purpose. I shouted again, the echoes died away, and again all was still. I then tried another house, and was at length answered by the cracked voice of a negro woman within. I told my business, that I had landed from the steamer, and was on my way to Pleasant-hill, and requested her to get up. I had been informed that lodging and refreshments were to be obtained here. A few minutes passed, and no sign of getting up, when again I shouted, and received the same answer,—"Sar? Iss, Sar." At last, after much exercise of patience, the old woman got up, and went to another house, and began to call—"Mas' James! Mas' James!" but Master James was still less inclined to turn out than the sable lady herself had been, and for a long time either could not or would not understand what was desired of him. All this, everything being so perfectly new to me, was more amusing than vexatious; it was not at all cold, and no inconvenience arose from remaining in the balmy air. When Master James tardily opened his castle door, rubbing his eyes, yet not half awake, I found that this lad, a boy of twelve years, son of the manager, was, with the exception of the negro maid, the only person on the premises. He tumbled into bed again, while she raked among the ashes and got me some breakfast, by which time it was daylight. My luggage remained all this time on the steps at the river's marge, perfectly free from risk, so lonely was the spot, until at daylight Master James blew his conch long and loudly to call the people; and soon a dozen "*black fellers*" appeared with their mules, to whom having given orders about my trunks, I set out for the country.

In the yard were some towering oaks, on which several Fox Squirrels *(Sciurus capistratus)* were frisking and leaping from bough to bough with great animation. A pair of the beautiful Summer Red-bird *(Tanagra aestiva)* were also chasing each other about the same trees. Though this is a gaily dressed little fellow, I don't think him so handsome as his congener, the Scarlet Tanager *(Tanagra rubra);* the fine contrast between the vermilion body and the jet black wings and tail of the latter pleases me more than the uniform scarlet coat of the former. Both, however, look very beautiful, as they play in the sun, among the quivering green leaves. With the day before me, I was not disposed to hurry on my journey, especially as so many charming things were every instant catching my attention, and enchaining my observation. Butterflies became abundant, especially the very beautiful little Hairstreaks *(Thecla),* species of great delicacy and beauty, whose hind wings end in one or two lengthened tags.* They are frisky little creatures, very fond of chasing each other through the air, and tumbling about with surprising quickness of evolution. When at rest, they often rub the surfaces of the hind wings upon each other, up and down alternately, and after a flight often return, like the flycatchers among birds, to the same spot from whence they departed; a projecting twig, or the topmost leaf of a bush. They were chiefly of one species *(Thecla falacer,* Boisd.), accompanied by several *Polyommati.* I did not find the *Theclae* numerous anywhere, but at that particular spot near King's landing.

Beautiful flowers, of varied colours and fragrant perfume, thronged the edges of the forest, and the road-sides: especially in the corners of the fences, which are almost wholly made of rails set up in the zig-zag fashion so general in the north, commonly called a Virginia fence. In the angles of these fences, there is always a dense and rank mass of vegetation; and many handsome flowers attain a luxuriance there which is not seen elsewhere. The beautiful Scarlet Woodbine *(Caprifolium sempervirens)* grew in profuse splendour among the bushes, its flowers being no less remarkable for fragrance than for elegance of form, and brilliancy of colour. I found that it possessed attractions not only for man; for, having gathered a spike, it was visited, even while in my hand, by a fine yellow Butterfly *(Colias Eubule,* Boisd.), which instantly began probing the deep tubular blossoms with its sucker; so eager was it to gratify its appetite, that without any trouble I caught it in my fingers.

Many romantic spots occurred in the course of my walk, especially where some little brook crossed the road, making, where it emerged from and again entered the forest, pretty shady glens, so sombre with the bushes, whose over-

*See engraving on p. 61.

arching tops touched each other overhead, and whose verdant and leafy branches seemed like an impenetrable wall, that the rays of an almost vertical sun were effectually shut out.

In these cool retreats—and I saw several such—the Emerald Virgin Dragon-fly (*Agrion Virginica*) delights to dwell. All the Dragon-fly tribe, as they are water-insects in their first stages, are observed to prefer hawking in the vicinity of water, as affording in abundance the prey which they pursue; but the open pond, or broad river, is most generally their resort. But he who would see the Emerald Virgin, must go to some such hidden brook as I have described; over which as it flows silently, in a deep soft bed of moss of the richest green, or brawls over a pebbly bottom, with impotent rage, three or four of these lovely insects may be seen at almost any hour on any summer-day. It is, indeed, a fly of surpassing elegance and beauty; the male especially, whose long and slender body is of a metallic green, so refulgent that no colour can convey an idea of it. This green hue becomes a deep blue, if held so as to reflect the rays of light falling on it, at a very obtuse angle,—a property common to the green hue of many insects, and some birds. The eyes are glossy, round and prominent; the wings broad, filmy, and minutely netted, of an uniform purplish black. The female might easily be supposed to be of a different species: it is much duller in colour, the body being nearly black, having little of the bright green reflection; the wings are browner, and they are all marked with a rhomboidal white stigma, near the tip, which is wholly wanting in the male. Their mode of flight is graceful, but rather slow, so that they are easily captured; and they will not leave these their favourite haunts, even though pursued. I have no doubt they are born and die within the limited space of a few yards.

The refreshing coolness of these wild woodland bowers was so tempting that I could not resist taking refuge in them from the burning heat without; and thus I contracted an acquaintance with these "demoiselles." I encountered a stream, however, of higher pretensions—Mush-creek—which I crossed by means of a very primitive bridge, the trunk of a tall forest-tree, which had been cut down so as to fall across. On this tree, basking in the sun, lay a large snake, of a dusky brown hue, about four feet in length, which, on my disturbing it, instantly plunged into the middle of the stream, and dived to the bottom. As the water was turbid, I saw no more of it. It was, no doubt, the species commonly called the Copper-belly (*Coluber porcatus,* Bosc.), which is numerous, but harmless. I afterwards observed a snake, probably of the same species, swimming swiftly in a clear stream, close to the surface, but entirely submerged; occasionally it stopped, protruding its head and neck above the surface to look about.

In the fields of some large estates through which the road led, I saw for the first time, negro-slaves performing the labours of agriculture. They were ploughing between rows of cotton, which was just appearing above ground. The ploughs appeared to me to be rude and ineffective, the share doing little more than scratching the soil: each was drawn by a single mule.

It was revolting to me to observe women engaged in this laborious occupation, whose clothing—if the sordid rags which fluttered about them deserve the name—was barely sufficient for the claims of decency. Poor wretches! whose lot is harder than that of their brute companions in labour! for they have to perform an equal amount of toil, with the additional hardships of more whipping and less food. But perhaps you will say that I am not yet competent to speak on this subject:—perhaps I am not, therefore I defer it till a longer residence here has given me opportunities of more mature observation.

To return, then, to the wild and the free: within a neglected pasture-field lay the carcase of a hog, which already diffused far and wide an odour anything but delectable. On this delicate morsel a pair of those obscene but useful vultures, the Turkey Buzzards *(Cathartes aura),* were regaling themselves; but, on my approach, they threw out their sable wings, and, lazily rising, flew slowly and heavily to a neighbouring tree, where, out of danger, they could still keep their banquet in view, and from whence they doubtless descended as soon as the coast was clear.

Both raspberries *(Rubus idaeus)* and strawberries *(Fragaria Virginiana)* I found ripe on the banks beside the road; but I understand they are now going out of season. I was the more pleased to see them, as being old acquaintances, and reminding me of the north.

Beguiled by these not very important but pleasing observations, a few only of which I have attempted to recount to you, rendered tenfold more interesting by the charm of absolute novelty that attended everything here, the day waned away unperceived. When I arrived at the hospitable mansion of my friend, the afternoon was considerably advanced; and I found that I had accomplished the tortoise-pace of one mile per hour. Here, however, I am at length, writing to you these rough notes of my woodland ramble. If it afford you half as much pleasure to read it as it afforded me to walk it, I shall feel well repaid. I regret that I had not arrived here a couple of months earlier; the opening of the spring is the most interesting season of the year, when, after a suspension, more or less absolute, of activity and life, all nature springs into fresh existence: the gate of Eden is, as it were, re-opened, and birds, insects, and flowers, renew their Creator's praise. I can well believe that the hunter's boast to his mistress is scarcely exaggerated:—

> "When our wide woods and mighty lawns
>   Bloom to the April skies,
> The earth has no more gorgeous sight
>   To show to human eyes." —Bryant

The commencement of this activity I have unfortunately missed: I have come in the very height of the spring, if it be not already verging into summer. However, be it mine to notice what still remains to be observed, instead of regretting that which is past, and which cannot be recalled.

Letter III

Dallas, June 1, 18—

You are aware that my intention in coming south was to open a school. Schools here generally are not private enterprises, as in the old country, but the ordinary mode of procedure is as follows. Some half-dozen planters of influence meet and agree to have their children educated together, each stipulating the number of pupils to be sent, and the proportion of expense to be borne, by himself. These form a board of trustees, who employ a master at a fixed salary, and, though they allow others to send their children at a certain rate, are yet personally responsible for the whole amount in the respective proportions of their stipulated subscriptions. I found no difficulty in obtaining an engagement of this kind, and have undertaken, at a liberal remuneration, the charge of about a dozen "young ideas." My schoolroom is a funny little place, built wholly of round, unhewn logs, notched at the ends to receive each other, and the interstices filled with clay; there is not a window, but, as the clay has become dry, it has dropped or been punched out of many of these crevices, so that there is no want of light and air, and the door, hung on wooden hinges, and furnished with a wooden latch, scarce needs the latter, for it remains open by night as well as day. The desks are merely boards, *split,* not sawn, out of pine logs, unhewn and unplaned, which slope from the walls, and are supported by brackets. The forms are split logs, with four diverging legs from the round side, the upper side being made tolerably straight with the axe. Some wooden pegs, driven into auger holes in the logs, receive hats, &c. A neat little desk, at which I write, and a chair on which I sit, are the only exceptions to the primitive rudeness of all our furniture, and the pupils are, mostly, as rude as the house,—real young hunters, who handle the long rifle with more ease and dexterity than the goose-quill, and who are incomparably more at home in "twisting a rabbit," or "treeing a 'possum," than in conjugating a verb. But more of them when I get better acquainted with them.

The situation of the school is singularly romantic; a space of about a hundred yards square has been cleared in the forest, with the exception of two or three lofty oaks which are left for shade. On every side we are shut in by a dense wall of towering forest trees, rising to the height of a hundred feet or more. Oaks, hickories, and pines of different species extend for miles on every hand, for this little clearing is made two or three miles from any human habitation, with the exception of one house about three quarters of a mile distant. Its loneliness, however, is no objection with me, as it necessarily throws me more into the presence of free and wild nature. At one corner a narrow bridle-path leads out of this "yard," and winds through the sombre forest to the distant high road. A nice spring, cool in the hottest day of summer, rises in another corner, and is protected and accumulated by being inclosed in four sides of a box, over the edges of which the superfluous water escapes, and, running off in a gurgling brook, is lost in the shade of the woods. To this "lodge in the vast wilderness," this "boundless contiguity of shade," I wend my lonely way every morning, rising to an early breakfast, and arriving in time to open school by eight o'clock.

Such a morning walk in such a clime, at such a season, you may easily imagine is not performed without multitudes of objects to catch the eye and delight the mind of an observant naturalist. A cloudy day seems to be almost an anomaly; and, even by the time the sun is two hours high, his rays are oppressively hot, scorching one's back and head like a fire; yet there is a freshness in the morning air in the woods, while the dews are exhaling, which is delightfully pleasant. Many birds which, during the heat of the day, are sitting among the thick branches of the "piny woods," with open beaks, as if panting for breath, are at this early hour busily hopping about the fences and roads, and trilling forth their sweet melody. But stay; suppose you just transport yourself (in imagination) to Alabama, and spend the day with me. I will be your *cicerone,* will point out to you all the birds and insects, and tell you "all about 'em;" and, as Hood's school-boy says, "I'll show you the wasp's nest, and everything that can make you comfortable."

Well, then, here I receive you at old Buddy Bohanan's gate, and am very glad to see you. Walk in; we are just going to breakfast, though it is but six o'clock. The "nigger wenches" have brought in the grilled chicken and the fried pork, the boiled rice, and the homminy.—"Hold!" you say, "what is homminy?" Ah! I forgot you were a stranger; homminy, then, be informed, is an indispensable dish at the table of a southern planter, morning, noon, and night. Indian corn is broken into pieces by pounding it in a mortar to a greater or less degree of fineness, as coarse or fine homminy is preferred, and this is boiled soft like rice, and eaten with meat.

Here is another article of southern cookery with which I presume you are un-acquainted,—*woffles*. You see they are square thin cakes, like pancakes, divided on both sides into square cells by intersecting ridges: but how shall I describe to you the mode in which they are cooked? At the end of a pair of handles, moving on a pivot like a pair of scissors, or still more like the net forceps of an entomolo-gist, are fixed two square plates of iron like shallow dishes, with cross furrows, corresponding to the ridges in the cakes; this apparatus, called a woffle-iron, is made hot in the fire; then, being opened, a flat piece of dough is laid on one, and they are closed and pressed together; the heat of the iron does the rest, and in a minute the woffle is cooked, and the iron is ready for another.* They are very good, eaten with butter; sometimes they are made of the meal of Indian corn (as so little wheat is grown here as to make wheat-flour be considered almost a luxury), but these are not nearly so nice, at least to an English palate. Neither is "Indian bread," which you will see at every table; this, too, is made of corn meal; it is coarse and gritty, does not hold together, having so little gluten; yet this is eaten with avidity by the natives, rich and poor, and even preferred to the finest wheaten bread. Such is the force of habit in modifying or creating tastes. I have somewhere read of a gentleman who had been brought up on the sea-coast of Scotland, where a species of seaweed is commonly eaten; and such was the taste which he had acquired for it, that in after-life, when residing far away, he was in the habit of procuring this weed to be transmitted to him, from a great distance, as an indispensable article of his diet.

The little negro-boy, who has a bunch of peacock's feathers in his hand, which he continually waves over the food, and over every part of the table, is appointed to keep off the flies, as these insects are so numerous here that they would other-wise settle on the food and spoil it. But I beg your pardon; while I am talk-ing, you are eating nothing. Be bold; though strange, you'll find it all good. For drink, here is coffee, new milk, sour milk, and buttermilk,—the last two are great favourites, but I dare say you, like myself, will decline them both: the sour milk is thick, and eaten with a spoon, so that perhaps I was wrong in call-ing it drink. Tea is almost unknown; coffee is the staple for morning and eve-ning meals. Here, too, is honey, fresh taken from the "gum," and here are vari-ous kinds of "preserves."

*I believe both the article and the name claim a Dutch parentage.

No more? I fear novelty has taken away your appetite; but, however, if you have really done, we will be going. I will just get my butterfly net and be with you; I always carry it.

Yonder is the chief of our feathered songsters, the leader of the American orchestra,—the far famed Mocking-bird *(Turdus polyglottus).* He is hopping about the rails of the fence, playing at bopeep, sometimes on this side, sometimes on the other, with great activity and animation. Probably his nest is not far off, for he is by no means shy of building around the homestead. His colours, black, white, and grey, are strikingly and elegantly disposed; but his voice is his transcendent recommendation. He does not choose to let us hear his melody just now, but it is ravishingly sweet, and though I am not competent myself to assert, yet good judges have asserted, that it is fully equal, if not superior, to that of the nightingale; like which it is often heard charming the still hour of night.

I see you are surprised at the rustling noise and motion that occurs among the dry leaves on either side, at almost every step. It is caused by the nimble feet of little lizards, which dart along like lightning as we approach, to the shelter of the nearest log or stone, under which they may hide: they move so quickly that it is very seldom we can catch a glance of their bodies; we trace them only by their motion and their sound. There are three or four species, the most common of which is called, by a strange misnomer, the Scorpion *(Agama undulata);* and it is this species which so rapidly scuttles along under the crisped leaves. It is about six inches long, of which half is tail: above, it is greyish, with darker bands; underneath it is palish, with a patch of bright blue under the throat, larger in some (I think, males) than in others. It is covered with prominent scales, each having a sharp ridge, which gives it a rough appearance. They are very abundant, and may be often seen chasing each other about some old log, running by little starts, now on the top, now on the sides, and now on the bottom, it being all the same whether the back be upward or downward. Though perfectly harmless, it has the reputation of being highly poisonous, which has probably given rise to its ominous name.

But swift as is this species, it is surpassed by another kind *(Tachydromus sexlineatus),* a lizard of great beauty, appropriately called the Fast-runner. It is by no means so common as the "scorpion," but the boys struck and killed one the other day, which they brought to me. It is slender, but about nine inches long, of which the tail is more than six. The body is dark brown, with a palish stripe down the back; three lines of bright yellow run down longitudinally on each side, and a fourth reaches from the head to the foreleg, passing through the ear; the stripes become indistinct on the tail: the under parts are white.

I laid this specimen on the window-sill of my chamber, in the evening, about fifteen feet from the ground; and in the morning found a black line extending from it to the earth all down the wall, formed by innumerable ants of a very minute species, and my lizard almost wholly devoured. These insects must have had very acute perceptions, to discover prey at so great a distance; or else, as is more probable, there must have been intelligible communications made from the one who perhaps accidentally discovered the food to others, and from them in succession to the whole multitude.

Since I am speaking of ants, I may mention another instance of their voracity: I had several caterpillars and chrysalids that I was rearing in a breeding-box: on opening it the other day, to my chagrin I found it occupied by a legion of these little black ants, which had killed all but one chrysalis, and partially devoured them. My preserved specimens of insects I find almost impossible to secure from them: they find them out in the store-boxes, even when these are inclosed in a trunk; and making their way through the keyhole, or beneath the lid, commit great havoc. The only effectual resource is to imbue each insect, as soon as killed, with a solution of corrosive sublimate; after which the ants will not touch it.

There is a Hare, or Rabbit, as everybody here calls it *(Lepus Americanus);* and indeed, in size and appearance, it is so much like our own rabbit, that it does seem rather unnatural to call it a hare, though perhaps the latter term is more strictly correct. It is a timid little creature, but rather curious withal. On our approach it runs a little way into the woods with erected scut, then suddenly stops, turns round, stands up on its legs, and, straining its long ears forward, gazes at us, then runs a few yards further, and again turns, till, having satisfied its curiosity, it hurries away to some hollow tree, creeps in at the little hole at the bottom, and there considers itself safe from its many adversaries, little dreaming of the hunter's twisting-stick. The young ones are very pretty, innocent-looking little things; one was brought in the other day by one of the children, who found it in the woods; it nestled in my bosom so confidingly, that I felt sorry it had been caught, and so let it run again.

The twisting-stick I mentioned just now is a curious mode of taking furred animals out of hollow trees, logs, and similar places. I lately saw it put into operation, but do not desire ever to witness it again. A hunter's dog had tracked and driven a rabbit to his hole in the bottom of a hollow hickory-tree. As the hole was too small to admit the hand with convenience, the negroes were set to cut down the tree, which was soon effected. When it fell they watched the butt to see that the rabbit did not run out; but it did not make its appearance. The hunter then got some long slender switches, and, probing the hollow, found that the rabbit was at the further end, several feet up the trunk. He now commenced turning the switch round in one direction a great many times, until the tip of it had become so entangled in the animal's fur as to bear a strong pull. He then began to pull steadily out, but the rabbit held on as well as it could, crying piteously, like a child. At length, however, it was pulled down; but the skin, which in these animals is very tender, was so much torn that it was quite painful to behold it. Almost all kinds of hunting, being accompanied with torture to the poor animals pursued, must be considered cruel; but this mode struck me as more than ordinarily barbarous and shocking.

Let us stop here awhile. Here are several species of butterflies, revelling, with multitudes of bees, wasps, and other insects, on the thick beds of Hore-hound (*Marrubium vulgare*), which abounds on each side of the road, and which is now in full blossom, and on the singular, but beautiful disks of the Passion-flower (*Passiflora caerulea*), which trails its long stems, and entwines its tendrils over the ground. Here is a very handsome kind, the Zebra Swallow-tail (*Papilio Ajax*). This beautiful butterfly is remarkable for the elegance of its shape, and the unusual length of the tails of the hinder wings, which sometimes project an inch and a quarter beyond the wing, although the butterfly is rather small for a *Papilio*. It is marked with alternate transverse bands of black and yellowish white, with a spot of bright scarlet, and three azure crescents on the hind pair. The under surface has two scarlet spots, and a band of the same colour. The larva is said to feed on the Swamp Papaw (*Anona palustris*). The chrysalis is short and thick, shaped almost like the body of a pig, with a sharp thorax. Its colour is dusky brown, with pale lines.

And there are no less than three species of *Colias,* all pretty: one is of a bright saffron-yellow, with a common black border, unspotted—the Black-bordered Yellow (*C. Nicippe*). This is numerous in gardens, particularly in the morning. That large one now resting on a flower, opening its brilliant wings to the sun, is the Black-based Yellow (*C. Caesonia*). It is a strikingly-marked species, the

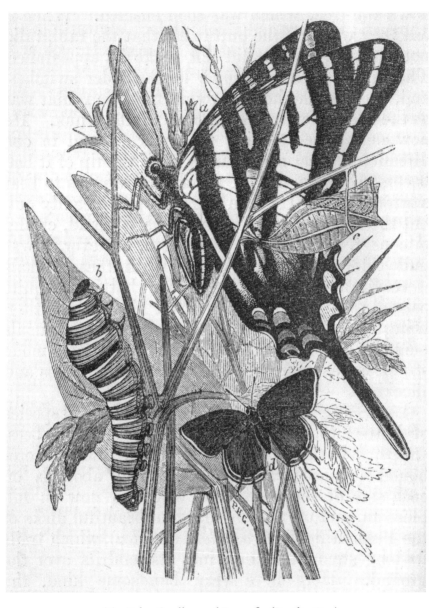

a. The Zebra Swallow-tail Butterfly *(Papilio Ajax)*
b. Its Caterpillar
c. Its Chrysallis
d. The Red-striped Hairstreak *(Thecla Pöeas)*
The flower is the Indian Pink *(Spigelia Marylandica)*

sulphur-yellow contrasting well with the broad border and basal cloud of deep black. Each wing has a silvery spot in the centre of the under surface, on which side the black is altogether wanting. And this pigmy, whose wings are scarcely more than half an inch in length, is the Black-banded Yellow *(C. Diara);* it is of the same sulphur-yellow as the last, with a black tip, and a broad band of the same running along parallel to the inner margin of the fore wings. The caterpillars of these butterflies have generally much resemblance to each other, being green, with white or yellow stripes; and the chrysalids, which in this genus are suspended by a girdle of silk around the thorax, as well as by the anal button, are like the larvae in colour.

But we will go on:—look at that conspicuous tree standing out from the edge of the woods just at the corner of two roads. It is a blasted chestnut; its bark has long fallen off, and left its limbs to bleach and dry in the summer sun. On the very topmost branch sits a Brown Thrush, or French Mocking Bird *(Turdus rufus).* Nearly every morning as I pass, I see him on that very twig; I have no doubt it is the same individual. Look at him, and listen to his warbling: in my opinion he is one of the sweetest of our songsters; I generally pay him the compliment of standing a few moments to hear him. Does he not seem in earnest, and full of enjoyment, with his broad tail spread like a fan and bent under the bough, his head elevated, and his spotted throat quivering with song, as he pours out his morning hymn of praise? He is fond of singing from an elevated point like this; but does not seem to frequent the shade of the woods.

Now we are going through a belt of stunted pine woods, mixed, however, with some hard-wood trees of slender growth: here the beautiful Cardinal Grosbeak *(Fringilla cardinalis)** delights to haunt. We hear its singular whistle on each side of us—"whit, whit, whit, whit," and there we catch sight of its brilliant plumage. Is he not a charming fellow? Look at his bright scarlet body, wings, and tail, his coal-black face and red beak, and his fine conical crest, now erect, and now lying flat: with what vivacity he hops from bough to bough, his glowing colour flashing out like a coal of fire among the sombre pine shades, then again hidden from sight; he cannot be still an instant. His vocal efforts are not confined to this monotonous whistle: that clear and loud song which we hear proceeding from the depth of the woods, and which, though not equal to that of the thrush, is yet

*See engraving on p. 67.

Ringlet Butterflies
a. The Blue-eyed Ringlet *(Hipparchia Alope)*
b. The Dusky Argus *(Hipparchia Eurythris)*
c. The Blind Argus *(Hipparchia Sosybius)*

highly melodious, is uttered by the Cardinal. Being easily raised, they are often caged, and are great favourites. Close to the school-house I know of the nest of a Cardinal, which I will show you by and by. It is in a young tree, about six feet from the ground, not very artfully concealed: there are two eggs in it, which are nearly as large as those of the quail. They are whitish, covered with brown spots.

See the little dusky butterflies characteristically called "Browns," dancing along in their peculiar jerking way, just over the tops of the bushes; they much resemble their congeners, the Meadow-butterflies *(Hipparchiae)* of our own country. They chiefly affect the glades and lanes of the woods, being not very often seen in the clearing; sometimes, however, they come into our gardens of a morning, but then they fly along close to the ground, beneath the shrubs, and in the shelter of the fence, as if shade were more congenial to their feelings than sunshine. Perhaps, as there is a correspondence and a harmony in all the divine works, there may be a reference to these retiring habits in the dull tint common to the tribe, and the want of those glowing colours so general among butterflies.

These are both small species; one is the Dusky Argus *(Hipparchia Eurythris)*, with two double-pupilled eyes in each fore wing, and one on each hind wing, besides a very minute eye in the angle of the latter; beneath, the hind wings have four eyes. The smaller of the two is the Blind Argus *(H. Sosybius)*, of which the upper surface is spotless brown, the under handsomely marked with a numerous series of eyes near the margin, and two transverse dark lines.

Ha! what have we here, crawling on your back? An intruder with whose acquaintance you may well dispense. It is a Tick *(Ixodes Americanus)*, and a singular subject it is. The trivial name, *Americanus*, is but a poor distinction, for two species at least, much resembling each other in size, form, colour, and habits, are common here. They are both flat, about one-eighth of an inch in diameter, of a dark reddish brown, but one has a white spot on the back and is round, while the other is oval. On the first day that I spent at my school, I was surprised by a violent twinge in my breast, just like the sting of a wasp, yet I could feel nothing with my fingers: the pain continuing, I examined beneath my clothes, and found one of these rascally ticks, with his rostrum so firmly imbedded in the flesh, that it was only after repeated efforts that I succeeded in pulling him off. Since then, scarce a day elapses without other polite attentions of the same kind, but I am informed this is nothing to what I may expect in a month or two, when the "seed-ticks" come about.

Look into the woods, in this direction:—yonder are two wild Turkeys *(Meleagris gallopavo)*, the finest bird that America has produced. Let us go nearer; we shall easily find the path again. They are both hens and have young, their alarm and anxiety for which cause them to make that loud calling, and to run round and round as if bereft of their senses. They are not eaten at this season, being very poor: no doubt if we could examine those, we should find them little but bones and feathers, and even of the latter no great quantity, the breast and belly being totally bare from sitting. If you will come a little way further into the forest, I will show you a very curious contrivance for taking turkeys. It is called a pen, and it is a common and very successful trap: this one was set up, "fixed," by some of my schoolboys in the winter, but it is not baited in summer, when the bird is not in season. It consists of an inclosure about ten feet square, made with rails resting on each other at the corners, covered also by rails. A hole or passage is dug, leading from some distance outside to the midst of the pen, under the bottom rail, the part next the rails, within the pen, being covered with a board, or

Turkey-pen

with sticks. Corn is then scattered around the hole and within the pen: the turkeys follow the corn, eating as they go, until they get into the pen; when, finding themselves inclosed, they endeavour to get out, running round and round, looking for an opening above, but are so stupid that they never think of getting out at the hole by which they got in, but remain there, until the hunter comes, who goes in and knocks them on the head. Many are sometimes taken at once in this way. I saw yesterday a number of eggs that had been taken from the nest of a wild Turkey; they were larger than hens' eggs, and rounder, but not so large as I should have expected from the size of the bird: their colour was drab, or pale brown, with darker dots.

But here we approach the august vicinity of that seat of learning, of which the presidential chair is occupied by your humble servant. This, Sir, is our "seminary," our "academy," our "establishment," our "*alma mater.*" Walk in, while I collect the urchins.

And now, as the declining sun indicates the approach of five o'clock, having dismissed our tumultuous boys, who have rushed from their restraint whooping and shouting at the return of liberty, we, with perhaps not less of enjoyment, will take our quiet walk homeward. We have yet two good hours of day, although the fierce heat of the high sun has in some degree abated. The day-fliers have not yet retired, for here is that widespread species, the Violet-tip Butterfly *(Grapta Caureum),* slaking its thirst at the edge of the brook. And just now I saw another northern species, the little Pearl Crescent Fritillary *(Melitaea Tharos),* which seems to be rather common.

The Turtle-doves *(Columba Carolinensis)* have been making the woods resound with their soft and mournful notes for some hours, but just now they are most garrulous in their melancholy. In truth it is a sweet sound; there is something inexpressibly touching in it, soothing our spirits and calming us into unison with the peaceful quiet of nature. It puts one in mind of the note of our own country's Cuckoo, so full of summer and all its pleasant associations; but the coo of the Turtle is softer, more deliberate, and consists of five syllables instead of two. They generally fly in pairs at this season, and often utter their coo as they sit on the road-fences, whence they frequently descend to the roads to peck among the gravel, or to bask in the sun and dust. They seem of a confiding nature, and to possess a large share of that gentleness and tenderness we are accustomed to associate with all the doves. As if conscious how much of a favourite it is, this sweet bird will scarcely leave the fence, or even the road, at the approach of a passenger. Its confidence, however, does not always protect it, for its flesh is a delicacy, and the gentle Turtle often becomes a victim to the rifle. Its flight when alarmed is very rapid, and attended by a loud whirring sound, which frequently betrays it in the woods to the hunter's unerring aim. Its shape is slender and elegant, the head is small and the tail long; the general colour of the upper parts is light blue, and of the under parts pale orange, the plumage reflecting, in a remarkable degree, those brilliant metallic hues which are more or less common to the whole pigeon tribe.

Here is a flower of great beauty, growing neglected and unnoticed in the corners of the rail-fence. It is the Indian Pink *(Spigelia Marylandica);* its spike of slender tubular flowers, brilliant crimson externally, and internally yellow, would alone entitle it to our admiration; but it has other claims to our regard, on account of its value in medical botany. But notice that heavy, thick-set butterfly, probing with its long tongue the deep nectar-tube of the corolla. Like the rest of its tribe,

Turtle Dove and Cardinal Grosbeak

for it is one of that extensive group commonly called Skippers *(Hesperiadae),* the White-spotted Skipper *(Eudamus Tityrus)* is more like a moth than a butterfly, and serves well to be one of the connecting links between the diurnal and the nocturnal Lepidoptera. It is very susceptible of alarm, flies swiftly, violently, and in a headlong manner, and has many of the motions of the Hawk-moths.

Now, as we plunge into this romantic little hollow, where the oaks and hickories meet overhead, and entwine their branches together, we seem to leave daylight behind us. And, as if to be quite in character, see the Barred Owl *(Strix nebulosa)* flying silent and ghost-like across our path, and now staring at us from yonder tree.

Here we emerge again into at least comparative daylight, though the sun sends nearly horizontal rays across the fields. Notice those birds, resembling swallows, which are mounting on the wing higher and higher and higher, screaming as they ascend, till, having gained a great elevation, down each plunges with closed wings like a stone, so that you think he will be killed by the fall, but just before he reaches the earth, he suddenly wheels round, and again mounts on the wing. The most singular part of the procedure is, that at the moment the bird arrests its precipitate descent, a hollow boom is heard, something like a heavy gun at a great distance, or the hoarse bellowing of a bull. The mouths of all this genus, for it is the Night-hawk *(Caprimulgus Americanus),* are very wide and capacious, though their beaks are extremely small, and it is doubtless to this fact that the sound is owing; the swift descent causing the air to rush into the open mouth, as into the bung-hole of an empty cask. They do not, however, always perform these manoeuvres in regularly continued succession: often, when high in air, they will rove about, or several will play together on the wing for some time before they precipitate themselves. The common people here generally call these birds by the name of bull-bats.

I see your surprise at the long whoops which begin to be heard from every quarter; be not alarmed; it is not the war-whoop of the wild Seminole, but a much more peaceful sound. The sun has set, and the negroes on the plantations have begun to call home the hogs. Some negroes from long practice have acquired great power of voice; they will utter a continued unbroken shout, lasting nearly a minute, which may be heard at the distance of a mile; and to me, in the still balmy evening, when softened and mellowed by distance, there is something pleasing and even musical in these sounds. The hogs are turned out in the morning to forage in the woods for themselves, and in the evening are summoned home by this call, which they well understand, to food and rest. I have been near hogs rooting and grazing in the woods, when suddenly the shout of the distant negro has pealed along the air; instantly they are all attention, every head is raised; they listen a moment, then all is bustle; with a responding grunt they scamper away towards home, and each races to be foremost.

The southern hogs are a queer breed; very singular creatures indeed; one does not often laugh when alone; but, really, when I have looked on these animals, with their sharp thin backs, long heads, and tall legs, looking so little like hogs, and so much like greyhounds, and have observed the shrewd look, half alarm, half defiance, with which they regard one, I have laughed till the water has run out of my eyes. From the amount of liberty which is granted them, and their consequent habits of self-protection and self-dependence, they are very wild; indeed, many are found in the woods which are as really wild, in every sense of the word, as any panther; perfectly ownerless, swift of foot, and fierce and strong withal. They have a peculiar colour (a dark brown), an appearance which distinguishes them from the owned hogs; and they are often hunted by the planters on horseback with hounds. They show good sport, sometimes leading a long and smart chase; but when close pressed, they stand at bay, and often inflict severe wounds with their sharp tusks upon the dogs that are not well trained; young dogs in particular frequently suffer for their temerity. When wanted for food, the rifleball puts the period to the chase, but the pigs are often marked on the ear, and turned adrift again. These marks are considered a token of ownership, and are always respected by those who make any pretensions to honour.

Now, then, that we are returned, as supper is not quite ready, perhaps you are not so fatigued but that you would prefer walking in the garden to sitting in the house. Although the twilight is fast fading into darkness, and therefore the brilliant tints and elegant forms of the flowers will be lost upon our unperceiving eyes, yet we shall not be without enjoyment: the sweetest fragrance is given out in the dewy evening; in the dusty, scorching, glaring day, we walk amongst the blossoms and admire their beauty, but wonder they are so scentless; but when night has begun to cool the atmosphere, and the exhaled vapours descend, then the air is loaded with perfume; from bud, leaf, and flower, from garden, field, and forest, the odours throng upon our senses.

The Guinea-fowls have ended their pertinacious clack, and have retired to their roost; the field-negroes have turned their mules into the yard; and the Mocking-bird is sweetly serenading his mate in the neighbouring wood. But here: look at this bush covered with blossoms; it is still light enough to discern their beauty, if you stoop down: the flowers are numerous, tubular, bright yellow, sometimes pink, sometimes both hues united. The plant is the Marvel of Peru *(Mirabilis jalapa),* called the Four o'Clock, from the singular habit of opening its flowers just at that hour. During the heat of the day they remain closed, the mouth or wide part of the corolla being curled inward, and appearing shrivelled; but about four in the afternoon,—and I have often been struck with admiration at the precision with which the hour is marked,—the blossoms begin to unfold, and in the course of a quarter of an hour all are widely expanded, and remain open all night. They are sweet-smelling, and their deep tubes make them a great centre of attraction to the large Hawk-moths which choose the morning and evening gloaming for their peregrinations; and it is partly for them that I have brought you to this bush.

We will be patient a moment:—there is one; I hear the humming of his muscular wings: be cautious! now I see him coming round the further side of the bush; we won't net him yet; we will watch his motions a few minutes, as well as we can for the dim twilight. He is suspended on the wing, just over the mouth of a flower into which his long tongue or sucker is inserted, probing to the very bottom, where the nectar lies: his wings are like an undefined film on each side, owing to the rapidity of their vibration, and by their motion make that shrill hum which so instantly discovers his presence. Now he is at another flower, having changed his position so quickly that it seems as if done merely by a volition, without passing through the intervening space. He stays three or four seconds at each blossom, visiting them in succession, if undisturbed, pretty regularly; not unerringly, however, as he often revisits a flower which he has just robbed. He never works in a resting position; I have never seen one alight; they always continue on the wing, and if alarmed, are gone like a thought.

This is the Tobacco Hawk-moth *(Sphinx Carolina),* a large but sober-coloured species. The usual food of the larva is the tobacco plant, on which it is found in considerable numbers, and it is therefore eagerly sought and destroyed; yet still the perfected moth is by no means scarce. I have also taken it from the tomato. The pupa is large, dark reddish brown, subterraneous in its habits, and is remarkable for a curious departure from ordinary structure, though this departure is not quite peculiar to it. If we take off the hard, shelly skin of a chrysalis, not very near its time of change, we find what appears to be a nearly homogeneous mass of white matter in a semifluid state, without any semblance of limbs, members, or organs. Yet all the parts of the future fly are there, perfectly separate and distinct, though not yet fully developed. In the outer skin, however, which has acquired consistency by exposure, the shape of the limbs and external organs is definitely marked. On the front of a chrysalis, we usually perceive in the centre, running from the head, half-way down the body, a double line, which covers the tongue; on each side of this are ranged three other folds, marking the positions of the three pairs of legs; these folds are broadest at the head, and taper to a point; then come the antennae, long and slender, one on each side the leg; in some moths, however, they are very wide and short; and outside them, the fore wings folded down on the breast, small of course, but still displaying the future form, and even the nervures; the hind wings cannot be seen, because they are folded directly beneath the others.

Now, as I said, the tongue usually lies straight down the middle of the breast, but in some of the larger Sphinges this organ is destined to be, in the future moth, of unusual length and size; and therefore, as in this species, it is not folded down with the other members, and covered only by the common skin of all, but has a separate skin or sheath, projecting from the head, with the tip (in some instances recurved) resting on the breast, looking very much like the trunk of an elephant. The tongue or sucker, when the perfect insect is evolved, is an organ well worth a moment's examination, as a beautiful instance of the modification of a part to adapt it to altered circumstances. Look here! I will unfold the apparatus, nearly two inches long, yet when rolled up in this beautiful spiral, curl within curl, scarcely larger than the head of the pin with which I am opening it. It is tubular throughout its whole length; and, what is singular, it is composed of two parts perfectly separable, you see, each part being a cylinder, yet when placed side by side, meeting in such a manner as to form a tube quite air-tight between the two lateral ones. It is this central tube which forms the sucking-pump; the outer ones being intended (so it is asserted) for the reception of air. In what way suction is performed, however, is still a mystery.

Now, in this long cylinder, who could detect the slightest analogy to the hard, toothed jaws of a beetle? yet, in fact, the two halves of the cylinder are neither more nor less than the two jaws, altered and modified to suit the necessities of the insect; for a Sphinx placed at the outside of a tubular flower, furnished only with a pair of short, hard jaws, would be in somewhat the same condition as the fox whom the stork invited to dinner; but as it is, who does not see the hand of God in all this?

But come; we will put away our investigations for the present, and take a little supper. The meal which we are accustomed to call "tea," is by Americans, universally, I believe, called "supper," and it is the final meal; there being but three in the day.

And now, as you have a long way to go tonight, you have need to spur your Pegasus. Many thanks for your company. Presto! Good night!

Letter IV

Dallas, June 10, 18—

A few nights ago, after all in the house had long retired to rest, not feeling disposed for sleep, I was sitting at an open window. We usually sleep with every window wide open, there being latticed blinds or shutters to prevent the intrusion of bats, birds, &c. It was fast approaching to midnight; the air, cleared by a recent thunder-storm, was most refreshingly cool and balmy; and gushes of fragrance rose from the garden that smiled beneath. It was not dark, for there was a "good piece of a moon" in the sky, whose rays fell on the tops of the almost boundless forest around, and nearer at hand were reflected by the diamond drops of rain that still glistened on the bushes. Everything was profoundly still, and Johns's sweet lines on Palmyra seen at midnight were running in my mind:—

"All silent now!—The starry wings
  Of midnight wrap the lonely plain;
The murmurs of the sleepless springs
  Alone disturb her solemn reign.
Oh! full of gorgeous gloom that hour,
  Where'er it falls, the wide world round!
It gives to every scene a power
  To stir the soul with thoughts profound;—
With thoughts that, like sidereal strains,
  Are all unheard the bright day long;
But, when night breaks their fountain-chains,
  Gush forth at once in mystic song!"

Suddenly I was electrified by the clear and distinct voice of the Chuck-will's-widow *(Caprimulgus Carolinensis)* in a group of trees in the garden, and not half a stone's throw from the window where I was sitting. I cannot tell you how much I was delighted with this sound. I had read of it often in other lands; it was invested in my imagination with a sort of romance, and to hear it with my own ears was one of the pleasures which I had eagerly anticipated in coming to this southern region. My mind was already in a state of quiet but high enjoyment, and was prepared fully to appreciate a long-wished-for gratification. I was almost breathless lest any sound should alarm the bird and drive it away, and my ears seemed to strain to catch every intonation uttered. It may appear strange to you that the voice of a bird should have such an influence, but such was the fact. The bird continued to repeat its call at intervals of two or three seconds for about half an hour. After it had been some time thus engaged, another answered, the two sometimes calling alternately, and sometimes together. A third, yet further off, soon joined them, after which the first ceased, and flew away.

The next evening, soon after sunset, I heard them calling in every direction, loud and fast, in the woods that surrounded the house. I was desirous to see as well as to hear them, and so walked cautiously into the woods. I found them very shy, however; for, notwithstanding all my precaution, they would most vexatiously cease long before I could get sufficently near; and though I tried one after another, with much perseverance, I tired myself without seeing a single individual.

The note of this singular bird is compared to the words "chuck-will's-widow," but "chuck-widow-widow," comes nearer to it; the first syllable uttered in an under tone, then a momentary pause, and the "widow-widow" repeated as rapidly as possible. If you take a slender switch, and wave it twice to and fro, so as to make it whistle as it cuts the air, you will have a very good imitation of it, except the preliminary "chuck." I have heard it rendered, "Jack married a widow," which is quite as good a translation as the received version, and has the advantage of meaning something intelligible. The bird is about the size of a pigeon, with a rather large head, and enormous mouth, though the beak is very small: the general colour is bright brown, sprinkled with innumerable spots and dashes of black and white, much like its congener, the European Night-jar *(C. Europaeus)*. Its food consists of large insects, which are abroad during the twilight and night, such as beetles, moths, &c. It lays two olive-coloured eggs, on the bare ground, without a nest.

On another evening, I was writing in my room, the windows being open as usual, when a tiny Boat-fly *(Notonecta),* scarcely more than an eighth of an inch in length, fell on its back on my paper. I took it up in my hand to look at it, but it flew away, and presently fell on the paper again. Did it mistake the white paper for the shining surface of still water? It flew away, and came again, many times in succession, flying in a circular, headlong manner, and invariably falling on its back; not coming down perpendicularly, but touching the paper at a very acute

The Chuck-Will's-Widow

angle, in the act of flying, so as to spin along the surface. From this curious fact I infer that these little insects fly chiefly by night, and that they fly as they swim, *with the back downward.*

In shaking bushes to procure caterpillars, I often shake off a pretty little lizard, of a bright pale-green colour, about five inches in length, of which two-thirds at least are tail *(Anolis bullaris).* It is nimble, but not nearly so swift as the other lizards; when shaken off, it soon runs up another bush, where it seems quite at home among the leaves. The Sassafras *(Laurus sassafras)* is its favourite resort. It feeds on insects: I once saw one with a brown grasshopper in its mouth: I should have thought it would need more agility than it appears to possess, to catch such prey as this; but probably it effects its purpose by creeping cautiously towards its prey, and then seizing it by a sudden spring, as a cat does a bird. I have observed that, when pursued to the end of a twig or branch, it will often leap to another at a short distance, and secure its footing without difficulty.

I had been inclined to consider the changes of colour attributed to some lizards a gross exaggeration, if not a mere fable: but I had recently the satisfaction of witnessing a change of this sort in the present species. The children had been chasing a little lizard about the logs of which the school-house is built, for some time; but it manifested great cunning and agility in avoiding them, creeping through the many crevices between the logs, being sometimes in the school and sometimes on the outside; they at length caught it, however, and brought it to me. It was all over of a brownish-black hue, except a line down the back, which was pale dusky. One of the lads told me that it was the little green tree-lizard, which had become black from being on the dark logs, and that it would turn green again if placed on a leaf. This I could not at all believe, though it certainly corresponded with that species in size, shape, and general appearance. But as it was easy to put it to the test of experiment, I let the lizard hop upon a small solitary plant in the sunshine, bidding some of the children watch it, without disturbing it. They soon brought it to me again, telling me that it was changing; and upon looking at it, I could distinctly perceive a tinge of green upon the black. Still incredulous, however, and thinking it might possibly be fancy, I put it into my desk; and about half an hour after, on opening it, I was no less surprised than delighted to see the lizard of a brilliant light green, the line down the back blackish; there was not the least hue of green in the black at first, nor was there any blackness in the green hue now; the change was complete. I sup-

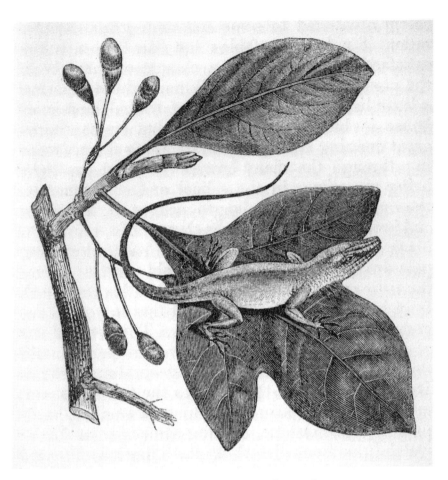

The Green Anolis, on a Sassafras Leaf

pose the black colour was not caused by the animal's being on the dark logs, but was the effect of anger on being chased.

When irritated, and also during other seasons of excitement, the skin of the throat is thrust forth, by a peculiar mechanism, to a great extent; this part then becomes of a bright crimson. The scales with which this lizard is clothed are very small, and scarcely observable. It is perfectly harmless, and is an elegant little creature, of very graceful and active motions, running and leaping.

There are in this neighbourhood many prairies—not the boundless prairies of the West, resembling an ocean solidified and changed to land, but little ones, varying in extent from an acre to a square mile. They are generally so well defined, that the woods environ them on every side like an abrupt wall, and one can hardly be persuaded that these prairies are not clearings made with the axe of the settler. The soil is a very tough and hard clay, and in wet weather the roads running through them are almost impassable, so adhesive are they to the feet of the passengers and the wheels of carriages. Multitudes of fossil shells are scattered over and imbedded in these prairies, but I know nothing of their characters or names. They are perfectly free from the least fragment of stone: I have searched over them in vain for a pebble large enough to throw at a bird. Several species of Thorn *(Crataegus)* grow in impenetrable thickets or in single bushes over their surface, and one or two kinds of wild plum, bearing a harsh sour sloe or bullace, are often mixed with them.

The plants growing on the prairie seem peculiar to it; the flowers abounding on it occur nowhere else, at least not in any plenty, and even many insects seem found only there. Many beautiful species of flowers grow on them. About a mile from where I reside, there is a nice little prairie-knoll (for though the prairies are usually quite level, they are not invariably so), which is one bed of herbage, almost one mass of flowers. Two species of Larkspur *(Delphinium azureum* and *D. staphisagria)* are common, both elegant flowers of a brilliant blue, and much like the common larkspur of our English gardens.

Another plant, still more beautiful, grows here, the Coral-tree *(Erythrina herbacea).* It is a low herb, with the leaves ternate, the leaflets brightly green, glossy, somewhat lozenge-shaped; the blossoms, growing in a spike, are papilionaceous, like the common pea, though it requires some examination to discover that they are so; for their form is very different from the usual shape. The banner *(vexillum)* is very long, slender, and almost tubular, while the other petals are small and inconsiderable: the whole flower is somewhat like a slender cylinder, cut off very obliquely, and curved up at the point, while from the cavity project the stamens, which are yellow, with the anthers bright green. The corolla and calyx, being of a most beautiful red, have a fine appearance, the long drooping blossoms looking very much like pieces of red coral.

A tall syngenesious plant, bearing a flower much like an aster, but with yellow rays *(Helianthus scaber),* is common, and two species of Swallow-wort *(Asclepias tuberosa* and *A. parviflora)* grow in groups or beds here and there. These latter bear large clusters of flowers, the former bright orange red, the latter white, both possessing much fragrance. They are also called milkweed, from the white glutinous fluid, highly acrid, which exudes from the stalk and leaves when broken, and also butterfly weed, because they form such an attraction to those brilliant insects. From this little hill an extensive, but not very pleasing prospect is visible, little being seen but the summit of an almost endless forest, varied here and there by the white smoke curling up from some dwelling hidden in its recess. Hither I frequently come to spend an hour entomologizing, and never fail to be well rewarded.

One of the most numerous of the many species that gaily flutter their brilliant wings in the burning beams of almost vertical noon, and contribute so much to the life and beauty of nature by their presence, is the Blue Swallowtail *(Papilio Philenor,* Boisd.). The upper surface of the fore wings is dull black, generally spotless, but the hind wings have a remarkable gloss, bright blue in one light and greyish green in another, with a row of white spots. Beneath, a row of large crescent-shaped spots of bright orange marks the hind wings, and one of round white spots the fore pair. The tailed appendages of the wings are short, sometimes being scarcely more developed than those of a *Vanessa.* I have taken these fluttering about the heads of the orange milkweed, their abdomens filled almost to bursting with the yellow nectar of these flowers, and so distended that the division of the segments are obliterated, and are discernible only by being bare of the scaly plumage. When in this state they seem unwilling to fly, but either remain at rest, or run to and fro over the blossoms, keeping their hind wings in a vibratory, quivering motion.

The Black Swallowtail *(P. Asterius,* Boisd.), found on the barren and ice-bound shores of Newfoundland, is also numerous here. It is a very elegant species, the black ground being relieved with macular bands of yellow, and on the hind wings by a series of bright azure clouds. The Archippus, too *(Danais Archippus),* with his broad wings of orange tawny handsomely striped with black, probes the mellifluous blossoms from morning to night, and is one of the most conspicuous flutterers on the prairie. But a more beautiful species than all these is the Green-clouded Swallowtail *(P. Troilus,* Boisd.). It is, however, rare, as I have only as yet seen a single specimen. The wings are black, the fore pair having a row of yellow-green spots at the margin, the hind pair having a similar row of crescents, and the whole disk sprinkled with a large cloud of bright green dots. Beneath, the hind wings have two rows of large crescent spots of bright orange, and a row between them of clouds of dots *(fasciae),* all of which are blue except the third from the hinder angle, which is green. Among those of humbler birth,—for these gorgeous swallowtails seem to be of royal blood, to have a presence that distinguishes them from the meaner herd,—I may mention the Painted Beauty *(Cynthia Huntera)* as one not inferior, though of a form more familiar to an English eye. It is so much like the Painted Lady of Europe *(C. cardui),* that one would be tempted to think it the same, a little varying on account of difference of food and climate, were not that species likewise found on this continent in nowise altered. This has the same tints as that, and distributed in a similar way, and particularly the same exquisite delicacy in the diverging and intersecting white lines and sober brown shades of the under surface, but it has only two eye spots instead of four.

Moths are likewise numerous, chiefly of the smaller kinds, but these I cannot attempt to particularize: there is one, however, too pretty to pass over in silence. It is the Pinkwing *(Deiopeia bella).* It is well known in many parts of North America, and among the flowers of these prairies it is particularly plentiful; we can scarce stir the tall rank herbage in any direction, but three or four of these pretty creatures, before unseen, scuttle out and flit away for a few yards, and then plunge down into the mazes of the leaves and stalks again: if repeatedly disturbed, however, they fly a good way before they again alight. The fore wings of this species, which is about an inch and a half in spread of wing, are marked with alternate transverse bands of white and orange-tawny, about a dozen in all, the white ones having a row of black dots in them: the hind pair are pink bordered with deep black. I have seen specimens in which the bands on the fore wings, which are usually tawny, were of a fine scarlet, but these are rare.

Perhaps you will say I am somewhat extravagant in my admiration of these insects, but really I think that any words of description are insufficient to do justice to their surpassing beauty. Take a butterfly into your hand and examine it yourself for a moment superficially; for though the internal organization would be equally instructive, we will not enter into that at present. Look at the richness of the colours. What brilliant hues! Note the burnished metallic gloss and the changeable glow of many of them; the soft velvety downiness of all. Look at the distribution of the colours; into what elegant forms are they thrown—lines, and bands, and spots, and rings, and eyes: think that the whole surface is a mosaic, the most minute, the most elaborate, and the most perfect, that can be conceived. Think that every atom of coloured dust is a feather of regular and prescribed shape, a feather having projecting points, and longitudinal ribs, and a little quill or footstalk, a socket into which it enters, and an organization by which it is fastened there! The subject is not new, and an allusion to it may seem trite, but I can never look at the shining motes that adhere to my finger after having touched their beautiful wings, or take up two or three upon the point of a needle, without feeling a fresh emotion of wonder and admiration. Then look at the structure of the wing itself, divested of its fairy plumes: composed of the most filmy gossamer, transparent, elastic, and firm withal; furnished with hollow ribs radiating to every part; possessing a wide-extended surface to compress a large column of air in flight, provided with powerful muscles to give it rapid and vigorous motion, and yet the whole so light that we can hardly hold it in our hand. Strength and buoyancy, the two great requisites for active aerial motion, are here in perfection. O Lord! manifold are thy works; in wisdom hast thou made them all.

There are prairies not very far distant of many miles in extent; the residents on which suffer greatly in dry seasons from the scarcity of water, a want that in a hot climate is peculiarly felt. There are no springs in the prairies, and the inhabitants depend on the rain-water, which, owing to the tenacity of the soil, does not soak into the ground, but accumulates in the hollows until evaporated by the sun. These hollows are sometimes large, and in winter, and during rainy seasons, form permanent ponds of considerable magnitude, but the water is of course very unwholesome.

I have heard sad accounts of the privations undergone by planters on these "dry and thirsty lands." Not very far from this neighbourhood there was a family, whose dependence was a large pond of this kind. The weather was excessively hot, and they were panting with thirst all day long, yet dared not use the water but in the most parsimonious manner. In any other circumstances it would have been rejected with loathing, for it was green, and stagnant, and lukewarm, and in one part of the pond lay the bloated carcase of a dead horse, to add to its flavour. This they were reduced to drink until it was absolutely impossible, when the only resource was to send the waggon and team with a large tub almost daily a distance of many miles, at a great expense of labour and time. When procured in this way, the water was so precious, that every mode of economizing it was practised; the scanty drop, in which the faces of the family were washed in the morning, served to wash the hands the whole day, and was in the evening given to the cattle; all that could be preserved from the necessary household lustrations was given to them likewise. The washing of clothes was performed at a distance, the garments being taken to the water; and in this miserable way they dragged on, until the weather broke up, and the rains afforded them a fresh supply.

There are two kinds of prairies distinguished here; the open prairie, which I have endeavoured to describe, and the wooded prairie, which is forest. I was spending the day a short time ago at a gentleman's plantation about half-a-dozen miles away, and happened to inquire if there were any prairies in that neighbourhood. I was told there was one very near, which I should find by going through the woods in a certain direction which was pointed out. I went and searched and searched, but no prairie could I see; nothing but endless forests. I returned, supposing I had missed the direction. In order to describe where I had been, I mentioned a little knoll in the woods where the trees were not quite so close to each other, and was informed that was the prairie; and then for the first time I learned the existence of forest prairie, which I should have thought somewhat of a misnomer. I believe the soil distinguishes the prairie; certainly I observed no outward difference between it and the other forest except that, as I have already said, the timber was rather less dense: none of the herbaceous plants and flowers that beautify the open prairie were to be seen. Very few flowers indeed grow in the depth of the forest in any circumstances; grandeur and gloom, not beauty, are the characteristics of these primeval shades.

Two birds have fixed upon the immediate vicinity of our house, as the scene of their domestic economy. One is the Gold-winged Woodpecker *(Picus auratus),* which has excavated a deep and commodious chamber in the blighted and decaying trunk of a girdled pine in the peach-orchard. One of the boys had discovered it, and in the dusk of the evening we went out to reconnoitre. He offered to show me the young ones, which I was desirous to see. We got a ladder (for the entrance was several yards high), and he mounted, having first thrown up a few stones to frighten the old bird, not caring to risk a welcome from her sharp beak. She rushed out, and took her position on a neighbouring tree, anxiously watching our motions. The boy pulled out one of the callow young, which I gently examined. It was nearly fledged; the young feathers of the wings being very conspicuous from their bright golden colour. It was not pretty; young birds never are. I soon put it back again, and afterwards, whether they were congratulating it on its return, or what, I don't know; but if you had heard the odd snoring or hissing that they kept up for some time, you would have thought the whole nation of snakes had been there "in parliament assembled." The anxious mother soon flew in again when we had removed our ladder, gratified, no doubt, to find no murder done.

This fine bird is as common here as in the north: he has many names, but "yellow-hammer" is that by which he is best known here. The bill of the genus generally is straight, grooved, and wedge-shaped, but in this species it is more taper, is slightly curved, and has very little of the wedge form, but is equally adapted for the supply of its wants, which is sought more on the ground than that of his brethren.

The other bird that I mentioned is much more diminutive, and has manifested a more familiar confidence in man. It is the Carolina Wren *(Troglodytes Ludovicianus)*. Mr. Bohanan is enlarging his house, by putting up an additional apartment; the frame is up, and they are clap-boarding it; and it is in this frame, in the angle of one of the beams, hidden from view below, that the bold little bird has determined to bring up her family. The talking of the carpenters, the grating of the saws, the hammering of nails, seem to give her very little inconvenience; she flies in and out all day about her business, with the most philosophical indifference, and nobody molests her. She has laid three eggs, profusely covered with red spots. She is just the same funny, inquisitive little thing that all the wrens are, peeping into every hole and corner, creeping into one end of a pile of logs or heap of stones, and out at the other, while the tail is carried bolt upright, with all the consequence imaginable. Her colour is plain, homely brown, as of the other species.

A large, heavy-looking beetle *(Passalus cornutus)* is common. It chiefly crawls by night, and in the morning we often see it in the paths, apparently overtaken unexpectedly by daylight, and not knowing whither to go. It inhabits the trunks of decayed trees, and is often found between the bark and the wood. On stripping off a piece of bark from a prostrate hard-wood log, I have found as many as four or five congregated together, so stupid and inert as scarcely to move a limb when taken into the hand. It is about the size of our English Stag-beetle, but it has not the enormous development of jaws that marks that insect; its affinity to the group *(Lucanidae)* is shown, however, by the form of the antennae. The head is marked by a short, blunt horn, curved forwards: its colour is deep brown, or black, highly polished, the elytra furrowed.

I have found two or three times a little beetle which has a very curious habit. It is of a yellowish-brown colour: the hindmost legs are unusually long, and these it can turn round in such a manner as to bring them forward; by this means it tumbles over and over in a very grotesque manner, when one endeavours to touch it, so that it is not easy to get hold of it.

Some little beetles resort to the heads of flowers, especially the syngenesious ones, among whose anthers they riot and revel, and almost cover themselves with the powdery farina. In their brighter colours and more active habits, and in a greater readiness to take wing, they seem more suited to the flowers they frequent, than the dark dorrs that nocturnally crawl over the earth. One little *Cetonia,* whose brown elytra are elegantly marked with white spots, gives out a very fragrant smell. Another *(Trichius delta)* has the thorax handsomely ornamented with a snow-white triangle. A third *(Tetraopes tornator)* is glossy crimson, with two black dots on each of the elytra, and four on the thorax. These three, with others, delight to bask on the prairie flowers, in company with the butterflies, beneath the beams of noon.

There is a handsome plant in the garden, trained over a lattice arbour, which it profusely covers with a luxuriant foliage of pinnate leaves. It is called the Virgin's Bower, but erroneously, as that name belongs to a species of *Clematis;* I believe it is rather *Glycine frutescens.* I have already intimated that it is a climbing plant, several stems as big as a man's thumb twisting round each other like a cable, so tight that a knife could scarce be thrust between. It bears a long and thick spike of flowers, of a pink or lilac colour, of pleasant odour. About a fortnight ago I observed in several places two or three of the leaves fastened together, and lined with a coating of silk, making a very snug tent; in each one of these leaf-tents was a singular-shaped caterpillar. It was long-oval, convex above and flat beneath, something like the common insect called a wood-louse, or carpenter *(Oniscus);* the head was oddly fastened to the body by a slender neck, which, as well as the head itself, was reddish brown, two large spots on the face being bright orange; the whole body was green, transversely wrinkled.

I took half-a-dozen of these to rear; in a day or two they ceased to eat, and began to change colour, as many caterpillars do just before going into the chrysalis state, turning of a pale pink or flesh-colour on the back, and becoming quite pellucid, so that the dorsal vessel was distinctly seen, with its alternate contractions and expansions, proceeding in regular waves from the tail to the head. Each then spun a girth composed of many threads of silk, placed side by side, and fastened at each end to two points within its tent, which, being completed, was passed over the head, until it embraced the fore part of the body; and thus it quietly awaited its transformation, gradually becoming more and more inactive and helpless. A day elapsed after the alteration of colour, before the spinning of the girdle, and after another day the skin was thrown off, and the soft white pupa was evolved, which soon, however, acquired consistency, and its permanent dingy tint, a greenish brown. They remained thirteen days in this state, and then produced the White-spotted Skipper *(Eudamus Tityrus),* which I had observed before on the flowers by the roadsides.

I have bred very many butterflies, and have universally found them, on first opening the dark box in which they had been evolved, perfectly still, and making no attempt to escape when touched with the fingers; but these Skippers formed a singular exception. Before the lid was half raised, all was scuffle and flutter within, the first intimation I had of their birth; though, as I had examined them every day, I knew by the discoloration of the pupa that the change was near. Before I could catch a glimpse of anything within, one dashed out like lightning, and if I had not shut the box, the other would have followed as quickly; I was obliged to get my gauze net, and cover the box while I opened it, or I could not have secured the specimen. The others, as they successively attained the *imago* state, each manifested the same wildness.

This tribe of Butterflies show their natural proximity to the Moths, as well by the position of holding their wings, as by other more prominent marks. Although like others they not unfrequently close the wings, the two surfaces being in contact, yet, far more commonly, they are held upward diagonally, the surfaces widely separated, and the hind pair almost horizontal.

The mode of clearing forest land for agriculture, called girdling, is almost universally practised here. An incision is made around the trunk of a tree with an axe, so that the inner bark is completely severed all round. The ascent of the sap being thus prevented, though no perceptible change is immediately manifested, death inevitably takes place in the course of the season. The scanty underbrush of scattered shrubs and slender saplings is torn up with an instrument called a grubbing hoe; and in the ensuing spring (a fence of oak rails having been run through the forest in the winter), this forest land is planted with Indian corn. No plough has turned up the soil, nor even a harrow scratched its surface; so soft and mellow is it with the accumulated vegetable mould of ages, that it needs but a hole to be made with the hoe, and the seed-corn deposited, to ensure an abundant harvest. No further trouble is taken with the trees; the branches decay and drop off piecemeal, and by-and-by the sapless trunks themselves, one at a time, come down with a crash, and scatter the earth beneath them.

This custom of girdling the trees instead of cutting them down gives the fields a most singular appearance. After the twigs and smaller boughs have dropped off, and the bark has dried and shrunk, and been stripped away, and the naked branches have become blanched by the summer's sun and winter's rain, these tall dead trunks, so thickly spread over the land, look like an army of skeletons stretching their gaunt white arms, clothed with long ragged festoons of Spanish moss *(Tillandsia usneoides),* across the field. They are not unattended with danger, but the risk of damage to the crop, and even to human life, is not considered to countervail the great saving of labour attending this mode of clearing; and they chiefly fall in the storms of winter, when the labours of the field are suspended. They form an unfailing resource for the Woodpeckers, all kinds of which, from the noble Ivory-billed to the little Downy, are incessantly tapping at their sapless trunks. The Red-tailed Hawk *(Falco borealis)* frequently chooses them as his watch tower, whence his large fiery eye gleams on his prey below, and now and then, as if impatient of rest, he flies from one to another with a sudden scream. But more especially the Turkey Vultures *(Cathartes aura)* are fond of sitting on them; for, being totally destitute of foliage to intercept vision, their topmost branches form a convenient observatory for reconnoitring the surrounding country.

I got up yesterday morning before sunrise, and went into the woods with a boy to see if I could procure any birds. We roused about fifty of these obscene vultures from an early breakfast on a deceased hog; they reluctantly enough took to wing on our approach, and settled in numbers together, in great black masses, on the branches of the dead pines around. When they rose—for if one moved all accompanied it—the united impulse caused large limbs to break off and fall with a thundering crash.

These birds are very unwilling to leave the vicinity of a carcase which they have discovered: they will continue to fly over the place, or sail far over head in widening circles, till an opportunity is afforded for them again to descend upon their prey. They make quick work with a carcase, and clean work too. The other day I was told of a hog in a neighbouring field, that had been but just discovered by the vultures: I wished to see them, but as it was close upon dinner time, I deferred it. On going to the spot after dinner, I found nothing but the clean-picked bones, the vultures having finished their dinner as well as I.

I have said that the dead trees fall chiefly in winter; storms, however, are not wholly confined to that season. Hurricanes of great violence occur not rarely at other times, before which the old tottering skeletons fly in all directions, and even the living forest-trees bow and fall. It is singular that these gusts, violent and terrific as they are, are limited generally to a belt of narrow width, but of varying length. I have been told that after the passing of one of these whirlwinds, which are very brief in their duration, its course may be traced for miles through the forest, having swept a lane for itself almost as effectually as if the settlers had been there cutting down the trees to make a road. On the approach of such a storm as this, the negroes in the field, warned by the blackening horizon, flee home for shelter; for exposure in a field of dry trees at such a time would be almost certain death. I witnessed a strong breeze the other day, but not violent enough to be called a hurricane. Every one in the house was collected at the windows overlooking the plantation, watching its progress with considerable anxiety. It was easy to trace it through field and forest, over the intervening valley, and sweeping up the opposite hills. The ragged Spanish moss flew out horizontally, like the fragments of a sail torn from the bolt-rope; we saw large white branches, careering through the air; old trunks riven, and splintered, and dashed to the earth, overturning others in their descent, and thus increasing the destruction. In less than a quarter of an hour from its commencement, the crash, the roar, the havoc had all ceased: the sky cleared; and you would not have known that the even tenor of the day had been broken, but by the effects which remained. In this case no damage was incurred, at least here, except the crushing of a fence or two, and the ploughing up of some of the corn and cotton in the field.

But I was going to tell you of my bird-seeking expedition yesterday at dawn of day. Besides the vultures, I was surprised to meet with very few birds indeed. I had supposed that at such an hour I should meet with very many; but perhaps I was wrong in going into the woods, instead of keeping near the edges. We by-

and-by discovered, however, what I thought well worth my trouble, a pair of those splendid birds, the Ivory-billed Woodpeckers *(Picus principalis).* They were engaged in rapping some tall dead pines, in a dense part of the forest, which rang with their loud notes. These were not at all like the loud laugh of the Pileated *(P. pileatus),* nor the cackle of the smaller species, but a single cry frequently repeated, like the clang of a trumpet. As it hung on the perpendicular trunk in full view, digging away with great force and effect, I thought this a very magnificent bird. It is the largest of all the tribe, being twenty inches in length, of a glossy black, broadly marked with pure white. The neck is long and slender, the head is crowned with a tall conical crest of the most splendid crimson, the eye is bright yellow; but the beak is his chief distinction. This is four inches in length, and a full inch in diameter at the base; it tapers to a sharp point, which is wedge-shaped. You would suppose it made of the finest ivory, highly polished, of great hardness, and beautifully grooved or fluted through its whole length. This is the male; the female exactly resembles it, except that her crest is of the same glossy black as the body. We succeeded in shooting both, which I skinned and dissected.

Wilson says, "The food of this bird consists, I believe, entirely of insects and their larvae:" but in this he is wrong. In the stomach of one of these, indeed, I found the remains of a large *Cerambyx,* but mingled with the stones of several cherries; that of the other contained nothing but cherries. The bird is usually called by the planters the Logcock, but no distinction is made between this species and the Pileated, both being known by the same name, although they differ materially. Neither species can be considered rare, but the Pileated is much the more common of the two; few days elapse without my seeing one or more, and hearing their loud cachinnations, as I wend my way to and from the school. They are not very shy, and it is not at all difficult to get near them; but they are cunning enough to keep on the opposite side of the tree. I have often been amused to observe the skill with which they keep the trunk or branch between themselves and me, moving round as I move, and now and then peeping the scarlet crown round the edge to reconnoitre. By concealing oneself behind a tree, however, and by waiting patiently a few minutes, one may have a fair sight of them. When far up a tree, they are not so cautious. The tail of all the woodpecker tribe, being used as a support in the perpendicular position so common to them, is very hard and stiff, and the shafts of the feathers are pointed, and extend beyond the

Ivory-billed Woodpeckers

vanes. These tips I have seen quite clogged up with turpentine resembling pitch, accumulated in the bird's frequent visits to the trunk of the pitch-pine.

A singularly interesting fact in entomology fell under my observation a day or two since. There is a small river called Mush Creek, which darkly pursues its tortuous course through the forests hereabout, and falls into Cedar Creek, a tributary of the Alabama. In several of its windings it approaches near to the schoolhouse, sometimes narrowed to a brawling brook, at other times widening into little still ponds and quiet bays. I was standing on the bank of one of these little smooth bays, whither I had resorted for the sake of the pleasant "shadow from the heat" (for it was about noon), idly watching the motions of a large Dragon-fly *(Aeshna)*. In the clear water there was a number of the young fry of some small fish, most of them not more than an inch in length, swimming in little shoals near to the surface. The Dragon-fly had been hawking to and fro over the brook some time; at length he dashed down into the water where a few of the fry were swimming, and made quite a little splash, but did not go under. He rose again immediately, but without success evidently, as he continued his hawking as before. The fry darted away in all directions from the intruder's attack, of course, but soon re-assembled and came to the surface as before. The Dragon-fly, not discouraged by failure, presently made another pounce, and now succeeded better, for he instantly settled for a few minutes upon a twig on the bank, as their manner invariably is when they take prey, to eat it. On the closest examination, I could discover nothing else in the water that could be supposed to be the object of his attack. The food of the Dragon-flies has been universally believed, as far as I am aware, to consist exclusively of insects, which are always caught in the air, though eaten at rest. The singular selection made by this individual is not less remarkable than the fact that it should venture into the water to obtain it. I have no doubt that young fish often form the prey of these insects in their early stages, when they are aquatic, as they are large and very voracious; and we know that the larvae of the greater water-beetles *(Dyticidae)* devour fish.

A few miles away, in a very unfrequented part of the forest, there is a shallow pool of considerable extent, perhaps covering three or four acres.It seems to have been caused by the accidental choking up of the course of a small creek, by the falling of a tree across it, the formation of the land on either side aiding the accumulation of the water. Evaporation is checked by the shadow of the dense and lofty trees around, the foliage of which spreads over the quiet water, and in a great measure shields it from the sun's rays; for the original course of the brook wound through the very heart of the tall forest.

A desolate scene is presented here to the visitor. One consequence of the accumulation of the standing water was the speedy death of the growing timber upon the whole area inundated; and majestic sycamores, and oaks, and chestnuts were in a short time prostrated by the high winds, and lay about on one another in all directions in the wildest ruin. These, as they fell, helped still further to choke up the water, and to increase its depth; while their broken, half-decayed trunks, covered with moss and parasitical plants, project from the sluggish surface, or form piers, which stretch away from the banks into the midst of the lake, and precarious bridges across different portions.

At first sight you are ready to conclude that no living thing is near. All is still and silent; the breeze that ruffles the leaves at the summits of the trees cannot reach here; scarcely a bird or an insect appears in an hour; the surface of the pond is unmoved and seemingly immoveable, for it is so covered with a dense coat of yellow-green vegetation, that you can scarcely tell where the land ends and the water begins, till the plunge of your leg half knee-deep into black, fetid, slushy mud, informs you of your *whereabouts.*

Yet, quiet and apparently desolate as this sombre lake is, it is the congenial home of some animals, and those not to be despised by man. It is true, if you approach noisily, kicking the stumps and breaking the twigs, you see nothing; nor will you be any the wiser if you move about the brink talking and laughing. But sit down on a log a few paces within the shadow of the forest, and remain quite silent, keeping your eyes on the surface of the pool, and especially on the fallen trunks that project from it. In a few minutes a little black head peeps from the mantle of green incumbent weed, and a Tortoise creeps noiselessly out, and takes up his position on one of the rotten logs. Glance over the pool; every log is tenanted by one or more of the same silent reptiles, not one of which was there a moment ago. But lo! while you look, another and another and another—nay, scores are crawling up upon the logs, so that in a quarter of an hour you may count them by hundreds, and others are still rising. They are of various sizes; some are as large as the crown of your hat, others are tiny creatures, not bigger than a half-crown piece, and of all intermediate dimensions.

My lads are familiar enough with them; they call them Mud-turtles or Terrapins, and say that their flesh is good to eat. Sometimes they shoot the larger ones

Turtles in a Swamp

with the rifle, aiming to strike them beneath the edge of the back-shell; and at others they lay traps of various devices, and lines with strong hooks baited with a piece of flesh. The rifle-ball is frequently turned by the horny shell of these animals, when struck at an angle; and hence this potent weapon is often unsuccessful, notwithstanding that the habits of the Turtles allow ample opportunity for the most careful aim. When out of water, they will sit for hours without moving, the foreparts raised, looking diagonally upwards, yet ready to drop on the slightest alarm into the water below. At the first crack of the rifle they disappear; every one has dropped silently down, not with a struggle and a splash, but so stilly, that you look round and wonder what magical art has made the host suddenly invisible.

I saw one shot and mortally wounded. It fell over on its back and rolled into the water, but could only feebly struggle, and had no power to turn, or to direct its movements so as to swim to the bottom. Hence with some difficulty it was dragged to shore. It was, as I had supposed, a species of *Emys;*—and I could not but admire the adaptation of the form for swift swimming, the carapace or back-shell being flattened, arching slightly in the middle, and thinned to an edge all round, so as to present as little resistance as possible to the water; and also the efficient protection which the integument affords against most ordinary casualties, the back and belly being encased in bony solid shields, and the neck and limbs covered with a loose skin so dense as to resist the edge of a knife. The strong, cutting jaws, shutting into each other just like the notched mandibles of a hawk, and the curved claws, likewise show how well furnished the creature is for taking its prey.

There are sometimes found in the swamps and in the wider rivers other Turtles of larger size and more formidable character, which I hear reports of, but have not yet been so fortunate as to see. The name of Snapping Turtle is given to one, but it is frequently called in books the Alligator Tortoise *(Chelydra serpentina).* It is said to be three feet in length, and as ferocious as the mailed leviathan after whom it is named. Concealing itself under the broad floating leaves of aquatic plants, it suddenly darts out its great head, and makes a snap at any intruder with fatal precision; while such is the force of the muscles which move the jaws, such the strength of their substance, and the keenness of their cutting edges, that any object less firm than metal is pretty sure to be divided. Instances have not unfrequently occurred of unwary persons having their fingers amputated at a single snap of this vicious creature. The allusion to the alligator in the name given to this animal, does not refer so much to this ferocity, as to the form, the stout limbs, and especially to the long and thick tail flattened sidewise, and surmounted by a saw-like ridge of stout elevated plates.

Another Tortoise of even greater size and equal ferocity is the Soft-back *(Trionyx ferox).* It is spoken of as rather rare, but as being occasionally met with in the Cahawba River, where its habit is to squat on fallen trunks and logs, like the Mud-turtle, watching for fishes, which it pursues and devours, as it does also ducks and other water-fowl. Its flesh is much esteemed, and hence it is captured for the table by those who are acquainted with its haunts. They bait a strong hook with a living fish, as it is necessary that the prey should be in motion to attract the Turtle. Care and caution are needful in landing the game when captured; for it darts its head in all directions, seeking to bite its enemies, and frequently inflicting severe wounds, from the remarkable suddenness and agility of its movements.

This large and fierce Turtle is chiefly remarkable for having only the central portion of the back covered with a shell of horny plates, the remainder of the upper parts being protected by a marginal flap-like expansion of leathery texture, the edge of which is free, and helps the animal in swimming; the feet also, which are armed with strong hooked claws, are furnished with large swimming flaps of like leathery substance.

Letter V

Dallas, June 16th, 18—

I am just returned from a pleasant ride to Cahawba; it was solitary indeed, but not the less pleasant for that. Human society that is not congenial is a greater bore than a total want of it; but nature is always congenial, and always conversible. The first part of the way lay through the forest, with nothing to be seen but tall pines on this side, and tall pines on that side. I quickly cantered through this, and came to the banks of Mush Creek, the same little stream that surrounds the school, but several miles nearer its outlet. The banks were high, but they had been cut away for the road to cross; most of the "creeks" have to be forded, few bridges being yet erected. When they are flooded by the winter rains, this is often an unpleasant, and sometimes a dangerous business, especially for ladies, as they are frequently so high that it is necessary to swim the horse; and to keep the saddle when the beast's back is entirely submerged, amidst his struggles with the foaming rushing flood, is by no means an easy thing. However, I had nothing of this sort to encounter, the water scarce reaching the stirrups.

The steep banks of this rivulet were ornamented with a very handsome shrub, the Oak-leafed Hydrangea *(Hydrangea quercifolia),* whose large sinuous leaves of dark green were admirably set off by its noble spikes of white flowers, thickly clustered like snowballs. Common and indigenous flowers are apt to be disregarded by horticulturists, even if beautiful; but this one, though by no means uncommon, seems to have its claims to notice acknowledged, and is a favourite in our gardens. It thrives most in low damp situations, and affects the vicinity of water.

By-and-by I came to some extensive plantations, in the immediate vicinity of King's Landing, where I had landed from the Alabama. Hereabout, on the sides of the road and in the angles of the fences, the Prickly-pear *(Opuntia———?)* was growing in abundance; it was a smaller species than that which I noticed on the shore at Mobile, not rising more than a foot in height, and the oval leaf-like divisions of the stem were also smaller. They were profusely adorned with the beautiful yellow flowers; but, warned by experience, I did not meddle with them. The tops of those receptacles from which the flowers had fallen were concave, and of a delicate pink hue.

On suddenly turning round a point of the forest, where the road was overflowed with water, forming a large pond, I surprised a Blue Heron *(Ardea caerulea),* which was standing, in the silent and motionless manner of the genus, on the very edge of the pool, intently gazing into the water, as if cut in stone. It was doubtless watching for water-insects and worms. On seeing me, it rose to flight, when it seemed all wings, and was soon lost in the deep woods. The Herons are shy retiring birds, delighting in the gloomy solitude of marshes, or unfrequented lakes, or where the large rivers flow through the untouched forest. Their form is gracefully slender, and their colour usually chaste and pleasing; that of the present species is a lavender-blue, the head and neck purplish.

A pretty moth which I had not seen before *(Callimorpha Lecontei)* was rather numerous: the wings are horizontal, white, fantastically marked into numerous divisions by bands of dark-brown, much more conspicuous in some specimens than in others.

Cahawba lies on the opposite bank of the Alabama from me, that is, the right bank as you go down. The Cahawba River empties itself into the Alabama just above it, so that the town stands on a point of land. This is a river of considerable length, and is navigable for some distance by steamers during the winter. The summer heats diminish the volume of all the rivers materially; even the Alabama is now so much shrunk, that steamers can no longer come up so far as this, so that water communication with Mobile is cut off for some months, except for very small boats.

I followed the road until it led me to the very water's edge. Cahawba was in sight, just before me, but the broad river rolled between; I was for a moment at a loss how to cross, but presently perceived a flat ferry boat on the opposite side, lying under the precipitous bank. I sent a shout across, and two old "nigger-fellers" began to shove their flat over. No house or inn was near to put up my horse, so I took him into a little wood, and tied him to a tree. This is a common practice; in the woods immediately round a place of worship, on a Sunday, we may see a hundred or more saddled horses usually tied by the bridle to a small hanging twig, and not to the trunk; the reason of which is, partly to give the horse more scope to move about, and partly because the elasticity of the branch, to the end of which he is fastened, yields to his movements, whereas, if tied to the trunk, he might by a sudden pull break the bridle and get loose.

The negroes ferried me over the romantic river, for which I paid a "*pic*" (*i.e.* a picayune, the sixteenth of a dollar, or half a "bit"), the smallest silver coin current. Cahawba was formerly the seat of government of the state, but it is now much decayed, and has a very desolate appearance: a few "stores," a lawyer's office or two, and two or three tradesmen's shops, with the usual proportion of rum-shops or "groceries," whose branch of business seemed scarcely to partake of the general decay, if I might judge from the number of customers in the verandahs—appeared to constitute the business of the "city." I found no temptation to linger here, and quickly returned.

In going, I had heard, from a wet marshy place beside the road, a continued and most deafening shrieking, extremely shrill and loud. When I came to the place in returning, the noise was still kept up, and my curiosity was much excited. I watched, and had reason to believe it was produced by a small dusky species of frog *(Rana clamata?)*, for, on approaching the spots whence it proceeded, it instantly ceased, at least there, and two or three of these frogs would dash into the water and dive. Wishing much to witness the act of uttering the sound, (which was no easy matter, for, as I have said, it ceased on the approach of a foot,) I crept cautiously to the edge of one of the little pools, in which I saw two or three frogs: they were very shy, and kept under water, but I waited patiently, quiet and motionless, a long time, taking care not to stir hand or foot. At length, one of them, taking courage, raised his head and half of his body out of water, sitting up, as it were, and resting on the toes of his forefeet, and thus uttered the piercing shriek, which had a kind of cracked or ringing sound, somewhat like that of a penny trumpet. When about to cry, he first fluttered the skin of the throat a few times, then suddenly inflated it, till it was like a blown bladder, perfectly round, as big as his head, which continued so all the time of the shriek, about four or five seconds. I saw him do it many times close to my feet: it was a very singular sight. The skin of the throat seemed, when thus inflated, like a thin transparent membrane.

I had always supposed that the food of the Lady-birds *(Coccinelladae)* was wholly confined to the different species of Plant-lice *(Aphides),* or at least to insects. We have a large species common here, which is yellow, with seven black spots on each elytron, and six on the thorax *(Coccinella borealis),* and I frequently find this species, sometimes congregated in groups amounting to a dozen, and sometimes single individuals, on the leaves of the water-melon *(Cucurbita citrullus),* on which they feed, gnawing ragged holes on the surface of the leaf, not at the edge.

The logs of which the school-house is built, being dry, the bark of course is loose and easily separable: on pulling it off, we see some curious little insects *(Lepisma),* which, on being exposed, run very swiftly, endeavouring to hide themselves from the light. They have no wings in any of their stages, being one of the few genera of true insects belonging to the order Aptera. The tail is composed of three slender bristles *(setae),* of which the external ones are held sometimes parallel to the central one, forming apparently but one, and sometimes diverging so much as to make two right angles with it. They are covered with powdery scales of a silvery lustre, in which respect they resemble the *Lepidoptera,* as also in the very slight tenacity with which these adhere, coming off upon the finger on the slightest touch.

One of the most prominent and most frequent of the sounds which strike a stranger here, and one which cannot fail to awaken the curiosity and excite the inquiries of even the most unobservant, is the call of the Quail *(Ortyx Virginiana).* All day long, from morning till night, we hear the words "Bob White," whistled with invincible pertinacity in every direction. The sound is exactly what may be produced by a person attempting to whistle these words, making the second syllable seven or eight notes higher than the first. It is loud and clear, and may be heard a long way off. The position of the bird, when uttering his call, may be the top of an out-house, or a pile of logs; but his favourite place is the topmost rail of the fence; for it is to the plantations he chiefly resorts, being rarely seen in the forest. I found a few days ago an egg of the Quail, lying on the bare ground in the midst of the public road; it was pure white, very sharp at the small end, almost conical. Though it generally makes a large nest, well covered over, I am told that it is not uncommon for it to drop its eggs on the ground, without any nest.

Wilson has some interesting speculations connected with this species. After speaking of some Quails, or Partridges, as he calls them indiscriminately, that had been brought up by a hen, he says:—"It has been frequently asserted to me, that the Quails lay occasionally in each other's nests. Though I have never myself seen a case of this kind, I do not think it altogether improbable, from the fact that they have often been known to drop their eggs in the nest of the common hen, when that happened to be in the fields, or at a small distance from the house. The two Partridges above mentioned were raised in this manner; and it was particularly remarked by the lady who gave me the information, that the hen sat for several days after her own eggs were hatched, until the young Quails made their appearance. The Partridge, on her part, has sometimes been employed to hatch the eggs of the common domestic hen. A friend of mine, who himself made the experiment, informs me that of several hen's eggs which he substituted in place of those of the Partridge, she brought out the whole; and that for several weeks, he occasionally surprised her, in various parts of the plantation, with her brood of chickens, on which occasions she exhibited the most distressful alarm, and practised her usual manoeuvres. Even after they were considerably grown, and larger than the Partridge herself, she continued to lead them about; but though their notes or call were those of common chickens, their manners had all the shyness, timidity, and alarm of young Partridges, running with great rapidity, and squatting in the grass, exactly in the manner of the Partridge. Soon after this they disappeared, having probably been destroyed by dogs, by the gun, or by birds of prey. Whether the domestic fowl might not by this method be very soon brought back to its original savage state, and thereby supply another additional subject for the amusement of the sportsman, will scarcely admit of a doubt. But the experiment, in order to ensure its success, would require to be made in a quarter of the country less exposed than ours to the ravages of guns, traps, dogs, and the deep snows of winter, that the new tribe might have full time to become completely naturalized, and well fixed in all their native habits."

Going home from school one evening, we saw crossing the path before us a very beautiful species of snake, which I suppose to have been the Scarlet Viper (*Vipera fulvia*, HARLAN; *Coluber coccineus*, SAY). The boys gave chase to it, and killed it; they called it the Blunt-tailed Mocassin Snake. It was bright scarlet, with transverse bands of black. I examined its head, and found that, by the rule given by Shaw, it should be harmless, as it had small teeth in the palate as well as in the jaw, and I perceived no poison fangs; but if I am right as to the species, it must have them: it has the reputation of being highly poisonous, but with the common people this accusation is so indiscriminately brought against all the tribe of serpents, that it is of very little weight; as I have found in most other instances of the kind, when I inquired if they had ever heard of any one who was bitten by it, they acknowledged that they had not, but "every body said that it was venomous." The children are very expert in discovering indications of the wild animals: they often show me a slight line in the dust across the road, where they say a snake has crossed, and they can even determine in which direction it travelled by a still more shadowy mark made by its tail.

I have sometimes thought, that the difference between the intellectual capacity of one individual and that of another, is much less than is generally supposed. There are certain conventional channels, into which we expect the mental energies to be directed, and if we do not find them in these, we are apt to conclude them altogether wanting. You shall take two boys in a school. One is the first boy in the first class; he repeats his lesson without a mistake; the pedagogue pats his head, and prophesies that he will be a councillor. The other of the same age, with the same chances, is the last boy of the last class; he perceives no agreement at all between the verb and the nominative case; you can scarcely convince him by argument that two and two make four. One of these is called a bright genius, the other is branded as a stupid dunce. But take these lads into the fields and lanes. The stupid one is expert at all games and exercises; is acquainted with every bird by sight; knows the colour, size, shape, and number of the eggs of each; can lay his paw upon all the nests in the neighbourhood; can ride, swim, trap a mole, shoot a hawk, hook a trout, like a professed adept. The genius is become a mope; he sees no pleasure in all this; can't learn it when he tries; knows as much about it when he leaves off as when he began; is out of his element—a fish out of water. The tables are turned. So it is with these boys of mine: they know little which in the cultivated society of crowded cities is thought worth knowing, or called knowledge at all; but in the sights and sounds of the wilderness, their trained eyes and ears, young as they are, read a language, which to the mere oppidan would be a sealed book, putting all his boasted learning at fault.

Of course provincialisms—slight peculiarities in dialect—are to be found in every part of a large country speaking the same language, and the inhabitant of one district has no right to assume any superiority over one of another who uses a phrase differing from his own. Still, however, in all liberality of allowance, the knowledge of such differences may be a legitimate source of amusement, and possibly of instruction. Let me tell you one or two idioms, in which the Alabamians rejoice. To "holler," is used to express any sort of noise as well as shouting; a carpenter-bee was buzzing the other day, and one of the children remarked "how the bee *hollers* in his hole!" To "whip," is to overcome, as we use "beat" in the same extensive sense. "He *whipped* me at leaping, but I reckon I can *whip* him at running." To "tote" is to carry; "I *toted* the *bucket,*" means "I carried the little tin pail in which the dinner was brought to school." A small river is a "creek," and a brook is a "branch." When I came first, I was inquiring for a neighbour's house, and was directed to pursue a certain path through the woods, till I crossed the *branch*. I looked out for some low branch of a tree that grew across the road, and searched in vain, of course. The sticks, straws, foam, &c., which accumulate by the side of a stream are designated by the expressive term "trash." In dress, trousers are "pantaloons," and a jacket is a "roundabout." I have been told of some "*severe* dogs," kept in this vicinity; and perhaps you have heard the joke about that "most severe pony," which is said to have been chased thrice round the field by a flash of lightning, and gained the race at last. When one wishes another to cease doing what is unpleasant, he requests him to "*quit* doing it," or else "*make tracks,*" that is, "go away." "Good," is used in the sense of "well;" "he writes good." "Right," in the old English acceptation of "very," thus: "it is a right pretty book." When one wishes to speak contemptuously of another, he either calls him "all sorts of a feller," or says, "he's no account." To learn a thing by heart is to "memorize" it. Inquiry is pronounced and accented "énquĭry;" idea is ídea; and other anomalies in accentuation exist, of which these may suffice. Still I have never heard an American fall into the blunder of calling a white egg, a "*wite hegg,*" as thousands of our countrymen do. But what has all this to do with natural history?—not much, in good truth, unless you class it under the head of "habits and manners of animals belonging to the genus *Homo*."

There are some insects which, without any particular or assignable reason, I have always had—ever since I cared anything about entomology—an especial desire to see. A living specimen of some of the larger species of *Cicadae* was of this sort. I have at length been gratified. For some time I have observed on the trunks of trees, especially pines, the empty pupa-skin of a very large species, very firmly attached by the claws to the bark of the tree, at some feet above the ground. From its position and shape, one might easily mistake it at first sight for the living pupa, but a nearer inspection shows the opening in the back and head from which the perfect insect has disengaged itself. And I have also found lately, in the sandy paths, round holes about two inches deep and an inch in diameter, each containing a living pupa of this species. I have taken two or three to endeavour to rear them, but they all died; one of them arrived so near its change as to show the discoloration which always immediately precedes evolution of the imago, and the skin of the back had even begun to split; but it died in the act, and was never perfected. The children had told me that they occasionally find the perfect insects in the summer, lying on their backs on the ground, from which position they are unable to rise. I hear their shrill ringing crink kept up unceasingly in the trees every day, generally high up among the branches. Once or twice I heard one on a low branch within reach, and carefully watched and searched with my eyes to discover the songsters, but found that with all my caution I could not get within several yards of the bough before they ceased, and they would not tune up again while I remained. Their song, though monotonous and pertinacious, is musical and cheerful, and therefore, to me at least, not unpleasing.

I have, at length, obtained one in the perfected state. I found it lying on the floor of the school, having just come in at the open door. It was lying on its back in the sun, and, as the children had described, vainly endeavouring, by fruitless kickings and strugglings, to regain a prone position, its feet being very short. It is a smaller species than the one which I had found in pupa, being only about three-fourths of an inch in length, and two inches and a half in spread of wing; the body is greyish green, spotted with black, the abdomen yellow; the wings are ample, perfectly transparent, colourless (except the nervures, and a few black dots), and glistening, very much like a thin lamina of talc. It is a pretty little creature. As I was examining it in my hand, contemplating the addition it would make to my cabinet, it suddenly stretched out its shining wings, and away it flew to the leafy branches of a tall hickory-tree. Its flight was straight, and somewhat heavy. The genus is commonly known here by the erroneous name of "locust."

The Purple Grakles (*Quiscalus versicolor*) are now numerous; in the evening they sit congregated together side by side, as close as they can place themselves, on the high branches of the dead pines that overlook the clearings. As they sit, they every now and then open their wings, uttering at the same time a querulous sort of low note.

What a most magnificent plant is the Trumpet-flower (*Bignonia radicans*)! It is a climbing shrub, embracing the trunks of the largest oaks to the height of thirty or forty feet, with handsome pinnate leaves, and spikes of splendid trumpet-shaped blossoms, each three inches in length, of a brilliant orange-red, projecting from a deep cup-shaped calyx of shining scarlet. The stalks are nu-

Ruby-throat Humming-bird and Trumpet-flower

merous, and the foliage so thick as to cover the trunk of the tree, from which the clusters of noble flowers profusely hang, clothing the dead and sapless oak with a verdure and a beauty not its own, and thus repaying with ample interest all obligations for the support it receives. In some fields, especially in low situations by the side of little streams, I have seen almost every girdled tree covered with the rich foliage of the trumpet-flower, and most of them in full blossom; altogether changing the character of those unsightly trunks, rendering them objects on whose beauty the eye delights to gaze. Sometimes the plant has entwined round an old broken stump of low stature; in this case, having risen to the height of its support, it begins to spread laterally, and soon forms a large round bush.

The Ruby-throat Humming-bird *(Trochilus colubris)* delights to visit these flowers; their deep capacious tubes are just the thing for him. We may sometimes see half-a-dozen at once round a single bush, quite in their glory, humming and buzzing from one flower to another, as if too impatient to feed; now burying themselves to the very wings in the deep corolla, sipping the nectar, or snapping up the multitudes of little flies entangled in the tube; now rushing off in a straight line like a shooting star, now returning as swiftly, while their brilliant plumage gleams in the sun like gold and precious stones.

There are other plants which climb up trees, sending out little rootlets by means of which they attach themselves to the bark. All such plants are indiscriminately called vines. There is one which is named the Cross Vine, from the singular circumstance of its stem, on the stripping off of its bark, spontaneously dividing into four parts, as if split crosswise into quarters. I do not know its specific name, but doubtless it is a *Bignonia.* I have already alluded to the ragged drapery of Spanish moss *(Tillandsia usneoides),* in which the withered arms of many of the girdled trees, and some living ones, are enveloped. It at first sight resembles the Tree-moss *(Usnea)* of the north; but that is a lichen, whereas this is a phenogamous plant. The whole plant consists of long thread-like filaments, thickly matted together about the boughs, and depending at the extremities; they are pale yellowish-green, especially near the tops where the young leaves appear, most of the plant being covered with a hoary greyish sort of down. The leaves sheath the stem, and each other at their bases, and project so little as scarcely to affect the general filiform appearance. The flowers are inconspicuous, closely set on the stem, without any footstalk, single, of a pale greenish hue. I am told that if a bunch be torn off, and flung into a tree, it will readily take root and spread widely and rapidly. Pursh says that its fibres, divested of their outside coating, make excellent mattresses, and are a good substitute for horse-hair. I have used the dry plant to stuff preserved skins, in lack of other material.

Perhaps of all that changeable race, the *Fungi,* there is none more changeable than a very curious species which is not uncommon on old fallen logs. It first appears oozing from crevices, on each side of which it spreads over a space of several inches. It then appears like a mass of very thick cream, which has been pressed through a hair sieve, and is sufficiently consistent to retain the irregularity of surface caused by the interstices; its colour is a brilliant gamboge-yellow. In about twelve hours, it has become much thicker and harder, but still soft enough to be squeezed by the finger; the inside is now nearly black, the surface alone being yellow. In twelve hours more it has changed to a mass of impalpable dry powder, of a dark olive-brown colour, which looks and feels like very fine snuff, the surface being of a dirty white or drab hue; so that no one who had not marked it would possibly recognise the creamy mass which he had seen twenty-four hours before.

Different species of Sensitive Plants are very numerous in the woods; a trailing spinous species *(Schrankia uncinata)* is very irritable; the slightest touch makes the leaflets close together instantly. It is called the Sensitive Brier. Others only close partially, and with much more slowness. The leaves are pinnate, the leaflets, which are numerous and even—that is, without a terminal one—are very singular in shape, the mid-rib dividing them into two very irregular and unequal portions. The flowers are in globular spikes, and resemble a little sphere of pink down, composed of fine filaments radiating from the centre, which are the long stamens of many small close-set blossoms. I have seen a much larger species *(Mimosa ——)*, a tree twelve or fifteen feet in height, whose globular flowers, an inch in diameter, and of a pink hue, were delightfully fragrant; this I think is rare, and I do not know that it possesses any peculiar irritability.

Just at this season the majestic Chestnut *(Castanea Americana)* is very conspicuous in the forest by its masses of pale mealy foliage, formed by the graceful pendulous feathery spikes of small flowers, their light downy appearance being caused by the flowers being composed of stamens and pistil without apparent corolla. These spikes first appear as slender strings, growing to the length of about six inches; at that time the unopened flowers, sixty or seventy on each spike, look like little flattened greenish tubercles, running in a spiral direction round the axis. Although these spikes are long, and contain many blossoms, no more than one or two produce fruit; indeed, it would be impossible for all to be fertile, for as the little blossoms are in close contact with each other, there would be no room for the growth of the fruit except by the destruction of many of them; for when full grown the fruit, or *burr,* as it is called, is two inches in diameter. The chestnut is one of the most common, and at the same time one of the most noble, of our forest trees. It grows to a large size, and frequently attains the height of a hundred feet. Its bark is fibrous and stringy, torn by the gradual increase of the trunk into longitudinal meshes, with lozenge-shaped interstices; it is of a hoary grey colour, and altogether bears a very close resemblance to that of the cedar of the north *(Thuja occidentalis)*. The leaves are like those of the Beech in shape and colour, long-oval with sharp teeth. The wood is red, and is fine and close-grained; yet is used for nothing, as it decays very soon, and is wholly unfit for fuel, smouldering away in ashes, and with difficulty kept alight at all.

There is an inexpressible grandeur in these primeval forests. Many of the trees are of immense magnitude, and their trunks rise like pillars from the soft and damp soil, shooting upward in columnal majesty; not, in general, gnarled and twisted and branched, like the trees of our own land, or as even these same kinds would be if growing in the open field, exposed to the influences of the sun and winds. The number of young saplings that at first sprang up together prevented the throwing forth of side-shoots; each struggled upward toward the light of heaven, each striving for the mastery over its fellows, for the possession of the space and the light which could be obtained right upward. To this end all the vegetative energy was directed; the sap was not wasted in lateral buds, or if such peeped forth, they withered for lack of light. But as all were engaged in the same struggle, the desired object still removed as the summits of the aspiring trees pushed upward; till the weaker, being left behind, died out one by one, and the mighty winners of the race at length found themselves comparatively few in number, and divided by vacant spaces sufficiently wide to allow of the expansion of lateral branches, and the formation of verdant crowns of interwoven foliage.

And thus we see the original forest. The ground is commonly clear of underwood to a remarkable degree, so that it is by no means unusual for hunters to pursue their game on horseback at full speed through these sylvan recesses. A few slender shrubs occur, of species that delight in the greenwood shade; and in some parts the trees are united by trailing vines and prickly creepers that clog up the way; but these are rather found in the woods of second growth than in the pristine forests.

To walk in the forest alone is a high gratification. The perfect stillness and utter solitude, unbroken, commonly, by even ordinary woodland sounds and sights, tranquillize and sober the mind; the gloom has a solemn effect, for there is no light but what penetrates through the green leaves far above our head; the range of vision all around is limited by the innumerable straight and smooth trunks, exactly alike on every side, in which the fancy becomes lost. The devout spirit is drawn upward in such a scene, which imagination presently turns into a magnificent temple, whose far distant roof is borne on uncounted columns; and indeed it is a glorious temple, one worthy of the Hand that reared it.

"Father, thy hand
Hath rear'd those venerable columns, Thou
Didst weave this verdant roof. Thou didst look down
Upon the naked earth, and forthwith rose
All these fair ranks of trees. They in thy sun
Budded, and shook their green leaves in thy breeze,
And shot towards heaven. The century-living crow,
Whose birth was in their tops, grew old and died
Among their branches, till at last they stood,
As now they stand, massy and tall and dark,
Fit shrine for humble worshipper to hold
Communion with his Maker. These dim vaults,
These winding aisles, of human pomp or pride
Report not. No fantastic carvings show
The boast of our vain race to change the form
Of thy fair works. But Thou art here—thou fill'st
The solitude. Thou art in the soft winds
That run along the summit of these trees
In music;—Thou art in the cooler breath,
That from the inmost darkness of the place
Comes, scarcely felt;—the barky trunks, the ground,
The fresh moist ground, are all instinct with Thee.
Here is continual worship;—Nature, here,
In the tranquillity that Thou dost love,
Enjoys thy presence. Noiselessly around,
From perch to perch, the solitary bird
Passes; and yon clear spring, that, midst its herbs,
Wells softly forth, and visits the strong roots

Of half the mighty forest, tells no tale
Of all the good it does. Thou hast not left
Thyself without a witness, in these shades,
Of thy perfections. Grandeur, strength, and grace,
Are here to speak of Thee."*

A large moth, the Purple Underwing *(Catocala Epione),* led me a wild-goose chase the other day. All the moths of this genus are beautiful, the under wings being generally dyed with brilliant crimson, scarlet, or orange, banded with black; in some however they are wholly black, as in the species before us, with a changeable purple gloss. The upper wings, in all, I believe, are finely variegated with sober colours, grey, brown, and black, in many waves and shades; and in this we see a wise ordination of Providence for their safety. Their usual resting place is the perpendicular trunk of a tree; and if the bright and conspicuous under-wings were visible, their retreat would be at once discovered; but when at rest, these are entirely concealed by the fore-wings, whose varied but sombre hues so exactly correspond with those of the bark as effectually to baffle the sight, unless the observer be very eagle-eyed. In pursuing these moths, particularly a very handsome one, whose hind-wings are scarlet, with two black bands *(Catocala Ilia),* I have observed and admired this fact, though as a collector I have been ready to wish they were a little more readily seen. They haunt the interior of the forest, and fly usually in the afternoon; the brilliant red of the wings is very visible in flight, and therefore their course is easily traced; they fly swiftly and suddenly, and on alighting on the trunk of a tree, usually a little out of reach, are perfectly at rest in an instant, so that they appear to vanish; for though I have watched them to a tree only a few yards distant, and have kept my eye fixed on the spot; on coming to it, I have looked in vain for the moth, and supposed that I have been deceived; but, to be sure, on reaching up to the spot with a stick, the red wings flash out, and away flits the moth to another tree.

There is a hymenopterous fly *(Scolia quadrimaculata)* which I have seen here occasionally, in the paths of the forest, towards evening. It is shaped like a bee, but is vastly larger, deep black, with four large yellow spots on the abdomen, placed in the form of a square; the wings have in a high degree that brilliant vio-

*Bryant; "Forest Hymn."

let reflection which is found in many species of this order; the legs are thickly clothed with coarse black hair. The first time I saw it, it was fluttering along the ground, half flying, half crawling, carrying a larva of a lamellicorn beetle in its mouth, as big and long as my little finger, indeed much larger and heavier than itself; I was told that it is in the habit of burying these in the ground. Doubtless, like many other similar insects, it stupifies the larva, without killing it, and then lays its egg in the hole with it, so that the young, as soon as hatched, finds its food thus ready prepared for it. The insect is somewhat clumsy in its motions, even when unencumbered; sometimes fluttering along the ground thus, a few inches at a time, so slowly as easily to be caught, at other times flying fairly enough, but with a heavy lumbering flight. I do not believe that it is poisonous, or, if it is, that it readily exerts its powers.

In the yard surrounding the school, is a hole in the sandy earth, in which sits a Toad *(Bufo musicus)*. The hole is just wide enough to hold him, but nine or ten inches deep. He stations himself just at the mouth, with his sapient head and brilliant eyes peeping out. If a stick is presented to him, he snaps fiercely at it, but if pressed, retires to the bottom of his cell, returning however to the mouth immediately. I presume his occupation there is to look out for any hapless insect that may chance that way. We dig him out and he hops away; very nimbly, considering he is but a toad.

Three or four species of butterflies have fallen under my notice since my last, which I had not before observed. Two of them are very little, the Red-lined Ringlet *(Hipparchia areolata),* and the Silver-spotted Ringlet *(H. gemma)*. They are much alike, both dusky on the upper surface, and beneath marked with a few eye-spots; the former has two reddish-brown lines crossing the wings; the latter, two or three dashes of silver on the under surface. Their caterpillars are green, with longitudinal stripes; and that of the former feeds, according to Abbott, on a grass-like plant, the drooping Andropogon *(Andropogon nutans)*.

Another species of this genus, the Pearly-eye *(H. Andromacha),* larger than these, and more beautiful, from the pearly iridescence of the inferior surface, is now common. It is interesting from its social and gamesome habits. A particular individual will frequent the foot of a particular tree for many successive days, contrary to the roaming habits of butterflies in general. Hence he will sally out on any other passing butterfly, either of his own or of another species; and, after performing sundry circumvolutions, retire to his chosen post of observation again. Occasionally I have seen another butterfly of the same species, after having had his amicable tustle, take likewise a stand on a neighbouring spot; and after a few minutes' rest, both would simultaneously rush to the conflict, like knights at a tournament; and wheel and roll about in the air as before. Then each would return to his own place with the utmost precision, and presently renew the "passage of arms" with the same result, for very many times in succession.

A fourth species is the largest living butterfly I have ever seen, being upwards of five inches from tip to tip of the expanded wings. I call it the Black Emperor Swallow-tail *(Papilio Glaucus);* it is a very noble fly, and forms quite a contrast to the dusky pigmies I just now noticed. Its colour is deep black, with two marginal rows of yellow crescents; and within them a row of larger azure crescents, which are obliterated towards the tip of the first wings; the second pair has a large cloud of azure dots in the centre. The under surface is much the same, but the black is more dusky; the crescents in the second wings are larger and tinged with orange, and the azure central cloud is wanting. It appears to be rare, as I have seen only two specimens of it, but one of which I succeeded in obtaining. This I caught in a garden just as the sun was setting, hovering over a strawberry-bed; the other was seen in the middle of the day, but in the dark shade of the woods; I gave chase to it, but it redoubled its speed, and was soon out of reach in the forest. I observed that it flew high, which butterflies do not generally do. The larva of this fine species is said to be in all respects like that of the Tiger Swallow-tail *(Papilio Turnus),* being of a fine green, with two eye-spots on the thickest parts of the body.

I have taken a single individual, in very shabby, weather-beaten condition, of another fine butterfly, the Red-spotted Purple *(Limenitis Ursula).* It is black, or rather a very deep purple, the hind-wings broadly banded with lustrous bluish-green, and marked with crescents of the same. The under surface, besides, has many spots of bright red. It very much resembles the Banded Purple of the north *(Limenitis Arthemis),* but it wants the delicate pearly-white band. It seems to replace that species in the south. The larva and pupa have a still more exact resemblance; the former is said to feed on the Green-wooded Whortleberry *(Vaccinium stamineum).*

And, while speaking of insects, I may just mention two or three others that I have recently seen, though I know little of them but their appearance. I took a few days ago, sucking some flowers beneath the burning beams of noon, a very pretty little creature, the Humble-bee Hawkmoth *(Sesia Pelasgus).* Having taken it in Canada, likewise, I presume it is widely scattered over the continent; though my northern specimen differs somewhat from the present. It looks very much like a humble-bee, the body being clothed with the same sort of down, and banded with black and yellow; the wings are perfectly transparent, except the margins, which are covered with dark brown scales. Like the Humming-bird Hawkmoth *(Macroglossa stellatarum)* of our own country, it is abroad (I believe exclusively) by daylight, and delights in whisking from flower to flower; its motions are swift and sudden. There is a beautiful flower now in blossom in the gardens, the Horned Poppy *(Argemone Mexicana),* which forms an attraction to these bright-hued insects. It is of a golden yellow, and has handsomely spotted, thistle-like leaves.

Among the soft decaying wood, beneath the bark of a fallen tree, I found many specimens of a very minute Earwig *(Forficula* ———?). Most of them were in larva; but one was in the perfect state, and very closely resembled in appearance our common European species, but for its minuteness, being less than one-fourth of an inch in length. The larvae of this genus have a far greater likeness to the imago than those of beetles, the forceps being present, and the shape identical; but the elytra and wings of course are absent.

There is another insect which I cannot pass over, for its very singular form. It is the Hair Spectre *(Emesa filum),* of a light grey colour, about an inch and a half in length, with long limbs, but so slender that the insect looks like a bit of grey thread, to which some bent hairs are attached. It moves slowly and awkwardly, often swaying backward and forward, as if balancing itself; but, from the length of its legs, it makes considerable strides. It has a sucker bent under the breast, in place of jaws, like the Bugs; and the thigh and shank of the fore-leg are armed with teeth or spines, as in the Mantes, which, on being doubled together, fit into each other. Such was its slenderness, that in endeavouring to transfix it for my cabinet, with a very fine pin, I cut it through and destroyed it. I have taken one since from a peach-tree, and it is occasionally seen on people's clothes after walking, but is not very common.

The woods are frequently enlivened by the antics of playful Squirrels, of large size. They especially haunt the tall trees that stand round the houses of the planters, or possibly they *seem* to prefer these trees because they are there more under constant observation. There are several species, of which the most common is the Fox-squirrel *(Sciurus capistratus).* He is a beast of some pretensions, a full grown male occasionally measuring fourteen or fifteen inches in length, exclusive of the tail, which is nearly as much more. Thus he greatly exceeds our little English species, whose manners Cowper so exquisitely portrays:

> "Drawn from his refuge in some lonely elm,
> That age or injury has hollow'd deep,
> Where, on his bed of wool and matted leaves,
> He has outslept the winter, ventures forth
> To frisk awhile, and bask in the warm sun,
> The squirrel, flippant, pert, and full of play.
> He sees me, and at once, swift as a bird,
> Ascends the neighbouring beech; there whisks his brush,
> And perks his ears, and stamps, and cries aloud,
> With all the prettiness of feign'd alarm,
> And anger insignificantly fierce."*

This description might almost have served for a portrait of our sylvan friend. He chatters, shows his teeth, and grunts at you from the security of some lofty branch; utters his short impatient bark; dashes round the trunk; threatens again from the opposite side; "whisks his brush," as the poet says, and declares, as plainly as action can speak, that he has a great mind to eat you up, only that you are so provokingly big.

Generally two or three play together, and it is very amusing to watch their manoeuvrings; to mark how they leap from branch to branch, to see them fly round and round almost with the agility of a bird; now they chase each other round and round the tree, dart up and down the smooth pillar-like trunk, in and out of the hollows; now they scamper along some horizontal bough till they reach the terminal twig, whence they take a flying jump to the neighbouring tree, fearless of the chasm that yawns between. All this is pretty play, but the merciless planter puts a tragical end to it. He comes up with his unerring rifle; the barrel drops into his left hand; the stock is at his shoulder; a momentary sight— crack!—down falls the gamesome squirrel, plunging through the green leaves, and plumps heavily on the earth. A drop of blood on each side, staining the white fur of the belly, shows that the fatal ball has passed right through. The planter

---

The Task, book vi.

The Fox-squirrel

loads again; as much powder as will just cover the ball lying in the hollow of his left hand, is the charge; the ramrod twice springs half out of the barrel, and again the rifle points upward. The other falls; and these two we carry in to furnish a dinner for the family. I admire, as they lie warm and flexible, yet motionless, in my hand, the soft thick fur, mottled grey on the back, and pure white beneath; the feet, the nose, and the ears, likewise spotless white, and the tail pencilled with long parted hairs of a delicate light grey. Truly it is a pretty little animal.

Occasionally we see Squirrels differing greatly from this in colour, but of the same size and manners. One is almost wholly black; another has the upper parts dark brown, and the belly rust-red; the latter is not uncommon. Both of these are considered by Dr. Bachmann, of South Carolina, as varieties of the Fox-squirrel.

Stewed, or made into a pie, squirrel is excellent eating; the fat is apt to be rank, especially of the males; the meat is white, much like that of the rabbit, but superior in flavour. Roasted I do not much admire it, as it is somewhat flabby.

There is a much smaller grey Squirrel, as common as the former, but haunting somewhat different situations. This is the Carolina Squirrel (*S. Carolinensis);* it is coloured nearly as the Fox-squirrel, but the grey coat of the back inclines to rusty. It is much less active and playful; frequents rather the dark sombre woods around the swamps and rivers, and hides under the long ragged tufts of Spanish moss *(Tillandsia)* that stream from the branches. Both kinds make a comfortable dray or nest in the fork of a tree; externally of twigs, sticks, and leaves, internally lined with moss and lichen. This is not only for the rearing of the offspring, but for the habitation of the adults, at least during the summer.

The value of the flesh to make or eke out a dinner is not the only motive which induces the planter to shoot these little truants. A rifle-ball, or a charge of powder, is worth more here than a pound or two of meat. They are incorrigible robbers. They appear to imagine that the planter's corn is sown exclusively for them, and fail not to make all the use they can of his liberality. Morning, noon, and eve, Squggy is in the corn-field; from the time that the young and tender grain begins to form within the enveloping sheath, till it has grown large, and hard, and yellow, and is housed (at least what remains of it) in the barn. But especially does the Squirrel like it (and unremittingly he pays his devotions to it) when the grain is of that plump but soft and pulpy substance that resembles cream; when the planter's palate, too, is particularly pleased with it, and when he plucks the ears, and, just parching them over the fire, brings them to table under the appellation of *roseneers, q. d.* roasting ears. This similarity of taste between planter and squirrel induces rivalry, and the result is as I have stated—*vae victis.*

Some time ago a very clever fellow announced that he had discovered an infallible preventive of the depredations of the Squirrels. So important a declaration was of course received with open ears; a considerable remuneration was collected for the secret, and the planters of the neighbourhood met him to be instructed. The sage received the cash, buttoned his pockets, and bowed. "Gentlemen," he said, "my scheme is simple, but effective. I have observed that the Squirrels invariably begin their attacks *on the outside row* of corn in the field. *Omit the outside row,* and they won't know where to begin!" The door was open—the speaker was gone—not waiting even for the applause, which his ingenious plan so much merited.

In the comparative solitude of these vast forests, the clearings are small compared with the immensity of the untouched wilds; the dwellings few and remote from each other; many of the occupations, and especially the amusements, which belong to the crowded inhabitants of Europe are here unknown. The wild animals are more familiar to man than his fellows; the planter often passes days, or even weeks, without seeing a human face except those of his own family and his overseer; his negroes he scarcely considers as human; they are but "goods and chattels." Self-defence, and the natural craving for excitement, compel him to be a *hunter;* it is the appropriate occupation of a new, grand, luxuriant, wild country like this, and one which seems natural to man, to judge from the eagerness and zest with which every one engages in it when he has the opportunity. The long rifle is familiar to every hand; skill in the use of it is the highest accomplishment which a southern gentleman glories in; even the children acquire an astonishing expertness in handling this deadly weapon at a very early age.

But skill as a marksman is not estimated by quite the same standard as in the old country. Pre-eminence in any art must bear a certain relation to the average attainment; and where this is universally high, distinction can be won only by something very exalted. Hence, when the young men meet together to display their skill, curious tests are employed, which remind one of the days of old English archery, when splitting the peeled wand at a hundred paces, and such like, were the boast of the greenwood bowman. Some of these practices I had read of, but here I find them in frequent use. "Driving the nail" is one of these; a stout nail is hammered into a post about half way up to the head; the riflemen then stand at an immense distance, and fire at the nail; the object is to hit the nail so truly on the head with the ball as to drive it home. To hit it at all on one side, so as to cause it to bend or swerve, is failure; missing it altogether is out of the question.

Another feat is "threading the needle." An auger-hole is pierced through the centre of an upright board; the orifice is just large enough to allow the ball to pass without touching; and *it is expected* to pass without touching. A third is still more exciting—"snuffing the candle." It is performed in the night, and the darkness of the scene adds a wildness to the amusement that greatly enhances its interest. A calm night is chosen; half-a-dozen ends of tallow-candle and a box of matches are taken out into the field, whither the uproarious party of stalwart youths repair. One of them takes his station by the mark; a stick is thrust perpendicularly in the ground, on the top of which a bit of candle is fixed either in a socket, or by means of a few drops of grease. A plank is set up behind the candle, to receive the balls, which are all carefully picked out after the sport is over, being much too valuable to be wasted. The marker now lights the candle, which glimmers like a feeble star, but just visible at the spot where the expectant party are standing. Each one carefully loads his rifle; some mark the barrel with a line of chalk to aid the sight in the darkness; others neglect this, and seem to know the position of the "pea" by instinct. There is a sharp short crack, and a line of fire; a little cloud of smoke rises perpendicularly upwards; an unmerciful shout of derision hails the unlucky marksman, for the candle is still twinkling dimly and redly as before. Another confidently succeeds; the light is suddenly extinguished; his ball has cut it off just below the flame. This won't do; the test of skill is to *snuff* the candle, without putting it out.

A third now steps up; it is my friend Jones, the overseer on the plantation where I am residing; he is a crack shot, and we all expect something superb now. The marker has replaced the lighted candle; it is allowed to burn a few minutes until the wick has become long. The dimness of the light at length announces its readiness, and the marker cries "Fire!" A moment's breathless silence follows the flash and the report; a change was seen to pass upon the distant gleam, and the dull red light has suddenly become white and sparkling. "Right good!" cries the marker; the ball has passed through the centre of the flame and "snuffed the candle," and whoops and shouts of applause ring through the field, and echo from the surrounding forest. This extraordinary feat is usually performed two or three times in every contest of skill.

A common exploit is "barking off" a squirrel. My worthy friend Major Vanner, the other day, at my request, performed this. A couple of fox-squirrels were playing far up on a towering beech in the yard, little suspecting what was coming "for the benefit of science." My friend went in, and brought out his trusty rifle; waited a moment for one of the little frisky gentlemen to be rightly placed, for it is needful to the feat that the squirrel should be clinging to the bark of the tree. The first shot was a failure; the squirrel fell dead indeed, but it was pierced with the ball, which was not the object. Perhaps the creature had moved a little at the instant, or perhaps the planter had been too carelessly confident; however, his mettle was up, and he took care that the second should be all right. The ball struck the trunk of the tree just beneath the belly of the animal, driving off a piece of the bark as large as one's hand, and with it the squirrel, without a wound or a ruffled hair, but killed by the concussion.

Letter VI

July 1st

You must not expect from me anything like a continuous narrative. "Story! why, bless you, I have none to tell, Sir!" My observations are slight and disjointed; peeps through Nature's keyhole at her recondite mysteries;—"passages in the life of a spider;"—"unpublished memoirs of a beetle;"—"notes of the domestic economy of a fly:"—and you must take them for so much as they are worth.

The Indian Corn *(Zea mays)* is in all its glory; few plants have a more noble appearance than the variety of maize cultivated here; the northern corn is a pigmy to it. It grows to the height of ten feet; the stem strong and thick, surrounded and partially enveloped in its large flag-like leaves, here and there the swelling ears projecting from the stalk, each enclosed in its membranous sheath, from the extremity of which the pendulous shining filaments hang out, called the silk, and which are the pistils of the female flowers; and the tall elegant spike of male flowers, called the tassel, crowns the whole. The full-ripe ears are often nearly a foot in length, and seven or eight inches in circumference; the grains are very closely set, and in growing pinch each other up into a square form; the *cob,* or pithy placenta, which remains after the grains have been shelled off, is as large as a full ear of the northern corn. It is now in that agreeable condition already alluded to, called "roasting-ear;" the grains being formed, but yet quite soft and pulpy. Some now go into field and gather the ears, and bite off the grains while raw, when they have a sugary taste; but they are more commonly used as a culinary vegetable, roasted at the fire, or boiled and shelled like peas, and eaten with melted butter. It is considered a delicacy; but as the ripening corn rapidly hardens, it lasts only a few days. Not only squirrels, but rabbits, bears, and many other wild animals, have a similar taste for roasting-ears, and do not scruple to indulge their partiality at the farmer's expense. Corn is almost the only bread-stuff raised here, the wheaten flour used being imported chiefly from the north. Cotton and corn divide the plantations.

The steep banks of many of the winding creeks and branches are densely clothed, for considerable portions of their darkling course, with tall canes (*Miega macrosperma*). When the country was first settled, the cane-brakes were much more extensive, and only penetrable by means of the axe. But many of them have been cut down; and the depredations of the cattle, which are very fond of the plant, eating off the tender and succulent shoots, keep down its growth, and prevent its attaining anything like the height and size which formerly characterised it. The whole plant has the appearance of a gigantic grass, with long, narrow, spear-shaped leaves, of a beautiful green, crowned with a bunch of seedy-looking flowers like those of a rush; the stalk or cane, when growing, is straight, green, and pliable; but, after being cut, soon becomes bright yellow, and, though elastic, acquires hardness and firmness, and makes nice walking-sticks, fishing-rods, &c. I have pressed these canes into the service of entomology, by cutting those of suitable size and length, and after drying them a few days, using them as handles for my butterfly-net, for which their lightness and strength make them very fit. It is said that when cane has been cut, and is so dry that it will burn, it is a holiday amusement of the negroes to set fire to a cane-brake thus prepared. The rarefied air in the hollow compartments of the cane bursts them with a report not much inferior to a discharge of musketry; and the burning of a cane-brake makes a noise as of a conflicting army, in which thousands of muskets are continually discharged. It rises from the ground like the richest asparagus, with a large succulent stem; and it grows six feet high before this succulency and tenderness harden into wood. When five years old, it shoots up its fine head of seed, like that of broom-corn; the seeds are large and farinaceous, and were used by the Indians as bread-corn.

In similar situations another plant is numerous, which gives a still more tropical air to the landscape: I allude to the common Fan-palm *(Chamaerops serrulata)*. It grows in the form of a low bush, without any stem, having many leaves. They are about two feet in diameter, affixed to a footstalk of about eighteen inches, from the end of which the leaf diverges in every direction, like a broad and nearly circular fan, folded in very regular plaits. Near the edge the plaits are divided, and each is pointed. The leaf is thick and leathery, but somewhat liable to split if forcibly unfolded. The cattle eat the tips of these leaves too, and spoil the elegant regularity of their form. Indeed, in summer, the poor creatures are hardly beset to procure a due allowance of proper food; they are turned adrift into the forest to browse on the twigs and shrubs, or to pick what they can get. It is not here as in our own country, or as in the north, where during summer the fields, the lanes, and even the roadsides, are profusely clothed with verdure, affording an ample supply of grateful food to the farmer's stock, and where the sleekness of their skins and the plumpness of their forms sufficiently attest their prosperous condition. But here grass is almost unknown; and nothing more strongly marks the distinction between this region and the one I have left, than the almost total absence of that green carpet in the fields, on the edges of the woods, on the borders of the streams, on the sides of the roads, in the corners of the fences, and in every place where one is accustomed to see it. There are shrubs, herbs, and weeds, in abundance; but none of them can supply the place of that soft, rich, velvety verdure, whose hue so delights the eye. It is true there is a native grass, which gives a good deal of trouble. One of the chief employments of the field-slaves during summer is, by hoeing between the rows of cotton, to destroy the grass; and one of the most common complaints among the planters is, that the grass is getting the upper hand of them. But it is a singular species, called Crowfoot-grass *(Cynodon dactylon),* bearing four or five diverging fingers or ears at the top of the stalk; a gaunt-looking plant, with sparse leaves, and apparently having no tendency to make a turf, at least under our burning sun. In winter, rye is sown for the cattle, and other substitutes for pasture are found; and, after harvest, those planters who raise a field of oats or wheat turn them into the stubble; this, however, affords but sorry picking; and at this season of the year the poor cows are very lean, and doubtless often go hungry. I missed the green grass very much when I came first.

When I see any insect, bird, or flower, that I have been familiar with in other regions, it affords me feelings of peculiar pleasure. The other day one of the children brought me that elegant and delicate little creature, the Star Crane-fly *(Bittacomorpha crassipes),* an insect common to Newfoundland, Canada, and this extreme. I looked on it quite as an old acquaintance, with feelings almost like personal friendship.

In the school-yard there are several towering oak-trees left for the purpose of shade. Examining the trunks of these the first day I saw them—which, as a good entomologist and true, I was bound to do—I found in one several round holes about half an inch in diameter, as if made by an auger; and from one projected the pupa-skin of some very large moth, being near three inches long. Some days after I found another in a similar situation, and after that another. As my curiosity was roused, I procured an axe, and with the aid of a young man began to cut away some of the wood of the tree, exposing many passages filled with excrement, and some of them lined with web. We at length exposed two very large caterpillars, one of which we unfortunately cut in two, as we also did a pupa nearly matured, about two and a half inches long. The remaining caterpillar was very wary, and I nearly lost my patience in trying to get hold of him. I had to chop very cautiously for fear of cutting him through like the others; and as fast as his hole was exposed, he retired further in; sometimes he would poke his tail just out; but on my touching him, he would instantly draw back. At last I managed to outwit him in this way: I began to batter the opposite side of the tree with the poll of the axe, and was pleased to see that at every blow he gave a start, projecting his hinder part farther and farther out of the hole, when I suddenly seized him with my fingers, and, maugre his utmost efforts and strong struggles, dragged him from his fortress into daylight.

I found it was the larva of a species of *Cossus,* very much like that of the Goatmoth of Europe, about three inches in length, of a livid reddish hue, thinly scattered over with fine hairs, with a hard horny deep-brown head. He was very fierce, seizing my hand with his jaws whenever I attempted to touch him, and jerking round his head with great spitefulness. It crawled very swiftly. I could not find that it had the sense of sight; for fierce and resentful as it was, when I placed my finger before it, even close to its head, it took not the least notice; but if I touched but the tip of one of the hairs, then it instantly raised its head and stretched open its jaws. Indeed, spending its life immured in the centre of a tree, sight would be perfectly useless to it. I did not detect the strong and subtle odour which distinguishes its European congener.

The economy of this and similar insects is curious. The egg is laid by the parent moth, on or beneath the bark of a living tree. The larva, as soon as hatched, eats its narrow passage into the heart, living on the particles of wood which it abrades. Of course its *ejecta* fill up the cell behind as fast as it proceeds, and thus it has no alternative but to go forward. Indeed, were it not so, it could not retrace its steps; for the diameter of the chamber is always but just sufficient for it to move comfortably in; and as it increases in size, it of course makes a wider passage; therefore, the excavation which contained it yesterday, would to-day be too straight to admit it.

This species appears to be slower of growth than most caterpillars, taking two or three years to attain its full size. Before it goes into the pupa state, it either opens the passage into the air or (which I think more probable) leaves an extremely slight lamina of wood unpierced at the very extremity, which the pupa can break with its head, or perhaps dissolve with some secreted fluid. From my finding the pupa in the heart of the tree, I presume that it waits until the time of exclusion of the perfected moth is near, before it comes to the edge; then works its way outward by means of a ring of little points directed backward, with which each segment of the body is furnished. On its arrival at the mouth, which appears (at least in all the cases I observed) to take place during the night, it projects the fore-parts until half of the insect is exposed; then the skin opens at the usual places, and the moth is evolved, leaving the empty puparium sticking in the hole.

I took the caterpillar home, and put him into a box, with some pieces of the wood of the tree; but he was sulky, and refused to eat. I kept him two or three weeks, and at last he died. I never saw him eat anything the whole time.

Here are some notes and dates, extracted literally from my journal, showing the progress of a wasp's nest:—

June 2d.—A middling-sized brown wasp (allied to *Polistes)* is building a comb, suspended, by a pillar of the same grey papery substance, from the eaves of the school, immediately over the door. It has been recently commenced, as I have but just observed it. It has seven cells.

5th.—The wasp's nest is progressing: this morning it has fifteen cells; yesterday it had thirteen. They are not all of equal depth. It appears that the wasp is not particular about finishing one cell before she commences another. The outside ones are the shallowest, however.

12th.—The nest has been stationary for some days past, as regards the numbers of the cells; but the old wasp has been busy in rearing the young, and in covering up some of the central cells. I suppose the latter contain pupae. How the grubs keep themselves from falling out, I can't think; for the position of the cells is perpendicular, the mouth downwards. I see to-day there are twenty cells, more or less advanced. The old one is almost always resting or crawling on the nest. She is very vigilant, always on the look-out, turns short round every now and then; and, if a stick is raised in the air, within a couple of feet of the nest, she flies towards it in a moment, as if to attack it. But I have forbidden the boys to molest her.

14th.—This morning I perceive the wasp has a comrade sitting on the nest: hitherto her labours have been performed quite alone. No doubt the stranger is one of her own progeny, newly hatched from pupa.

15th.—A second wasp was evolved, and on the

18th, a third; so that now four take their station on the comb, in no wise distinguishable from each other. After this, more were successively produced, but I ceased to take any further notes.

Simultaneously with this, another operation was going on in another part of the school-house, of a somewhat similar character. A large shining black Bee, very much resembling in size and appearance the beautiful Violet-bee *(Xylocopa violacea)* of Europe, but without the purple wings, was boring a circular hole, about one-third of an inch in diameter, in the under side of one of the logs of which the house was built. Being the first specimen of the species I had seen, I caught it and secured it for my cabinet. That was on the twelfth; but on the fourteenth, I discovered to my surprise that another bee of the same species had taken to the hole, at which she was labouring with great industry. The direction is perpendicularly upwards; and the bee gnaws away the particles of wood with her jaws, moving round and round as required. Tedious as this process seems, such was the assiduity with which she prosecuted her employment, that the hole, which had been on the previous day 1 1/6 inch deep, was now 1 5/12 inch. The abraded particles of wood fall profusely, like sawdust, from this hole, and from another being bored by the same species in one of the rafters. On the 18th it had attained the depth of 1 5/6 inch. When the bee is touched or otherwise molested during her work, she does not always come out, but sets up a shrill, ringing hum, which is very different from the common grave sound, and which every one must have noticed in any species of bee when touched. It was this sound, made by this identical bee, that the boy so felicitously designated "hollering."* This by the way. One day I was surprised to see another bee of the same kind go into the hole while the owner was at home and at work; and even when she found it was preoccupied she did not seem very willing to relinquish it. I should infer from this circumstance, as well as from the readiness with which the second bee appropriated it, on the death of the first, that they do not undergo the labour of excavating when they can find a cell already prepared. And I have seen other instances of insects apparently wishing to avoid unnecessary labour. Those species which thus drill round holes in wood, for the purpose of obtaining a secure and commodious nidus for their young, are appropriately called Carpenter-Bees.

The Sassafras-tree *(Laurus sassafras)* is exceedingly common in the forest,

Vide supra, p. 109.

principally in places where the light has free access. It sometimes grows to a tree of considerable size, but not very often. It is very beautiful as a bush or shrub, the leaves being of pleasing shape, and of a lively green hue, while the fruit is highly ornamental. It is an oval berry of a brilliant blue, seated in a shallow cup of a bright red hue at the end of a long footstalk. These are now appearing; the flowers, which are said to be yellow, I have not seen, as the plant blossoms very early, even before the leaves are developed. The latter are sometimes nearly oval, undivided, but more commonly there is a sinus on each side, dividing it into three lobes. And not seldom we see leaves here and there with a lobe well developed on one side, and the other side perfectly entire, the whole leaf taking the exact form of a woodman's mitten, the lobe being the thumb. Leaves of all the forms are often found on a single bush. Children are very fond of chewing the leaves and twigs, and particularly the root; the taste is agreeable, and the chewing communicates a pleasant warmth to the mouth; the root is especially warm and spicy. It is reputed to possess valuable properties in medicine, especially in cutaneous affections and chronic rheumatism.

The Spice-wood *(Laurus benzoin)* is a kindred species; the leaves, however, are rougher and more wrinkled, and the taste is not so pleasant. I think this is rather rare in this neighbourhood, as I know of only a few bushes, which grow in a swampy part of the forest, surrounded by long-leafed pines and willow-oaks. The berries of this species are scarlet.

There is a pretty little Butterfly common now, the Pale Azure *(Polyommatus pseudargiolus),* which so nearly resembles an English species *(P. argiolus),* as scarcely to be distinguished from it. Its colour is light azure-blue on the upper surface (with a broad black margin in the female), and, on the under side, much paler still, nearly white, with some small black dashes. In appearance and manners it much resembles the delicate little Hairstreaks *(Thecla)* with which it associates. Like them it appears to be very pugnacious, attacking with Quixotic knight-errantry any intruder, no matter how much bigger than itself. It is particularly gamesome a few hours after sunrise; taking its stand on some prominent leaf of a bush, it rushes out upon every butterfly that passes by; then they perform such swift and tortuous evolutions that the eye is unable to follow them: this lasts only for a few seconds; for having pursued the traveller three or four yards, the Polyommatus returns to the very same leaf to watch as before. All this, however, I believe is done in a spirit of play, and not with any warlike intent.

This constancy of resort to one individual leaf or twig is very singular and unaccountable: sometimes on my approach to one so situated, it has been alarmed and flown to a considerable distance, but, taking a flight round, it returns to the place; and presently there is the little thing alighting on the very leaf again. The playful pugnacity just noticed seems almost peculiar to the *Lycaenadae*. With the exception of the Pearly Eye *(Hipparchia Andromache)*, noticed in my last, which has the same habit, I do not recollect any instance in which I have seen it displayed by any of the other families of Butterflies.

I have just seen a pretty but very destructive little insect, the Peach Hawkmoth *(Aegeria exitiosa)*. It was in the woods; and as it flitted in a hurried manner from shrub to shrub, and crawled swiftly to and fro over the leaves quivering its antennae, and flirting its violet wings, I was again struck with an observation that I have before made,—how very *hymenopterous* many of the Aegeriae are! The similarity is not confined to shape, though this is striking in antennae, wings and body; the most usual colours are black banded with yellow, with white, sometimes with orange or scarlet,—all hymenopterous colours. The prevalence of purple reflections from the wings, and the angle with the body at which they are often carried, are hymenopterous; as are also their manners. Their flight is usually rapid, and in straight lines; they alight suddenly, and as suddenly depart; move by fits and starts, and in short are so much like the waspish tribes, that, notwithstanding the acquaintance with insects which some years' observation of their habits has given me, I have often been deceived. It was not until I looked at the *Exitiosa* very closely, that I discovered it to be a moth.

Most insects of this genus pass their larva state in the trunks of trees, either between the bark and the wood, or in the heart of the wood itself. This species inhabits the peach-tree, to which it is very injurious, often causing premature decay and death. The larva is white, as are most larvae which are habitually excluded from the light, whether residing in holes in wood, in cells of combs, or beneath the surface of the earth. The pupa near the time of its exit works its way to the circumference of the tree, like the *Cossus* I mentioned before, where it opens, the perfect insect entering upon a new existence, and leaving the exuviae of the pupa, its grave-clothes, lying at the mouth of its late sepulchre. It has now become a pretty fly, with wings perfectly destitute of plumage, but glossed with a reflection of bright steel blue, the body bright blue, with one band of scarlet.

A large dipterous fly *(Mydas clavatus)*, common now, is marked in a similar manner with a band of scarlet across the abdomen, a rather unusual thing among the two-winged flies. It is much like a *Musca,* but with a longer abdomen: the wings are dark brown with a purple gloss; it is about an inch and three-fourths in length, and two inches and a half in spread of wing. Of its habits I know nothing, save that it is rather dull of motion.

Not so a pretty Bee-fly *(Bombylius* ———?), which I caught this morning,— the first I have ever seen alive. I first discovered it by observing its shadow on the ground, quivering, yet stationary; and on looking up, saw this pretty fly suspended in the air, about two feet from the ground, without any motion, except the rapid vibration of its almost invisible wings. What its object could be in thus suspending itself in the sunshine over the bare gravelled road, I am at a loss to conjecture. In general form it is much like a flesh-fly; but it has a long straight proboscis projecting from the head, like that of a gnat. Its motions are very swift and sudden, shooting from one stationary point to another so rapidly as to be invisible during the transit.

A singular instance of voracity, or of deviation from ordinary appetite, has come under my notice. I had found while out, a large downy caterpillar of the Tobacco Hawk-moth *(Sphinx Carolina),* and soon after, I took a stout dragon-fly *(Libellula* ———?). I put both into the same box to bring them home, and, on opening it, found that the caterpillar, having taken a fancy for a change of diet, had ventured upon animal-food, and had actually eaten a large piece out of his companion's wing, including a good deal of the stiff and hard front rib: I should think he must have found it rather a dry dainty. I have occasionally before known a caterpillar to eat into the bowels of a living chrysalis, or to seize upon another caterpillar; and I once reared one which ate young earth-worms with great relish. Had the caterpillar any patriotic intention of avenging the atrocities perpetrated occasionally by the Dragon-fly race upon the Lepidopterous tribes?

Two species of Butterfly have occurred to my notice since my last: the Variegated Fritillary *(Argynnis Columbina)* and the Coral Hairstreak *(Thecla Mopsus).* The former is tesselated with orange, black, and yellow, which colours on the under surface (especially of the hind wings) are admirably varied with shades of soft rich brown. It is not deficient in beauty, though it wants the brilliant metallic spots common to many of its congeners. Two inches and a half is its usual extent; I have seen a specimen which measured three inches and one-tenth, but it was one of unusual size. It is as yet rare, and very difficult of approach. The Hairstreak is a little one; the hind-wings are of rather an unusual shape, running off to a point: the colour is dull brown, unspotted above, beneath marked with a row of round spots of bright scarlet, like a string of beads. These are rather common. Of the butterflies which I have noticed before, the Green Clouded Swallowtail *(Papilio Troilus)* and the Painted Beauty *(Cynthia Huntera),* are becoming quite common: the Blue Swallowtail *(Pap. Philenor)* is becoming scarce, and the Zebra Swallowtails *(P. Ajax)* are nearly all gone.

As one species goes out of season another comes in; so that there is a constant succession: and the fields and prairies are still enlivened and adorned with these beautiful fairy creatures.

An eye accustomed only to the small and generally inconspicuous butterflies of our own country, the *Pontiae, Vanessae,* and *Hipparchiae,* can hardly picture to itself the gaiety of the air which swarms with large and brilliant-hued Swallowtails and other *patrician* tribes, some of which, in the extent and volume of their wings, may be compared to large bats. These occur, too, not by straggling solitary individuals: in glancing over a blossomed field or prairie-knoll, we may see hundreds, including, perhaps, more than a dozen species, besides moths, flies, and other insects.

When contemplating such a scene thus thronged with life, I have been pleased to think of the very vast amount of happiness that is aggregated there. I take it as an undoubted fact, that among the inferior creatures, except when suffering actual pain, life is enjoyment; the mere exercise of the bodily organs, and the gratification of the bodily appetites, is the highest pleasure of which they are capable: for as Spenser says—

"What more of happiness can fall to creature
Than to enjoy delight with liberty?"

Fate of the Butterfly.

To look then on the multitudes of beings assembled in so circumscribed a spot, all pursuing pleasure, and all doubtless attaining their end, each one with an individual perception and consciousness of enjoyment,—what a grand idea does it give of the tender mercy of God, as a God of providence!

Let us extend the idea:—there are about one hundred thousand *species* of insects known; let your mind try to guess at the number of *indivduals* of each species in the whole earth, (perhaps if you count the clouds of musquitos and gnats that issue from a single marsh, in a single night, it may assist you in the conjecture,) think of the other less populous orders of animals, fishes, mollusks, testacea, animalcules, &c., &c., reduce *them* to individuals, and you may have some distant approximation to one idea of Him, who "openeth His hand and satisfieth the desire of every living thing." EVERY LIVING THING! I have often thought that no one can appreciate the grandeur, the sublimity, of this sentiment of the Psalmist, like the devout naturalist.

Letter VII

July 3d

You ask me whether the farms here are similar to such as you are familiar with. There are some peculiarities about them, and as all are laid out pretty nearly upon the same plan, a description of one will serve, with a little variation, for all. Of course the houses differ in their degrees of comfort and elegance, according to the taste or finances of their proprietors, but in general they are built double; a set of rooms on each side of a wide passage, which is floored and ceiled in common with the rest of the house, but is entirely open at each end, being unfurnished with either gate or door, and forming a thoroughfare for the family through the house. Various kinds of climbing plants and flowers are trained to cluster about either end of these passages, and by their wild and luxuriant beauty take away the sordidness which the rude character of the dwellings might otherwise present. The *Glycine frutescens* with its many stems twisted tightly together like a ship's cable, hangs its beautiful bunches of lilac blossoms profusely about, like clusters of grapes; the elegant and graceful Scarlet Cypress-vine* *(Ipomaea coccinea,)* with hastate leaves, and long drooping vermilion flowers, shaped like those of a convolvulus; the still more elegant Crimson Cypress-vine *(Ipomaea Quamoclit,)* whose flowers, shaped like those of the sister species, are of the richest carmine, and whose leaves are cut, even to the mid-rib, into a multitude of long and slender fingers; our own Sweet-brier, the Trumpet Honeysuckle *(Caprifolium sempervirens)*, whose deep scarlet tubes are the twilight resort of the sounding-winged Hawkmoths:

> "———and luxuriant above all
> The Jasmine, throwing wide her elegant sweets,
> The deep dark green of whose unvarnish'd leaf
> Makes more conspicuous, and illumines more,
> The bright profusion of her scatter'd stars."**

These, with other favourite plants, cover the rough logs and shingles with so dense a mass of vegetation and inflorescence, as effectually hide them from view.

*See engraving on p. 165.

**Cowper's *Task*, book vi.

When the air within the house is close and sultry, almost to suffocation, and the unmerciful rays of the sun, without, glare upon the head beyond endurance, it is a pleasant relief to sit in these halls beneath the shade, where too there is a current of air whenever there is a breath stirring. Here the southern planter loves to sit, or to lie stretched at full length; and here, particularly at the approach of evening, when the sunbeams twinkle obliquely through the transparent foliage, and the cool breeze comes loaded with the fragrance of a thousand flowers, the family may usually be seen, each (ladies as well as gentlemen) in that very elegant position in which an American delights to sit, the chair poised upon the two hind feet, or leaning back against the wall, at an angle of 45°, the feet upon the highest bar, the knees near the chin, the head pressing against the wall, so as now and then to push the chair a few inches from it, the hands (but not of the ladies) engaged in fashioning with a pocket-knife a piece of pine-wood, into some uncouth and fantastic form; the tongue discussing the probability of a war with the "British," and indulging a little national egotism, in anticipating the consequences to follow thereupon, "whipping the British" being, of course, assumed.*

Very many of the houses, even of wealthy and respectable planters, are built of rough and unhewn logs, and to an English taste are destitute of comfort to a surprising degree. There is one about a mile distant, belonging to a very worthy man whom I have often visited, which is of this character. I will try to give you an idea of it. It is a ground-floor house of two rooms. Fancy the walls full of crevices an inch or more in width, some of them running the whole length of the rooms, caused by the warping of the logs, the decay of the bark, or the dropping out of the clay which had been put in to fill up. There is no window in the whole house; in one room there is a square hole about two feet wide, which a

---

*This jealousy of "the British" shows itself continually; nor do the good people seem to imagine that it can be at all unpleasing to their guest, who is so unlucky as to be himself a "Britisher." Their ignorance of our peculiar manners and local relations, superimposed on this propensity, occasionally has a ludicrous effect. The other day the papers had, among the European news, an account of some trumpery factory row in Paisley or Glasgow; and one of my neighbours, a wealthy planter, and a very worthy man, called me aside to tell me, with a sympathy and condolence I fear not quite sincere, how "the Scotch had risen to throw off the British yoke!" The universal notion of Scotland, Ireland and Wales, is that they are conquered provinces, on a par with Poland, kept in a state of galling servitude by the presence of a powerful "British" army, and ever watching for an opportunity to assert their freedom as independent nations.

shutter professes to close, but as it is made of boards that have never felt either saw or plane, being merely riven by the aid of the broad-axe out of an oak log, you may guess how accurately it fits. A door formed of similar boards, rarely shut, at least from dawn till night, gives light and air to each room, though the crevices of the logs, and those of the roof, would afford ample light when both door and shutter were closed. You will perhaps wonder how a door can possibly be made of boards whose edges have never been made straight by the plane; the fact is, the boards are not laid edge to edge, but the edges lap over each other, as board-fences are sometimes made in England; to speak scientifically, the boards are *laterally imbricated.*

A bed-room has been added since the original erection; unbarked poles were set in the ground, and these riven boards nailed outside, edge over edge, by the way of clapboard; there is nothing of lathing, or boarding, or papering within, nothing between the lodger and the weather, but these rough, crooked, and uneven boards, through which, of course, the sun plays at bopeep, and the wind and rain also. It forms a lean-to, the roof being continued from that of the house. The lowest tier of logs composing the house, rest on stout blocks about two feet from the ground; beams go across from these logs, on which the floor is laid; the planks are certainly sawed, but they are not pinned to the beams, being moveable at pleasure; and as the distance between the lowest logs and the ground is perfectly open, the wind has full liberty of ingress through the seams of the floor, as well as in every other part.

The roof is of a piece with the rest; no ceiling meets the eye; the gaze goes up beyond the smoke-burnt rafters up to the very shingles; nay, beyond them, for in the bright night the radiance of many a star gleams upon the upturned eye of the recumbent watcher, and during the day many a moving spot of light upon the floor shows the progress which the sun makes towards the west. But it is during the brief, but terrific rain-storms, which often occur in this climate, that one becomes painfully conscious of the permeability of the roof; the floor soon streams; one knows not where to run to escape the thousand and one trickling cascades; and it is amusing to see the inmates, well acquainted with the geography of the house, catching up books, and other damageable articles, and heaping them up in some spot which they know to be canopied by a sound part of the roof.

There is a fireplace at each end of the house, a large open chimney, the fire being on the hearth, which is raised to a level with the floor; the chimney itself is curiously constructed; simply enough however, for the skeleton of it is merely a series of flat slips of wood, laid one upon another in the form of a square, the ends crossing at the corners, where they are slightly pinned together, the square contracting from five feet at the bottom to little more than one at the top. As this frame-work proceeds, it is plastered within and without with well-beaten clay, to the thickness of two or three inches. This is considered a sufficient protection against the fire; for though, on account of the clay here and there dropping off, the slips of wood often ignite, and holes are burnt through, yet the clay around prevents the fire from spreading, and these holes are regarded with a very exemplary philosophy. I should have observed, however, that at the bottom of the chimney, and more particularly at the fire-back, the clay is increased in thickness to more than a foot. Add to this description a ladder of three steps at each end of the passage, from the ground to the floor, and you have my worthy friend's hospitable mansion.

Now poor and mean houses may be found in every country, but this is but one of the many; it is not inhabited by poor persons, nor is it considered as at all remarkable for discomfort; it is, according to the average, a very decent house. There are some, certainly, much superior; but these are frame-houses, regularly clapboarded, and ceiled, and two, or even three stories high, including the ground-floor. They are mostly of recent erection, and are inhabited by planters of large property; these have comforts and elegancies in them which would do no dishonour to an English gentleman.

The towns and villages partake of the same rude and make-shift character. The Americans, in commencing a hamlet or village, always look forward to its becoming a city; and hence the plan is laid out with an amplitude and grandeur that seems ridiculous, when contrasted with the immediate filling up of the blank; for they are content to put up with the meanest huts for present use. Nothing like attachment to a particular house, estate, or town, exists in an American's breast; he always expects to sell his "improvements," and "move" to some other region; hence his residence has always a temporary character; and those thousand little conveniences and amenities which we delight to accumulate around us, and which are so many links to enchain us to a given spot, have no temptations to him. The accompanying sketch will give you an idea of the shops and

Pleasant Hill

groceries of Pleasant Hill, "our village," which may, for aught I know, be a populous city in half-a-dozen years.

The house in which I am residing stands in the middle of a large yard, formed partly by a fence of rails and posts, and partly by the offices and outbuildings, such as the pantry, kitchen, spinning-house, dairy, &c.; these are distinct buildings, formed of logs, and always more or less distant from the house. Two or three of the negro-houses are likewise usually placed in the yard, that hands may be called on at any moment if needed, the general range of huts being out of sight and hearing of the house. Little black children, stark naked, from a few weeks old to six or seven years, at which age they go out to the field, play, or grovel about the yard, or lie stretched in the glaring sunbeams, the elder ones professedly taking care of the younger or more helpless. Here of course they are early inured, by kicks and cuffs, to bear the severe inflictions of the lash, &c., which await them in after life. The pigs and fowls entertain very little respect for the negro children, with whom there is a perpetual squabbling; and what with the scolding of the youngsters, the squealing of the pigs, the cackling of the guinea-fowls, the gobbling of the turkeys, and the quacking of the Muscovy ducks, the yard does not lack noise. Of these last *(Anas moschata)* there is always a troop of all ages and sizes; it is the only duck *patronised;* the "English duck," as our common species is called, being kept only as a curiosity. The greater size of the former, approaching to that of the goose, is a recommendation, but it is far inferior in beauty, and, in my opinion, in flavour, to the common kind.

A very great ornament, indeed a *sine quâ non* in a planter's yard, is the Pride of China, commonly called the China tree *(Melia azedarach).* It is deservedly a favourite, for it possesses many claims to admiration; the leaves are pinnate, like those of the ash and laburnum, with many leaflets of a beautiful deep green hue; in spring the pretty lilac or pink flowers appear in racemes, having a delicate odour, and these are succeeded by round green berries, which in autumn turn of a bright yellow, and the skin becomes shrivelled. It grows rapidly, but does not attain a great altitude. It is said to be a native of Persia.

Shade is a luxury in this hot climate, and therefore trees are in much request around the house; the oaks, and the sycamore, seem to be generally preferred, doubtless on account of their dense and massy foliage. The latter, the Button-wood of the northern states *(Platanus occidentalis),* is indeed a noble tree, probably the most noble of our forests. Growing in the rich black soil of the deep swamps, the accumulated vegetable mould of uncounted ages, it acquires a diameter and an altitude which entitle it to be called the forest king. Here it often shoots up its columnar trunk to the summit of the surrounding trees, before it begins to branch; and then its tall pyramidal head of foliage towers far above, appearing when viewed from an elevation, like a tree growing on the surface of the forest. It is sometimes subject to remarkable swellings and distortions of the trunk; I have seen some, hollowed by decay, as capacious as a small room, while from one side up shoots the fair green trunk, like a tall chimney. I have been told of one not far distant, in the hollow of which, it is said, a man may turn round, with a rail on his shoulder (a rail is from ten to fourteen feet in length); I have not, however, seen this tree myself, but I consider it as by no means improbable.

The leaves are of a fine green, six or eight inches in width, somewhat triangular, with projecting pointing lobes, indented or heart-shaped at base. They hang in broad dense masses, with large intervals of dark shadow, giving by the fine contrast of light and shade, a very picturesque effect to the tree. In spring the leaves are thickly clothed on the under surface with a subtle down, easily displaced, which being blown about in the air, is by some persons considered injurious to health. I believe it to be a groundless prejudice; but yet, I have been told, it has been the cause of the destruction of many fine trees, of late years, in the northern cities, in whose streets, particularly in those of Philadelphia, it had been planted in rows, contributing much to their beauty, at least. The *aments,* or catkins of flowers, take the form of little hard balls, like marbles, which in the course of the summer grow to an inch in diameter, perfectly round, hanging from long peduncles. These have given the name of Buttonwood to the tree. They fall in autumn and winter; and, parting asunder, the seeds of which they are composed are wafted about by aid of the plumy egret with which they are furnished. The trunk and large branches are remarkably fair and smooth, of a pale green, approaching to white, and like its congener, the European Plane, its bark has the singular property of separating and throwing off the epidermis every year, in broad thin laminae. The smoothness of the trunk offers a strong temptation to the possessor of a pocket-knife to carve his name on it, but the successive rejections of the epidermis in a few years entirely obliterate the inscription. The wood of this fine tree, though close-grained, susceptible of high polish, and beautiful from the size and brightness of its medullary rays, is yet almost altogether neglected, as it is very liable to warp, and speedily decays. The roots, when fresh from the soil, are of a brilliant red, but the tint soon fades.

I must mention two other trees of our yard, not so much for their own personal importance, as on account of the visitors they are in the habit of receiving. The first is, I believe, the wild cherry of the north *(Cerasus Virginiana),* but whose small black fruit seems, either from partial cultivation, or from the influence of a sunnier sky, to be much ameliorated. Though still of no mention as a fruit, it is sweet and luscious, deprived of that bitterness which makes the northern berry so unpalatable. To the taste of the smaller Woodpeckers, however, it would seem to be highly agreeable; so irresistible is the temptation, that not only our familiar acquaintance, the Red-headed *(Picus erythrocephalus),* pays particular attentions to its clusters, but even those shy and retiring species, the

Red-bellied, and the Yellow-bellied *(P. Carolinus,* and *P. varius),* are almost daily to be seen on the higher branches, particularly in the early morning. All these birds have the head more or less marked with brilliant metallic red, scarlet in the last two, but in the first more inclined to crimson: in either case making excusable the mistake of the Irish emigrant, who on his first sight of one of these birds engaged in "tapping the hollow beech-tree," exclaimed in unfeigned astonishment,—"Arrah, Paddy! see the craythur, batin' his face to pieces agin a tree, an' his head all in a gore o' blood!"

The appropriation, to certain genera of animals, of particular colours, generally following more or less closely a definite arrangement, is not the least interesting nor the least curious of the very many branches into which the vast science of natural history ramifies. The glossy black spotted with white, of the back and wings, and the bright red of the crown, in the genus before us, as well as the meteoric gleams, and gem-like flashes of one to which I shall presently allude, are scarcely less characteristic and distinctive, than the wedged beak and horny tail of the one, or the tubular tongue and falcate wings of the other.

There seems something recondite in this: the modifications of form which the bodily organs assume, we can generally connect with some obvious end; we see and admire the beautiful adaptation of the form to the instincts and habits of the animal; the wedge-like beak to chisel away the hard wood of the tree, the barbed tongue to fetch out the ensconced grub, and the horny tail to support the perpendicular position during the act;—but what bearing have the peculiar tints of the plumage on the mode of life?—is a woodpecker better fitted to get his living because he is clothed in black and white and scarlet? I dare not say he is not: for though I can trace no possible connexion between the colours and the instincts, the constancy of such an appropriation, evidently anything but arbitrary, or unintentional, and the wide prevalence of the principle in all the orders, convince me that it is not a reasonless or accidental circumstance. Others may perhaps see more deeply into the matter than I can, and may discover another link in that mighty chain, which, traversing all orders of being, compels us to recognise in each the All-wise God.

But to return: the other tree to which I alluded as a denizen of our dry and sandy yards, is one cultivated for the beauty of its appearance, the Althea. It rises to the height of twelve or fifteen feet, with a full, spreading body, profusely covered with pink flowers, much resembling those of the hollyhock of our gar-

Ball Chafer

dens, but rather smaller. These trees or shrubs are an unfailing resort of the Humming-birds, which every day through the long summer, flock to their blossoms, and hang and sip round and round, always there, but never still; so intent on their pursuit as to allow you to approach directly under them, if you go cautiously. I have mentioned these fairy creatures before, but if I were content with only a single passing notice, you would fail to acquire a commensurate idea of their abundance with us, and of the part they take in filling a southern landscape. In every part of the garden we may see them at all hours of the day, flitting to and fro, coming and going, making the very atmosphere alive with their gaiety and radiance.

An object, that cannot fail, although small, to arrest the attention even of the most incurious, is the Ball Chafer *(Phanaeus carnifex)*. It is a short, square-built, thick-set beetle, a little smaller than our English cockchafer: the abdomen and the elytra are metallic green, the top of the thorax, which is elevated, is rough but glittering, and much resembles in appearance, burnished copper. On the head is a tall horn, like that of a rhinoceros, recurved over the thorax. The indefatigable exertions of this little creature are directed to the appropriation and removal of the dung of other animals, chiefly of horses and cattle. This humble but useful object it effects in an amazingly short space of time. No sooner is the material dropped than the chafers congregate to it from all sides, and after flying around it a few times, narrowing the circle at each gyration, alight on it, close their elytra, draw up their folded wings, and instantly commence operations. Plunging his head into the mass, each labours to separate an irregular portion with his jaws, of about an inch in diameter; this is done in a very few minutes, when, turning round, he begins to push the lump with his hindmost pair of feet, crawling along backwards, as it proceeds, upon his anterior and middle feet. In rolling, it soon becomes quite globular, when of course it rolls with more facility. When many are engaged together, as is usually the case, I have often seen them leave the ball they are rolling and begin to roll another, indiscriminately, as if they had no notion of property in their work. And sometimes two may be seen rolling one ball, apparently not by consent, but as if unconscious of each other's efforts, when the mutual rollings over and over of ball and beetle are very amusing. Neither could I ever perceive that any particular ball was propelled in a determinate direction; from the very erratic course pursued, I conclude that the object of the beetles is merely to scatter the balls, so that all shall not remain in one spot. But as their labours take place chiefly, of course, in the middle of the most frequented highways, where their balls would inevitably be crushed, it is not improbable that one object of their instinct may be the removal to a place of greater security. I believe, but I cannot say from my own personal observations, that these balls are the repositories of the eggs of the female, which I suppose are laid in them after they have reached their destination, and that then they are buried in the earth, to afford nutriment to the grub when hatched. Whether the labourers are exclusively females, I cannot decide, but from the difference occurring between individuals working together in colour, development of the thorax and frontal horn, &c., I incline to think both sexes are engaged in this duty. A kindred species of about the same size, but all over of a dull black *(Coprobius volvens),* labours peaceably in company with these, in exactly the same manner: and I believe the habits are common to some European species.

I may add to these notices, that, so effectually do these scavengers perform their task, that in a few hours no remains, nor even a vestige of the original matter, can be traced, save sometimes a round hole in the earth, and a darker tint of the soil around.

There is a peculiarity in very many beetles of this great tribe *(Lamellicornes)*, which is as singular as it is unaccountable. I allude to the prominences so often found on the thorax and head, resembling horns. They are often of great size and strength, generally more or less curved at the tips, but being immovable except as that division of the body which carries them is moved, it is difficult to conceive any mode in which they can be used. In some the frontal horn of the head may, by the motion of the head itself, be brought to meet one which projects from the centre of the thorax, as in a very large and fine species *(Dynastes Tityrus)*, which is found, though rarely, with us. The specimen which I have obtained is of a yellowish grey, with black irregular spots on the elytra, and is the largest beetle I have ever seen alive. I have no reason, however, to conclude that the horns are ever used in this way; and in many of the species, in which, though largely developed, they occur only on the thorax, the points can never make the slightest approach to contact. Whatever other office they may hold, there can be no doubt that they are marks of sexual distinction, being much less developed in the female than in the male, thus bearing no distant analogy to the true horns of many of the ruminant mammalia.

These remarkable prominences are, I believe, wholly confined to the Lamellicorn tribe, which formed the vast genus *Scarabaeus* of Linnaeus. I have before me a fine example of thoracic development in a living specimen of *Oryctes Maimon*. It is larger than any English beetle, though, perhaps, not so *long* as some specimens of the Stag Beetle *(Lucanus cervus)*, which it resembles in colour, being of a deep chestnut, highly polished. On the thorax are three horns, each about half-an-inch in height, one in front, and one on each side, all curving towards each other at the tips. The head bears none. I have seen individuals having these processes in all degrees of development from the size I have mentioned, down to projections so slight as to be scarcely perceptible above the general surface, so that the difference is not *wholly* sexual.

This insect has just astonished me by a proof of its vast strength of body. Everyone who has taken the common dorr in his hand knows that its limbs, if not remarkable for agility, are very powerful, but I was not prepared for so Samsonian a feat as I have just witnessed. When the insect was brought to me, having no box immediately at hand, I was at a loss where to put it until I could kill

Oryctes Maimon

it: but a quart bottle full of milk being on the table, I clapped the beetle, for the present, under that, the hollow at the bottom allowing him room to stand upright. Presently, to my surprise, the bottle began slowly to move, and glide along the smooth table, propelled by the muscular power of the imprisoned insect, and continued for some time to perambulate the surface, to the astonishment of all who witnessed it. The weight of the bottle and its contents could not have been less than three pounds and a-half; while that of the beetle was about half an ounce, so that it readily moved a weight 112 times exceeding its own. A better notion than figures can convey will be obtained of this feat, by supposing a lad of fifteen to be imprisoned under the great bell of St. Paul's, which weighs 12,000 lbs.; and to move it to and fro upon a smooth pavement by pushing within.

Perhaps some analogy to the highly developed processes mentioned above may be found in the spinous projection of the thorax in many of the *Longicornes,* a family containing the largest species of beetles yet discovered. I am not aware, however, that these spines ever take the semblance of horns. A rather large species of this family *(Prionus imbricornis)* occasionally flies into our open houses in the evening, attracted, I suppose, by the light. It resembles, in general aspect, an English species *(P. coriareus)*. The antennae are long, thick, and deeply serrated; the elytra are chocolate brown; the thorax and head deep black. The eyes are largely developed in this genus, often occupying the greater portion of the head, and sometimes almost the whole of it, meeting and touching each other at the crown, as in the present species. The development of an organ is generally ascertained to bear a marked relation to the economy and wants of the animal; in the predatory *Cicindelae* and *Carabi,* for instance, the large and prominent eyes give an extent of vision that materially aids them in discovering prey. But the Prioni are not predaceous; their instinct leads them to the pine forests, where they bore holes in the timber by chiselling the wood with their conical jaws; the eggs are laid, the young grow up and become pupae in the heart of the tree, from whence the perfected beetle issues to pursue a similar course. Acuteness of vision appears not to depend on the *size* of the compound eye, which merely affects the extent of the visual horizon, but upon the *depth and number of the optic tubes,* whose convex extremities form the facets of the eye. These tubes in the Longicorn beetles are by no means numerous, in proportion to their extent of surface, but few and large; so large as to be quite visible in the greater species to our unassisted sight, the large eyes being perceptibly netted, like those of the dragon-fly, while the eyes of other beetles appear to the naked eye quite smooth and shining. It would seem, then, that a wide range of vision is granted to these insects to enable them to discover the trees suited to their wants, but that no great discrimination being required as to what particular spot of the trunk shall be attacked, they need not and have not this sense minutely distinct and accurate.

Some very fine Lepidoptera have fallen under my observation lately. The Arched Swallowtail *(Papilio Calchas)* begins to be frequently met with; it is about four inches and a-half in spread of wing; black on the upper surface, with three rows of yellow crescents on the front pair, and on the hind two rows, and a broad band of yellow across the middle. Beneath, the front pair are as above, but the hind wings have the band divided into large and regular crescents, forming a third series, and all the rows are beautifully tinged with orange; there is also an intermediate row of azure fasciae. The anterior margin of the fore wings is unusually curved, causing these wings to assume a rounded form. This fine insect is not noticed by Abbott, nor is a yet nobler species, the Yellow Emperor Swallowtail *(Papilio Thoas),* which measures, when expanded, five inches and a-half. The ground colour of this is black, with a very broad macular band of buff-yellow, crossing the base of the hind wings, and running on to the tip of the fore wings;

there is a similar band likewise common to both pairs, which follows the course of the outer margin at some distance from it. The tails are yellow, with a black border. Beneath, the ground is yellow, on which the nervures are broadly traced in black, and three or four similar black lines run along the middle area of the fore wing; a narrow black band crosses both pairs near the outer margin, containing a series of azure crescents in the hind pair. The contrast between the prevailing colours of the upper and under surface is very observable, as the insect floats carelessly along, slowly flapping its voluminous wings, or rests half expanded to sip the slushy mud in the stable-yard: when it has a magnificent appearance. It seems to be rare, as I have seen but a single specimen. Boisduval gives a figure of its larva, which is of large size, and, from a singular distribution of its colours, reminds one of a piebald horse. The tints are arranged in about seven large patches,—two white, four black (viz. two on each side), and a large brick-red one behind the head. I have never met with it myself, and know not its food.

From the largest of our butterflies, I come, by a contrast quite unintentional, to speak of the very least, which I am but just now acquainted with. It is the Red-striped Hairstreak *(Thecla Poeas)*, a most active, vivacious little creature, measuring exactly one inch in expanse. The hind wings have each two thread-like appendages in the form of tails, which, though found in many species of the genus, are more developed in this than in any other of ours which I know. The upper surface is black, with a blue gloss; the under side soft brown, with a transverse band of scarlet. It is fond of skipping about the bushes at the edge of the forest during the brightest hours of sunshine, or walking to and fro on a leaf, rubbing the two surfaces of the hind wings together, when erect; but with so delicate a contact, that not an atom of the feathery bloom is rubbed off or displaced.

I may not omit to mention the capture of that very fine insect, the Great Plane-tree Moth *(Ceratocampa imperialis)*, though I can give but a meagre account of its economy. My specimen is a female, measuring five inches and a-half in spread of wing, and was found lying motionless on the ground, beneath the lofty sycamores on the swampy bank of Mush Creek. It is exceedingly inert (as are many female moths, especially the thick-bodied *Sphingidae* and *Bombycidae),* allowing itself to be handled without any resistance or attempt to escape, so that I should hardly know it to be alive, but for the slight adhesion of the tarsi, when the feet are touched. The colour is pale buff, each of the wings having a round purplish spot in the centre, and a band proceeding from the tip to the inner margin of the same hue; there are also very many scattered dots, the whole being softened, or, as it were, blurred. The male I have seen only in cabinets; it is smaller, adorned with brighter purple, and more of that hue; the antennae, which in the female are thread-like, are, in the male, feathered through half their length. Abbott gives a figure of the larva and pupa; the former is about four inches long, and thick in proportion, tubercled, with tufts of hair on the back; the colour is sometimes green, but usually tawny. It feeds on the sycamore, liquidambar, oak, and pine. The chrysalis is large and blackish, with a forked tail.

The mere enumeration of species, in general, possesses little interest to any but the scientific collector; it is not altogether useless, however, as the formation of local faunas materially contributes to accurate ideas of the geographical distribution of animals. This must be my excuse for occasionally giving the names of insects which I have met with, even when I can supply no other information about them. I have lately caught *Milesia ornata,* a large dipterous fly, handsomely and singularly marked with black, upon a bright yellow ground; *Amphipyra pyramidea,* a moth, which I have taken in Canada, and which is a native also of England; *Sphinx pampinatrix,* a pretty little olive-coloured Hawk-moth, which sat vibrating her wings as if shivering, on a bush in the garden, one evening, and which I netted without difficulty, as she would scarcely leave the spot.

A few evenings ago, while twilight was yet bright, there was a most unusual concourse of Bats, flying in circles a few yards from the ground, around the stables and horse-yard. A multitude of minute dipterous flies were in the air, probably recently evolved from the dunghill, forming, no doubt, the centre of attraction to the bats, which had congregated in some scores. By getting on a wall, I readily obtained two, capturing them in my butterfly net; they were of one species, of a bright tawny hue *(Lasiurus rufus).* They continued their pursuit till night hid them from view.

In an unfrequented path in the forest, I have several times seen that lovely little creature, the Indigo bird *(Fringilla cyanea).* As it has always been in one particular spot, and as one evening I saw the drab-coloured female in company with him, I have no doubt they have a nest thereabouts. They hopped restlessly about the shrubs, often coming within two yards of me, as I stood observing them, but my collecting mania was not strong enough to induce me to molest them. As they hopped about, they frequently uttered a single "chip," which Wilson most accurately describes as resembling the sound made by two pebbles struck together.

When the male was alone one day I heard his simple song, "weesy, weesy, weesy, che, che, che, che." It frequently darts down from the stalk of some weed or herb to pick up an insect, and then hops up to its place again, alighting on the perpendicular stem, not, however, as a woodpecker alights on a tree, but across it, as if it were horizontal, one foot being immediately above the other; rather a constrained posture, one would suppose. I have seen this too often, to suppose it an accidental occurrence; it is doubtless the habit of the bird.

Of course, in coming to the south, my curiosity was excited to see the far-famed Tulip-tree, but with regard to the flowers, I have been a little disappointed. Here and there a single tree shows a good mass of yellow bloom, but in the forests and swamps, where it is most abundant, the blossoms are not numerous. However, the visible qualities that we most admire in flowers are, individual size and beauty; and, examined as individuals, the flowers of this tree are worthy of admiration. They bear a close resemblance to tulips in size and colour, but are rather less bell-shaped, and shallower; the petals, six in number, vary in tint, but are chiefly yellow, with a red base, containing five or six pale longitudinal streaks; they have the advantage of the tulip, in possessing a fragrant odour.

The tree itself *(Liriodendron tulipiferum)* is one of the most magnificent in our forests, often attaining the height of a hundred and twenty feet, being thus second only to the giant sycamore. It is here universally distinguished by the name of Poplar; but, in some of the States, I believe, the appellation of White-wood is given to it. It delights to grow, in company with its noble rival, in the deep bottoms of valleys, and in the solemn swamps which border our great rivers. These swamps must not be confounded with marshes; the soil is firm, and in general, though damp, is not wet, except when overflowed by the spring freshets. The Tulip-tree does not thrive in a soil habitually wet. When growing in situations where the branches have space to expand, they ramify in a very beautiful and regular manner, and, as the foliage is abundant, large and massy in its character, and of a rich deep hue, the tree, independent of its floral pretensions, is one of great beauty and splendour. The leaves are of a very singular, but elegant form, sometimes eight inches in width, fixed at the end of a long petiole, somewhat fleshy, smooth and glossy, growing alternately on the stalk. There is remarkable peculiarity in their manner of growth; the young unexpanded leaves curiously folded up, grow within two large leaf-like bracteae, forming an oval sac, which, as the young leaf grows, swell, and at length burst, and are left on each side of

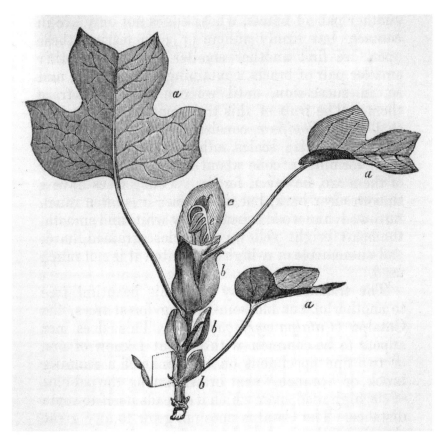

Twig of Tulip-tree

the leaf-stalk, as represented in the accompanying engraving. There is a succession of these; if we examine a young twig, perhaps we find two or three leaves
(a a a) already expanded, and as many pairs of these bracts *(b b b)* at their bases;
the twig is terminated by a pair *(c),* which are convex outwardly, and whose edges
are in contact with each other; if we cut off one of these (as at *d*), we expose the
next leaf folded together, and bent downward *(e),* and, beside it, another pair
of bracts, whose edges not only are in contact, but firmly adhere *(f);* on tearing
these open, we find another smaller leaf, and another smaller pair of bracts, containing a similar set, and so, in succession, until we can no longer trace them.
The fruit of this tree somewhat resembles that of the *Coniferae,* consisting of a
great number of thin greenish scales, adhering to a placenta, or axis, forming a

cone about six inches long; few of them are, however, fertile. Young trees have a smooth clear bark, but in old ones it is often much furrowed; the wood is beautifully white and smooth, the heart bright yellow; it is close-grained, hard, and susceptible of a high polish, but it is not much used.

The transition is easy from this beautiful tree to another of our blossom-bearing forest trees, the Catalpa *(Catalpa syringaefolia)*. This does not appear to be common with us, but I know of one or two fine specimens on the banks of a running brook, or "branch," that brawls among the pebbles of the high road, over which it spreads itself to some distance. The Catalpa does not grow to any great size, but it has a broad top of spreading boughs. The flowers, which have now disappeared for some weeks, were large, growing in clusters, like those of the trumpet flower *(Bignonia radicans)*, which they much resemble also in shape, but are not quite so long. They are of a delicate white, spotted on the inner surface with yellow and pink dashes. Though numerous, they are not very conspicuous at a distance. A long cylindrical pod succeeds these flowers, which is at present green, but which, when ripe, will become dark brown. The leaves are very smooth above, but clothed with down beneath; they are shaped like those of the Lilac, but are very much larger. The bark is smooth and of a greyish white, or hoary appearance.

Letter VIII

July 5th

I have just been assisting (at least, so far as looking on) at a very interesting operation,—the taking of a wild bee's nest. The incident is, I am told, one of frequent occurrence, the honey-bees often sending forth a colony at swarming time, which seek a new abode for themselves. Even the little boys have their eyes open, and their attention awake to the motion of the forest bees, watching their flight, and often following the direction they have taken in hopes of seeing others, which may serve as so many finger posts to guide their track, till at length the increasing numbers of bees thronging the air announce the proximity of their home, when a little searching with a practised eye soon traces the industrious insects to their very hole; and the urchin, having carefully marked the spot, comes home with the triumphant intelligence that he has found a "Bee-tree." A tree of this kind, in which a swarm had hived, having been discovered yesterday, I went with a friend and a couple of negroes to see them cut it down. They carried two axes, a bundle of loose cotton, to make a smoke with, and a "gum," or square box, to hive the swarm; the possession of the bees being not less desirable than the acquisition of the honey.

We soon arrived at the spot, which was in the forest, a few yards only from the high road, and at no great distance from the house. My attention being directed to a large and tall tree of the long-leafed pine species *(Pinus palustris),* I perceived, far up in the branchless trunk, a round orifice, about which several bees were clustering, going out and coming in, departing and arriving to and from all points of the compass. The men lighted a little fire, stripped, and commenced felling the tree, one on each side. The trunk was thick, but the negroes were skilful and sinewy, and plied their axes until the perspiration streamed profusely from their glossy shoulders. Not a stroke was given in vain, and very soon the columnar trunk was supported only by the slender interval left between the two deep notches, as if balanced on the edge of a prism. Still, so little was the preponderance of either side, that the bushy head quivered in the sky with a tremulous motion for several seconds, before we could determine to which side it would incline; at length it slowly bowed, groaned, cleft the air with a roar, and plunged with a deafening crash among the bushes and saplings, snapping its own stout limbs like glass, and scattering the moist earth far over the leaves on every side.

One of the men ran immediately to the hole of the hive, which was about three inches in diameter, perfectly round, and smooth, worn by the continual passage of the bees, and coated from the same cause with a white substance, probably wax, bleached by the sun and rain. Having lighted a handful of cotton, smothering up the flame in the midst of it, he held it close to the orifice, blowing in the dense choking smoke, to prevent the bees from coming out, which they had already begun to do in some numbers, alarmed, doubtless, by the downfall of their house.

While he was doing this, the other was gathering green leaves from the chestnuts, oaks, and hickories, which he cleverly rolled up into a solid cylinder. This, when large enough, was thrust into the entrance of the hive to stop it up, while they opened it in another place to extract the combs. The next proceeding was to discover the situation of the comb, which could only be ascertained by repeated trials, cutting into the trunk in different places. Aware that the hive was above the entrance, they first cut a notch on the opposite side from the orifice, and about two feet above it; but as soon as the axe had penetrated the hollow, the bees began to hum and cluster to the light, whereby the men knew that they had not reached the top of the nest. Preventing, therefore, the egress of the imprisoned bees at this opening, by holding the smoking cotton there, until it could be closed by another stopper of rolled leaves, they made a new trial about two feet higher. Here, however, the bees were as thick as before; so, having closed this also in the same manner, they made a third cut still higher, and at length discovered that they had reached above the top of the nest.

One of them now blew the smoke into this orifice, while the other having fixed the "gum," and supported it by props over the original entrance, drew out the stopper of leaves, in order that the bees, being driven out by the smoke blown in at the other end, might take refuge from the annoyance in the new hive, and thus render the seizure of the honey more easy. But the bees did not seem to manifest that decided preference for the new lodging over the old one that the negroes desired; so they, becoming impatient, proceeded to split off the longitudinal chip or section of the trunk, contained between the first two cuts, supposing that by so doing they should expose the mass of comb to view. As they peeped in, however, by lifting up one edge, before the piece was quite detached, and perceived that the comb was not there, they did not split it off, but tried the upper chip: here, at last, they exposed the long oval combs lying one over another as the fallen tree now lay, but side by side, and parallel to the sides of the trunk when it was erect.

The men now began to cut out the comb with their knives, disregarding the bees, which crawled about, manifesting little disposition to sting, seeming "more in sorrow than in anger;" but probably in reality stupefied and disabled by the effects of the smoke. We all feasted on the honeycomb, which was full to overflowing of rich, clear honey, nearly as transparent and colourless as water, indicating that the swarm was young. A good deal of the comb was either dry and empty, or contained the young bees in different stages of their growth; some being in larva and pupa, others perfected, but with their members yet soft and white.

The men now removed the "gum" from the original entrance, and placed it over this main opening, blowing in smoke at both extremities, but, as they had taken out most of the comb, I did not remain to watch the result; a great many of the bees were flying off when I left. They had, previously to commencing operations, rubbed the inside of the gum with salt and peach-leaves, the smell and taste of which are believed (with what foundation I know not) to be attractive to these insects. Not one of us was stung, except one of the negroes, and he before they began to cut into the hollow.*

The silence of night, which has become proverbial in other countries, in this is but a poetical fiction,—at least in summer time. A large species of Gryllus, called provincially the Katedid *(Pterophylla concava),* fills the air with its nightly music, such as it is. Multitudes of them lodge in the trees around us, and no sooner has evening waned into night, than they tune up with their cracked notes, and keep up an incessant ringing during the whole night, until morning dawns, when they all become silent. This sound has been heard but a few weeks, beginning not gradually, but, as it were, in all places at once, or nearly so, and bursting forth into full and vigorous chorus. This is, I suppose, to be accounted for by a very interesting and remarkable fact, that the majority of individuals of any

---

*I have little doubt that the wild bees of Alabama are, as believed, colonies of the species domesticated there; but whether that species is identical with our *Apis mellifica,* I am not sure, and I have now no means of ascertaining. I think it not improbable, however, that the domestic bees of different countries may be found to consist of several species.

particular species of insects attain the perfect state almost simultaneously, even to a degree of precision scarcely credible; so that a brood seems suddenly to have started into existence, where not a single individual had been previously seen. The ringing crink of the Orthopterous insects is made only by the perfected individual, being, it is believed, the sexual call of the male.

I think it will give you a pretty correct notion of the tone and character of the particular concert in question, to fancy a score or two of people with shrill voices, divided into pairs, each pair squabbling with each other:—"I did!" "you didn't!" "I did!" "you didn't!" the objurgation maintained with the most amusing pertinacity, and without a moment's intermission, on every side of you. The performer is a large and handsome Gryllus, of a bright green hue, somewhat resembling the great green Grasshopper of England, in size and general appearance, but the outer wings *(hemelytra)* are dilated and oval, and very convex externally, the pair taking nearly the form, when closed in a state of repose, of a blown bladder. The antennae are of uncommon length and slenderness; but the most singular part of the conformation is the musical organs, which are situated one at the base of each *hemelytron,* and forming a part of it, which is turned, at a right angle to the rest, over the back, so that the one shall partly overlap the other. The organ consists of a hard glassy ridge in front, which, on being crossed by its fellow, creaks sharply, making the crink that is heard in the trees. There must, however, be three distinct but rapid crossings to make the whole sound represented by the word "Katedid," which it can produce as quickly as one can pronounce the word. Occasionally it gives but a single impulse, which we may call uttering only one syllable of the word, but usually the three are heard, then an interval of a second, and again the word, and so on. Behind this ridge there is a transparent membrane, which appears tightly stretched over a semi-circular rim, like the parchment of a drum, and which, no doubt, increases the sound by its vibrations. The insect I found would creak freely, when held in the fingers, provided it were held by the thorax or head, so as to allow the *hemelytra* free power of motion; though these are only partially opened, the bases being a little separated without affecting the position of the whole. But for the well-known fact, that the males alone of these creatures are musical, I should have supposed the specimen I have been describing to be a female, for the extremity of the abdomen was furnished with a large sword-shaped organ curving upwards, resembling an oviduct. I presented to it some house-flies, which it readily took from my fingers, and devoured with great gusto, though I should apprehend its diet, in a state of nature, must be wholly vegetable. I had an opportunity of comparing the sexes together, for last evening a female flew in at my open window. I can find little difference between it and the former, except that it entirely wants the membranous drum, and glassy ridge at the base of the front wings; this part, which has the same form, and which laps over in the same manner as in the other sex, is of exactly the same texture, colour, and general appearance as the rest of the *hemelytra.*

It is a trite observation, but not the less wonderful, that habit renders us insensible to the agreeable or disagreeable qualities of those sensations which we are constantly experiencing; when the Katedids commenced their nocturnal serenades, I found it impossible to sleep, and bewailed my hapless fate in the prospect of disturbed repose throughout the summer; but perpetual reiteration has so blunted my perceptions, that I now not only disregard the annoyance, but am actually unconscious of its existence, save when the mind accidentally reverts to the subject. I need scarcely say that there are many conditions of human life in which the power which the mind thus possesses (trifling as it appears in the present instance) of accommodating itself to circumstances, is a most kind and merciful ordination.

"There's mercy in every place:
 And mercy, encouraging thought!
Gives even affliction a grace,
 And reconciles man to his lot."

Feeding on the acrid milky leaves of a very beautiful flower, the Butterfly weed *(Asclepias tuberosa),* I found, a few weeks ago, a fine caterpillar of the large black and orange butterfly *(Danais Archippus).* It had a tigrine appearance, being marked with transverse bands and stripes of yellow, white, and black, and was adorned withal with four flexible fleshy horns or tentacles, two on the shoulders, and two on the rump. A day or two ago, it hung itself up by the tail, from a little conical knob of silk, which it had skilfully spun, thread over thread, on the roof of its box; an apparently trivial circumstance, yet so decisive as to show indubitably to which of the two great divisions of the butterfly tribe it was to be referred. The pupae of butterflies are, I believe, invariably suspended, or at least tied; but while those of one great section are loosely hung from a little button, as in the specimen before us, those of the other have, besides this support, a slender but strong girdle of silk, which, passing round the body near the head, binds them generally in a horizontal position, and allows them little scope to swing about. It is a remarkable fact, that the Butterflies which are evolved from the former position, have the first pair of feet so short as to be useless as instruments of locomotion, while those using the latter mode, have these feet resembling the middle and hindmost pairs in form and office. This association of characters is invariable; yet we cannot perceive the most distant connexion between the presence of a girdle in the pupa, and the development of the feet in the imago.

But I was going to advert to the change of form, which takes place in the transition from the caterpillar to the chrysalis state. Those persons who are aware of the fact that such a change occurs, but have never observed the process, are apt to imagine that the chrysalis comes forth in the form in which they see it, all hard and horny from the bursting skin of the caterpillar, as the armed Minerva from the head of Jupiter. But in truth, the change of general form is gradual; beginning before the disruption of the skin, and mainly going on after that skin has been thrown off. The former part of the alteration consists in a gradual obliteration of the annulose divisions, a rounding and shortening of the body and a perceptible approximation to the form of the matured pupa, especially in the Moth tribes. But the change of form which the evolved pupa undergoes is most conspicuous in the suspended butterflies; and I have never seen it more remarkable than in this of the Archippus, although I have observed the metamorphosis of many species; and I may here remark, by the way, that there are few processes in nature more interesting to be witnessed than the transformations of a butterfly. In this case the abdominal segments were at first much elongated, being distinctly separable, as in the caterpillar; those of the thorax, on the contrary, were contracted, while the wings were small, thick, and wrinkled; their extremities being free, for a purpose we shall presently discover. The whole skin was soft, moist, and pulpy, and the colour bright green, with alternate yellow bands. In a few hours, the abdominal segments had contracted into the form of a smooth, blunt cone, all traces of the divisions being lost, except where a fine line, scarcely perceptible, marked their position; the thoracic segments had much lengthened, and the wings now occupied the half of the entire length; their tips, which before were free, had stretched beyond their first boundary, far over the abdomen, and were now fixed in the general outline. The whole surface was become tense, hard, and glossy, and the hue an uniform greenish white, with a few gilt dots. I may add, that the amusing act of taking hold of the sloughed skin with the abdomen, while the tail was thrust out to feel for the silk button, was performed just as the common Vanessae of our own country, the tortoise-shell, the peacock, &c. would do it: by observing which, most of the preceding remarks may be readily verified.

The chrysalis in question produced the imago in eight days, but under circumstances worthy of narration. Having accidentally let fall the box containing it, the fragile shell of the chrysalis was broken off, leaving the anal joint and tail-like process attached to the silk. It was, however, too near its exit for any wound to be made in the body of the enclosed butterfly, though some liquid was discharged. This occurred in the morning; in the course of the day, the chrysalis began to assume the colours and marks of the Archippus butterfly, or, to speak more correctly, these tints began to be visible on the contained insect, through the increasing transparency of the pupa-skin. The next morning, early, I looked at it, just as it was bursting into its new life; it attained its perfection in the usual way, in about half-an-hour, without any injury from its accidental fall; having been but eight days in the pupa state. Whether from the caterpillar's having been bred in confinement, I know not, but the butterfly is the smallest individual of the species I have ever seen.

A day or two since I had the pleasure of discovering, in a little hollow, beneath a decaying log, a nest of our commonest lizard (*Agama undulata*), vulgarly called here the Scorpion. I conclude that such was the case, from the circumstance of a lizard of this species being in the nest when I first observed it. As the reptiles never, that I know of, sit on their eggs, or visit them after their deposition, I presume that these had just been laid by the parent. The eggs were four in number, oval in shape, and about half-an-inch in length, of a dull dirty white. The shell, or envelop, was tough, like a leathery sac, and upon cutting one open, first there issued a quantity of clear glaire, and then the yelk, which in consistence and colour much resembled the brain of birds, being white with reddish streaks.

The spring is peculiarly the season of flowers, and comparatively few are now seen. Some, however, appear in succession, a few of which I shall notice. In neglected pastures, the tall, well-known, and widely-spread Mullein (*Verbascum nigrum*) has begun to develop the earliest of its pretty blossoms. Bearing many flowers in its lengthened and closely-set rachis, it continues in bloom a long time, and it is singular that it usually shows its open flowers at the two extremities of the spike, while the central ones remain unexpanded. Of course these in their turn open, and the peculiarity ceases. There is something noble in the appearance of this tall plant; and its flowers are elegantly spotted with red, on a bright yellow ground. The leaves are large, and thickly clothed with soft woolly down. It is even more abundant with us in the open situations I have named, than in the north, and frequently affords a resting place for such birds as the Fly-catchers *(Muscicapae)*. The lovely little Blue-bird *(Sylvia sialis)*, that universal favourite, I have often seen watching on this plant, in the same manner as those birds do, for flies and other insects, and occasionally warbling forth his sweet but unpretending notes, or flitting from one stalk to another through a whole field; the bright azure blue of his back and wings making him very conspicuous in the sunbeams.

In the garden of a planter I lately saw the Indian Shot *(Canna angustifolia)* in flower. From the habits of the proprietor, it is not at all probable that any of his garden flowers would be exotics, as the place was deep in the solitude of the forest, and so recently reclaimed, that the stumps of the trees still remained undecayed in the garden. I have little doubt that the plant was originally found very near, if not exactly on the site where I saw it. It is a singular plant; the leaves are large, oblong, and deeply plaited longitudinally; the stem is angular, and bears many handsome flowers, whose sword-shaped petals are bright scarlet, varied with yellow at the base. They are succeeded by a rough, oval, pale green capsule, containing a few black seeds, perfectly round, and so hard as to have given the name of Shot to the plant.

In the woods a delightful odour is diffused to a considerable distance from the abundant racemes of white blossoms pendent from the Sorrel-tree *(Andromeda arborea)*, whose leaves, like those of the Oxalis of our own country, are agreeably acid. I will here notice a fact that I think I have observed, though I have never seen it alluded to by any writer, that if a person stand at a small distance from any flower of strong perfume, he will distinctly perceive variations in the intensity of the odour, as if it were projected from the flower in irregular waves or gushes. In the open air this might plausibly be attributed to varying currents of air, but I have observed it in a room, where it could hardly be dependent on such agency.

The Comfrey *(Commelina erecta)* is now in blossom, but it is not common in this neighbourhood. I have observed but one or two plants of it, in the shady woods. The leaves are pointed ovate, with longitudinal veins, of a very pale green: the flower, which is of peculiar formation, proceeds from a semicircular sac, formed, as I suppose, by the union of a pair of bracteae; when this is pressed, a clear glutinous fluid is squeezed out, in which the flower must have been bathed before its expansion. When full-blown, however, this sac is crowned by two large roundish petals, of a light blue, standing each on a thick neck or stalk; beneath these are two membranous sepals, much smaller, and quite white. From the centre stand up four nectaries, on long slender filaments resembling stamens, so that I know no flower more likely to puzzle a student endeavouring to find its name in the Linnaean system. Only a single blossom is seen on the plant at one time, which is produced in the morning, and shrivels in the course of a few hours; but a new one is evolved on the next morning, and thus a succession continues for a considerable time.

Another beautiful and fleeting flower is the Tree Primrose *(Oenothera fruticosa),* which grows on the sunny edges of the woods, in the corners of fences, &c., rising to the height of several feet. The flower is large, of a brilliant yellow.

Two species of Banner-pea *(Vexillaria Virginiana,* and *mariana)* are trailing on the ground, or creeping up other plants in the forest. They are papilionaceous flowers, much alike, and resembling a sweet pea, the banner *(vexillum)* being much enlarged; the colour is a delicate lilac. The stems are scarcely thicker than a thread, though very long; the leaves are ternate, or set in threes.

Large tracts of waste land, neglected fields, &c., are now covered with the glowing scarlet blossoms of *Zinnia multiflora,* which, standing in dense masses, have a showy effect, something like that of a bank covered with the common scarlet poppy in England. Beautiful as it is, however, it is too common to be admired; it is nothing but a weed, having not even the consideration of a familiar name.

One more plant, and Flora is dismissed. I know nothing of its pretensions to beauty or fragrance, but allude to it on account of its very remarkable economy. It is the Venus's Fly-trap *(Dionaea muscipula),* an appropriate name, as far as it expresses its office, but why dedicated to the goddess of love I am not aware. The plant is small; the leaves grow, like those of the primrose, on the ground, the stem being undeveloped, and are furnished at the end of each with an appendage, like another smaller leaf, the two lobes of which turn upon the mid-rib, as upon a hinge, and close together on being touched, like the erected wings of a butterfly. The edges are armed with stiff spinous hairs, which lock into one another, and prevent the escape of any unfortunate insect captured by this curious trap. On tickling the surface with a straw, we can at any time cause the leaf instantly thus to shut up; but on close investigation its irritability is perceived to reside in a few hairs, not more than three or four, which are scattered over the surface; for if these be avoided, the leaf may be tickled all day to no purpose, but the moment one of them is touched, though ever so slightly, the magic effect is produced. When the plant grows old, the divisions bend backward, and then the glandular hairs lose their irritability.

I sometimes feel rather disappointed that I am able to do so little, either in collecting, or in making observations out of doors, seeing that there are so many things, particularly in Entomology, worthy of being observed and recorded. But the fact is, the sun's heat is so intense, being almost vertical, and rarely shadowed by a cloud, that it is scarcely prudent to expose oneself to it during the middle part of the day. Gentlemen, who ride on horseback (none walk), usually carry an umbrella, as *locum tenens* of a parasol; but to pursue swallow-tailed butterflies, with a net in one hand and an umbrella in the other, would be not quite "the thing." There is, moreover, a degree of bodily languor and weakness induced by excessive perspiration, which depresses the mind and blunts scientific zeal, if not strongly combated. Of the prostration of strength arising from this cause, you may form an idea from a single fact. Sitting down in my room alone to write, without any previous exercise to warm me, almost undressed, I had not written half a page, when I found, where my hand had lain, a little pool of water on the paper, as much as a teaspoon could contain, the exudation from my hand alone during those few minutes. The morning hours, therefore, are the only part of the day that can habitually be rendered effective to science; for very few insects or birds, comparatively, are abroad in the evening, except the night-fliers. My usual plan is, to take a long walk through the forest in the morning, before the sun is very high; and in the heat of the day, if business permits, arrange my captures, write, or paint insects and flowers.

Letter IX

Peaches are now ripe; and beneath our sunny skies they acquire a luscious fla-vour that no wall can impart in a colder climate. So highly is this fruit esteemed, that every farm has large tracts planted with it, as orchards, to one of which the slaves have liberty of access when they please—a politic concession, whereby the planter hopes, by the sacrifice of a portion of his produce, to save the remainder. There are many varieties common, differing greatly in their qualities and in the season of their maturity.

Whole fields are also devoted to the culture of the different species of mel-ons and gourds. The botanical appellation of these fruits, a berry, seems some-what startling, when we think that some of them, the Water-melon for instance, often attain the length of two feet in the greatest diameter; yet such they are, and when examined, indeed, a melon does possess a very great resemblance to an enormous gooseberry. The Gourd, or Calabash *(Cucurbita lagenaria),* is cul-tivated, not to be eaten, for which it is not at all fitted, but to be used for uten-sils of household economy. The leaves are roundish or heart-shaped, downy, and toothed at the edge: the fruit is woody, of a remarkable shape, like a long tube, swelling at the end into an oval globe. A slice is cut off from one side of the di-lated part, the pulp and seeds are scraped out, and the woody shell is hung to dry, after which it is used as a ladle, or a drinking cup, or in many other ways. One singular use to which it is applied is that of birds'-nests; several gourds are frequently hung around a tree whose branches have been lopped, to entice the Purple Martin *(Hirundo purpurea)* to occupy them as breeding boxes; a prac-tice learned, I believe, from the Indians. Some persons exercise their ingenuity in ornamenting the outside of the household gourds with carved lines and figures.

The Musk-melon *(Cucumis melo),* the species chiefly used in England, is grown rather extensively with us, but is not so general a favourite as the Water Melon, the peculiar odour being to some persons rather disagreeable. It is, however, one of the handsomest of the family.

The Water-melon *(Cucurbita citrullus),* is deservedly esteemed; as I know not a more cooling or delicious fruit in the heat of summer. I am not aware that it is known in England; I have never seen it exposed in the London markets, but all through the Union it is highly prized and easily obtained; even as far north as the State of Maine and Canada it finds its way, the south supplying an almost inexhaustible quantity during the season. The very negroes have their own Melon "patches," as well as their peach orchards, and it is no small object of their ambition to raise earlier or finer specimens than their masters. The plant is distinguished by having the leaves divided into five lobes, which are deeply cut into rounded sinuations: the fruit is usually oval, but sometimes oblong, and not unfrequently pear-shaped. The rind is smooth, dark green, usually marked more or less distinctly with longitudinal stripes of a lighter hue. The flesh is very spongy, generally white, but often tinged with a delicate pink or crimson: the central part, in which the numerous seeds are lodged, has often struck me as bearing a strong resemblance to snow saturated with water, and when put into the mouth, melts deliciously away like snow into the sugary juice, of which the delicate cells are full: and though perhaps *not quite* so cold as melting snow, it may be considered as the best realization of the French princess's brilliant idea, of "ice with the chill taken off," especially when "drawn from the obscure retreat" of the underground cellar, to which they are usually consigned, for at least a night, to cool after being gathered. A cart-load is brought home from the field, nearly every evening, to supply the demand of the family for the next day; for during this torrid weather, very little business but the eating of water-melons is transacted. If a guest call, the first offering of friendship is a glass of cold water as soon as seated; then there is an immediate shout for water-melons, and each taking his own, several are destroyed before the knife is laid down. The ladies cut the hard part, near the rind, into stars, and other pretty shapes, which they candy as a conserve for winter.

With these are interspersed occasional plants of the little Smell Lemon *(Cucurbita ovifera?)*. The fruit is about the size of a small orange, perfectly round; its appearance is beautiful, the hue being bright glossy red, with stripes of yellow running round, like the meridian lines on a globe. The smell is very fragrant, and hence they are often placed on ladies' work-tables; they are not eatable, and I know of no other good qualities that they possess than their beauty and perfume. Children are fond of carrying them in their pockets, and tossing them about as playthings. I have seen what I suppose to be the same species in some of the London shops, particularly at a fruiterer's in the Poultry, where it was ticketed as "Queen Anne's Pocket Melon." Now and then the Prickly Cucumber *(Cucumis anguria)* is seen growing in a melon field, but I believe merely as a curiosity, the globose fruit being covered with sharp spinous processes, standing up like those of a hedgehog.

The fruits of many of our forest trees are now fast approaching maturity; and I will take this occasion to describe some remarkable species that I have not yet introduced to you. There is, within a few yards of me, a fine tree of the Three-thorned Locust species *(Gleditschia triacanthos),* often called, from its singular fruit, the Honey Locust. It sometimes grows two or three feet in diameter, but this is much smaller. The trunk is usually twisted, and shows longitudinal cavities, opening upwards: this part, as well as the larger branches, is studded with stiff and long thorns, often in formidable clusters, and each armed with smaller spines growing from its side. The leaves are bipinnate, long, and containing very many small, oval leaflets; and being of a pleasing green, give a particularly light and elegant character to the foliage. From the smaller branches hang enormous pods, which are about a foot long and one or two inches wide, flattened, and irregularly curved, of a light reddish brown hue when ripe. The inner surface of each division of this legume is coated with a thick glutinous pulp, as sweet as sugar, giving the name to the tree; the pods are often chewed for this substance; the seeds, which are many in number, hard and brown, are arranged side by side, as the common pea.

A very singular appendage is found on a common species of Elm, called the Wahoo *(Ulmus alata).* The smaller branches and twigs have the bark dilated on two opposite sides into a flat edge, about a quarter of an inch wide, of a tough elastic texture, much like cork in appearance, which extends through their whole length, much more regularly than in the English Elm.

One of our commonest trees is the Sweet Gum *(Liquidambar styraciflua),* which grows to a large size both in swamps and in dry woods. Its foliage much resembles that of a maple, the leaves being five-lobed, but the lobes are more regular than in that genus, and finely toothed. They are of a beautiful green hue, and give out, when rubbed, a fragrance something like that of the lemon-tree, but inferior. In the angles formed by the main nerves, which diverge from the base of the leaf, there is a little mass of down, which is characteristic of the genus. The flowers are inconspicuous, the barren and the fertile ones being on distinct branches: the latter succeeded by a singular fruit, consisting of numerous capsules agglomerated into a ball of an inch and a half in diameter, from which the points of the capsules project in every direction; it hangs from a petiole two or three inches long. These globes are green, but become yellow when ripe, and then the capsules burst, and allow the exit of little winged seeds, like those of the ash. The bark of old trees is full of deep furrows: if wounded in summer, it distills a fluid gum or resin in very small quantity, possessed of an agreeable fragrance. The wood being strong and tough, and of close texture, is sometimes cleft into rails, and used for building, but having little durability, it is not much valued.

This must not be confounded with the Sour Gum or Black Gum *(Nyssa sylvatica),* a tree of a very different genus. This thrives best on the high grounds, where it becomes a noble tree of seventy or eighty feet in height. The leaves are long-oval, rather crumpled; the fruit, from which it derives its commonest appellation, is a beautiful oval berry of a deep blue, generally arranged in pairs at the end of a long pink footstalk. They look very tempting to the eye, but like the apples of Sodom, they are nauseous to the palate, for though the first taste of their acidity is agreeable, they are found to be intensely bitter. The berry contains a largish flattened stone, marked with longitudinal lines. The wood is exceedingly hard to split, the fibres being singularly interwoven, like a braided cord—a very remarkable peculiarity of this genus. There is a joke current of a poor Irish emigrant, who having engaged himself to cut and split fence rails, unfortunately selected a Sour Gum-tree as the subject of his dissective power; but having toiled all day with indomitable perseverance, he accomplished the manufacture of but a single rail.

The Cotton Plant *(Gossypium herbaceum),* to the cultivation of which so very large a portion of our fields is appropriated, is now adorned with its beautiful blossoms, and even a scattered pod here and there already shows the invaluable material which is to become a source of prosperity and preeminence to nations. The cultivation of this plant is *the agriculture* of the State, all other crops being subordinate, and even maize being raised only for home consumption. The fields are ploughed in autumn and spring, with ploughs of very rude and inefficient construction, drawn by mules, the usual beasts of draught for all farm purposes. The cotton seed is sown early in spring, in drills or rows, between which the ground is carefully and repeatedly hoed by the slaves during the summer, to eradicate the Crowfoot Grass *(Cynodon dactylon),* and other weeds. The plant usually appears above ground in the latter part of May, and grows to the height of four or five feet; but as it is an annual, and a tender one, it dies in the autumn. The leaves are lobed like those of the vine, and the blossoms are large, and much resemble a single Hollyhock; they have the remarkable property of changing their colour: the flower when it blows is of a pure yellowish white, with a red spot at the base of each petal, as in the common Hibiscus; this colour it retains during the first day, but towards evening a very slight tinge of pink is perceptible here and there; on the morrow the whole blossom has become deep pink, and on the third day it drops. The flower is enclosed in a calyx, which is again enclosed in a cup-shaped involucrum of three bracts; these are large, and cut into long teeth; so that on the whole it has a noble appearance. It is succeeded by an oval green fruit, which attains the size of a hen's egg, and contains many seeds, enclosed in four divisions, and enveloped in the cotton, whose individual filaments grow as long hairs from the skin of the seed. If an unripe capsule be opened, it will be found full of the white cotton, but saturated with moisture, much compressed, and possessing little elasticity. When ripe the capsule opens, by the separation of the four sutures at the vertex, when the snowy-white cotton speedily dries, and by its elasticity projects till it forms a mass nearly as large as one's fist, just as it appears when it comes to the manufacturer.

A not unfrequent plant in our gardens is the Adam's Needle *(Yucca aloifolia),* which is, about this season, crowned with its magnificent spike of large, white, lily-like flowers, very much crowded. The leaves of this plant are lanceolate, stiff and hard, terminating in a point as sharp as a needle, and as they radiate in every direction, the lowest pointing downwards, the topmost ones upwards, and the middle ones standing out horizontally, it is next to impossible to get one's hand to the trunk, or rather stipe, without being wounded. The earlier leaves in succession decay to their bases, which are left sheathing the stem, in the same manner as in the palms. Whether in bloom or not, it is a highly ornamental plant. I have no doubt it is a native, though I have not had the good fortune to find it wild; but its congener, the Bear's Grass *(Yucca filamentosa),* is not uncommon by the sides of little streams, and in shady places. It differs from the preceding, in the stem being altogether undeveloped, the leaves being more broadly lanceolate, and having their margins furnished with contorted filaments; these are the outermost fibres of the leaf, which detach themselves for the length of an inch or two, and curl up like slender tendrils. In the time of flowering, which is rather earlier than this, it shoots up a flower-stalk to the height of four or five feet, crowded with noble white blossoms, much resembling those of the former.

I must now announce the fashionable arrivals in the insect world. A handsome Chafer *(Gymnetis nitida)* flies in some numbers around the peach-trees during the heat of the day. Though it rarely appears before July, it is called here the June Bug, the term bug being universally misapplied by the Americans to beetles. It is about the size of the common Rose Chafer *(Cetonia aurata)* of England, to which it bears a general resemblance; but the soft rich metallic green of the present species is far superior in brilliancy to the hue of the other; a good deal of the splendour, however, vanishes as soon as life is extinct.

The Tiger Swallow-tail Butterfly *(Papilio Turnus),* so numerous in Canada, and extending even to Newfoundland, has lately come under my notice; and a still older acquaintance, the Admirable, or Red Admiral of English collectors *(Vanessa atalanta),* a denizen also of both the northern countries I have just named, as well as of most parts of the Old World. Here, however, it appears to be a great rarity, and the former is by no means common.

I have taken specimens of a large black Click Beetle *(Alaus oculatus),* marked with irregular white dots, having on the thorax two large oval spots, which are velvety, and intensely black, surrounded by a white edge. As the insect is more than an inch and a half in length, these spots render it very conspicuous.

The latest novelties in the butterfly *beau monde* are the following: the Blue-eyed Ringlet *(Hipparchia Alope),** a large and fine species, having the upper surface of a soft, sober, brown hue, with a great patch on the fore wings of a yellowish white, in which are two large black eyelets with azure pupils, and an obscure eyelet near the angle of the hind pair. Beneath, the colours are much the same, but the eyelets are brighter, and there are four in the hind wing, and the brown ground is beautifully marked with transverse dashes of black. The Pale-clouded Ringlet *(Hipparchia* ———?), an undescribed species, I believe, is much like it, but smaller, having the brown upper surface darker, the patch smaller and yellower, and only the front eyelet present in either surface, much reduced in size. On the hind wings the four eyelets of the under surface are reduced to two (with, however, a slight indication of the other two), and the one on the upper side is

*See Engraving on p. 63.

hardly visible. It may possibly be the male of the preceding. They bear a resemblance, particularly the latter, to our English Meadow Brown *(S. Jurtina)*, but are handsomer. They are wary, and fly swiftly, chiefly affecting lanes in the forests, but occasionally coming into the gardens early in the morning. The third which I notice is one which, in the enthusiasm of my first acquaintance with it, when after a hard chase in the burning sun I captured it, appeared the most splendid butterfly I had ever seen, and amply repaid me, by the triumph of possession, for my fatiguing pursuit. It is the Vanilla Fritillary *(Argynnis vanillae)*. Though it has appeared but a few days, it has already become rather numerous. The upper surface is deep orange-tawny, in some males almost vermilion, with a few black spots, and the nervures dilated into black stripes. But it is in the under surface that the superlative glory of this most lovely insect is seen. The front wings are deep scarlet, with the tip yellowish brown; the hind wings are of this brown tint, and both are adorned, but particularly the latter, with many large and irregular spots of bright white, which have all the lustre of silver; each spot is surrounded with a black edge, that seems to set off its beauty—a beauty of which the silver spots on some of our English Fritillaries can give but a faint idea. Slight traces of this metallic brilliance even appear on the upper surface, as silver pupils to the larger black spots of the fore wings. The caterpillar of this exquisite creature is said to feed on the flesh-coloured Passion flower *(Passiflora incarnata)*.

A fourth is the Snout Butterfly *(Libythea motya)*, remarkable for the great development of the palpi, which are lengthened into a snout, as in some small moths, projecting nearly half an inch from the head. In other respects it is much like a little *Vanessa*. The wings are orange, with brown margins; the tip of the first pair is brown, containing three large white patches; beneath, the first pair are as above; the second are dark brown.

Add to these, two little sable urchins, regular "chummies" in appearance— the Sooty Skipper *(Hesperia Catullus)*, and the Banded Skipper *(H. Phylaeus)*; but they are too ugly to be worth any other description, than that they are blackish brown, with a few white dots.

I have also obtained some very fine moths: the Green Emperor *(Saturnia luna)* is a very remarkable as well as beautiful species. It is large, measuring nearly five inches in breadth; the wings are of a pale pea-green, with a half-shut eyespot in each; the hind pair are elongated into a long tail-like process, as in the swallow-tailed butterflies, which extends more than an inch and a half from the outline of the wing. An eminent naturalist observes, that "the lower wings of the Lepidoptera, when thus unusually lengthened, perform the same office in flight as the tail does among birds, for we find that all the swiftest flying butterflies have what are aptly and justly called swallow-tailed wings." I am not aware, however, that the present species affords any exception to the generally heavy flight of the thick-bodied family to which it belongs: the specimen which has come under my notice was particularly slow and tame (although a male), but as both the tailed processes were much shortened by being weather-beaten, it would not be fair to draw a conclusion from it alone. I suppose, without breeding the insect from pupa, it would be rare to meet with a perfect specimen, these long tails being, from their fragile nature, particularly liable to injury.

Two specimens of another species of the same genus, the Corn Emperor *(Saturnia Io),* were lately given to me; one of which flew into a house in the evening, the other was flying in the shade of a large tree in the middle of the day. Both are females; they are four inches and a half in extent; the fore wings dark red, with two dusky bands; the hind wings yellow, with two concentric semicircular bands, the outer red, the inner black, and a very large, round, deep black eyespot in the centre, having a linear white pupil. The male of this moth differs remarkably; his fore wings being bright yellow, with a few spots and dashes of dark red; the body also is yellow; the hind wings are like those of the other sex. The larva is said by Abbot to feed on the maize, dogwood *(Cornus),* sassafras, &c.

A very splendid, but I believe undescribed species of *Catocala,* a genus commonly known by the appellation of Crimson Underwings, has lately occurred. It far exceeds in beauty, as well as in size, the Scarlet Underwing, formerly noticed, being four inches and five-sixths in spread of wing; the fore pair of a soft rich brown, with lighter shades, crossed by two very sinuous lines of intense black; the hind pair brilliant crimson, with three black bands, and an indented pale margin. I know nothing of its habits; my specimen was observed resting with closed wings on a rafter in a house, during daytime; I carefully put my insect net over it, and on touching it, it suddenly opened its bright hues, and darted off in the headlong manner common to the genus, but unfortunately for itself, plunged into the bag of the net. From the perfectly uninjured state of the plumage, I conclude that it was but just out of pupa.

It has been supposed that the strong and offensive odours produced by some insects, are intended as a means of defence. From certain circumstances, however,

Moths
a. Corn Emperor *(Saturnia Io)*
b. Green Emperor *(Saturnia luna)*
The flower is the Scarlet Cypress-vine *(Ipomoea coccinea).*

I have reason to think, they may be connected with the reproductive economy, at least in that wide family to which I allude, and in which a peculiarly rank odour is so general, if not universal. Two large plant bugs *(Pentatoma,)* on being disturbed, diffused suddenly their rank odour, in a degree far more pungent than I had ever before smelt; it even caused my eyes, though at a considerable distance, to smart like the exhalations from a cut onion.

Everybody knows how liable the Common Dorr and the Humble-bee of our own country are to be infested with parasitic mites or ticks, to so great an extent, indeed, as often to be almost covered with them, while the poor exhausted creature is utterly unable to defend itself against their attacks, and at length dies. Mr. Rennie, in his "Insect Miscellanies," speaks of having seen butterflies and dragonflies burdened in the same manner. I have lately observed a parallel fact, in the case of a little dragonfly *(Libellula Berenice),* which I found much infested with minute scarlet mites, beneath the abdomen. But there is a much more interesting fact, which I forgot to mention when speaking of the Ocellated Clickbeetle *(Alaus oculatus),* viz. that one of these beetles was molested by *great numbers* of the curious little creature, *Chelifer.* It resembles a very tiny scorpion without a tail; and these, which I found, ran backward as readily as forward. That these little insects are fiercely predaceous has been long known, but not (at least that I am aware,) that they are gregarious, or parasitical.

The continuation of the species seems to be the chief end of individual insect existence: an instinct which almost triumphs over death itself.

"Naturam expellas furcâ, tamen recurret." Moths which have been pinned by the collector before the deposition of their eggs, in conformity with this instinct, hasten to deposit them on the setting board, and I have seen one of the Ghost Moths *(Hepialidae),* which eject their eggs to a distance, immediately on being pinned, begin to shoot forth her little black eggs with great rapidity, as if aware that she had not long to live, and anxious to make the most of her time. So, a rather large, but extremely delicate *Ephemera,* which I caught about dusk in the garden, a few evenings ago, on being pierced, protruded her eggs in a very singular manner, not one by one, but all together, in two long rolls, stuck side by side, leaving the abdomen suddenly empty, or filled only with air. In this case the situation was peculiarly inappropriate; for, at liberty, the fly would have sought some pool or stream, and deposited her rolls of eggs in the water, of which the genus is an inhabitant in its first stages.

Ever since I arrived in the State, I have observed a very handsome Locust abundant. I first noticed it at Mobile, where specimens were as numerous as here; hitherto they have been only in the larva, and a few latterly in the pupa state, of various sizes. The colour in these stages was glossy black, with stripes of scarlet. About a week since, I observed that several had attained the imago state, and were become very large and thick, the females being as much as three inches in length. The parts which before were scarlet, are now yellow, namely, the margins of the abdominal segments, some dashes on the head, and a stripe down the thighs. The wings and wing-sheaths are small, and unfit for flight; the former are bright crimson, with a black margin; the latter black, with a beautiful network of crimson nervures. The species, which appears to be allied to the true Locusts, is, I believe, *Romalea microptera*.

Two species of *Lucanus*, the Deer-beetle *(L. dama)*, and the Elk-beetle *(L. Elaphus)*, now crawl across paths in the evening. They replace our English Stag-beetle, which they very closely resemble, in size, colour, and form. The former has, however, rather shorter, and the latter much longer, jaws in proportion. The latter is also more slightly built, and has the head broad and flat, and raised above the thorax, like a very short pillar. The female of one of them, I know not which, is scarcely to be distinguished from the female of *L. cervus*.

A pretty, but offensive bug, the Chequered Bug *(Hammatocerus Purcis?)*, is found crawling on plants, in gardens, &c. The thorax is black, with a red margin, and the abdomen, whose edge extends beyond the incumbent wings, is marked with alternate bands of black and scarlet; the head is long, and produced into a narrow neck.

I visited again, a day or two since, the little prairie knoll, which I have already mentioned, and which was a month or two ago so profusely clothed with flowers, and swarming with insect life. I expected to find insects equally numerous, though the species should be changed; but I was much disappointed. The *Asclepias*, and all the other former flowers have disappeared, and though there are some new ones in their places, there are but very few butterflies. The pretty Pink-wing Moth *(Deiopeia bella)* was still abundant, flitting to and fro among the herbage, and hiding, when pursued, among the stalks of the grass. Returning, I observed a large stout Asilus *(A. Polyphemus?)*, densely clothed with yellow hair; to my surprise, it carried one of the black Pill Chafers *(Coprobius volvens)* in its mouth, and flew with apparent ease, notwithstanding its burden; an effort of strength which I should think, considering the relative size and weight of the two insects, truly herculean, and far beyond that so often quoted of a lion carrying off a young bullock: the insect was flying, not crawling. I have since observed this powerful and predaceous fly carrying insects heavier than itself, on several occasions, and so well are its instincts recognised, that it has obtained the common name of the "Bee-catcher."

Letter X

August 1st

There is a plant now abundantly in blossom, which grows in neglected fields and such-like places, in company with the *Zinnia*, covering, like it, large patches of ground with a dense mass of vegetation, two or three feet high. It is *Cassia occidentalis.* It has pinnate leaves, with many narrow leaflets; a bright yellow flower, succeeded by a pod like that of a sweet pea, which contains seeds hard and unpleasant to the taste. From its local name, Florida Coffee, I infer that these seeds are roasted, as an imitation of the Mocha berry, but such a use seems unknown here. The caterpillar of the Cloudless Sulphur Butterfly *(Colias Eubule)* is said to feed on this plant. I may remark that this gay butterfly, which was among the first that I noticed, still continues plentiful. Another kindred species, but a very little one *(Xanthidia Tucunda),* the Black-banded Sulphur, which was common in May and June, is become scarce, though it has not yet disappeared. I will describe it, for a reason which appears in the note. It is an inch and three-eighths in extent, sulphur-yellow, with a black cloud at the tip of the first pair, and some black irregular spots running into each other, at the margin of the second. But its distinguishing character is a broad band of black, running along the inner margin of the fore wings. Beneath, the first pair are yellow, with a dusky tip; the second greyish, with innumerable specks. Another species, of as nearly as possible the same size, has but recently appeared, but is become quite common; the Black-edged Sulphur *(Xanthidia Delia).* It is marked very much as the preceding, save that the band at the inner margin of the first wings is altogether wanting. Beneath, both pairs are yellow, with pink fringes; numerous specks, and a few larger black dots, are scattered over the surface.*

*Boisduval, in his beautiful *"Histoire et Iconographie des Lépidoptères de l'Amérique,"* has figured the Black-banded as the female of *Delia,* but in this he is mistaken, as I have caught *Delia* in circumstances which enable me to determine the male and female with precision. The sexes of this species differ in nowise from each other, except that *the male* is of a slightly brighter yellow, and has rather more of the black margin to the *hinder* wings. No trace of the band appears in either sex. This error is the more unaccountable, since he gives the Black-banded again, as the *male* and *female* of *Tucunda,* which is correct. I have little doubt, also, that his *Thecla favoninus,* and *Thecla hyperici,* are identical.

The Rattlesnake *(Crotalus)* is quite common, but though well known to be poisonous, is not much dreaded. The retreat of this reptile is usually a hollow tree, which has an entrance near the ground: when pursued, he makes for his hole and ensconces himself within; but his pursuer, if he be a chance passenger, and have not time or means to get him out, just blocks up the hole, by driving in a stout stick, or a stone, marks the tree, and calls at the nearest house to give the information. This is quite a conventional practice; such a notice was left at our door the other day, and I accompanied a young man to the place pointed out. He collected a good heap of dry bush and leaves around the hole, and then taking out the plug, set fire to the mass, in order to smoke out the tenant; but we watched in vain: either our customer was sulky, and chose to die, like Sardanapalus, in his palace, or else he had previously made his exit by crawling up the inside of the trunk, and out at the top. That snakes have the power of crawling up perpendicular surfaces, I had lately a very curious proof. I was engaged one afternoon quietly reading, in a room which was only clap-boarded, without being ceiled within, when, turning my head, I saw just above me a snake mounting the wall, about eight feet from the ground. I was a little alarmed, and gave a start which frightened my visitor, and he fell and escaped: I regret that in my surprise I did not notice the species. The only assistance afforded him in the ascent, was from the projecting edges of the clap-boards, about half an inch wide, that overlapped each other.

To return to the Rattlesnake. The hollow horny appendages to the tail, which are commonly called the rattles, are said to be cast annually with the sloughed skin; and it is inferred that, "*consequently,* no inference as to the age of the animal, can be drawn from the number of pieces which compose the rattles." I confess this appears to me to be a *non sequitur,* for is it not quite possible that one may be added to the *number* annually, without involving the actual perpetuity of the preceding ones? I cannot decide the fact. A young one that I killed in the garden (probably *Crotalus durissus),* had but three rattles: now as these appendages are often found much more numerous, it is evident that the increase must take place at some time or other, and it seems to me more likely to occur at the sloughing of the skin, that is, annually, than either oftener or seldomer. I may remark of the specimen which I killed, that its colour was purplish brown, marked with a red-brown streak down the back, and somewhat irregular bands of black; the tail was black, and an inch and a half in length, exclusive of the rattles: the total length was about twenty inches.

A Lizard of a bluish colour puzzled me not a little, owing to its tail not being more than an inch in length: I should have supposed that it had been broken off, an accident to which these reptiles are very liable, but that, short as it was, it tapered to a point. The creature was crawling about the logs of the house, and was very wary, so that I could not examine it; it was much like the kind vulgarly called Scorpion *(Agama undulata),* but seemed somewhat thicker. An observation, however, of Dr. Harlan's, in the "Journal of the Academy of Natural Sciences," threw light on the matter: it was to the effect that the Skinks, a family of lizards, have the power of reproducing the tail, when it has been accidentally broken off, and that the new tail is of a blue colour. The tail of the one under notice was undoubtedly in the process of reproduction, and perhaps the wariness of the animal might have been induced by the experience of injury, and consequent suffering.*

The chief enemies of the lizard tribes are the smaller and more ignoble birds of prey. Owls catch them in their evening wanderings, for I have found the stomach of an owl crammed full of the bones of small lizards. But I rather think that our lizards are almost exclusively diurnal in their habits, and therefore must be exposed to the predatory assaults of the weaker Hawks. The Swallow-tailed Kite *(Elanus furcatus)* is one of these, a bird of more than ordinary elegance, which has recently appeared with us, and may now be seen nearly every day associating in little groups. Their habit is to sail round and round on the wing in wide circles, sometimes at an immense elevation over the lofty woods; at other times they swoop down towards the bushes and herbage of the fields, and sweep to and fro among the trees; doubtless in pursuit of prey, for an attentive eye may now and then observe them raise one foot to the beak with a rapid movement, and deliver something to the mouth.

The appearance of these birds in the air is very beautiful. The fine contrast of the colours, pure white on the head, neck, and whole lower parts, and deep glossy

*Since this observation was recorded, I have had many opportunities of noticing phenomena analogous to the above: the power of renewing the tail is common to most, if not all, Saurian Reptiles.

black on the back, wings, and tail; the size of the bird, a full-grown male measuring two feet in length, and nearly five feet in spread of the expanded wings; and the remarkable elegance of its figure, produced by its slenderness, its small head, and the great length of its pointed wings and tail, in which it exceeds the swallow—all combine to attract admiration. The grace of its motions, too, in the air, is admirable; it continues to sail about for hours without resting, apparently without effort, now coursing around our heads, now chasing its fellows in amicable play, and presently mounting in spiral circles to the loftier regions of the air, as if it had forsaken this sordid world, and would wing its way to some distant sphere.

The children, who are familiar with this charming bird, say that several of them build every year in a gloomy pine swamp not far off. I know the place, a sombre dismal tract, bordering on both sides a sluggish stream that falls into the Alabama, where tall rugged pine trees rear their lofty heads, and spread their sable foliage, and toss about their gnarled arms, festooned with those pendant rags of Spanish moss that chill the spirit, and seem the very essence of desolation. On one of the tallest of these old pines, at the very summit of the tree, there is a great bundle of sticks and moss, which the lads tell me is a kite's nest of the present season, though now deserted, and already the worse for summer storms.

I have just obtained a specimen of a bird nearly related to this, and which might, indeed, be supposed by a stranger to be the same species in imperfect plumage. The colours and their distribution are much the same as in the preceding, but they are less pure, both the white and the black inclining to grey. Its size too is smaller, and the tail is but slightly forked. This is the Mississippi Kite *(Ictinia Mississipiensis);* a much less common bird, but of nearly the same habits and manners. My specimen was brought down by the unerring rifle of a friend the other day, while pursuing the same graceful evolutions in flight that I have mentioned as characteristic of its more elegant cousin. The food of both species is described to me as consisting mainly of the larger insects and the smaller reptiles; the *cicadae* that sit on the trees and fill the air with their deafening crink; the large dragon-flies that hawk to and fro over the fields and pools; the locusts and katedids that jump about the herbage and shrubs; the savage brown wasps that build huge nests of grey paper on old trees and posts, and many species of beetles, form the insect-diet; while nimble lizards, small slender snakes, and frogs afford a frequent and agreeable variety. The contents of the stomach in my

Mississippi Kite confirmed, in part, at least, this report; for it was stuffed with a couple of cicadae, and a large dragon-fly, mercilessly crumpled up, to be sure, but otherwise little damaged.

In one of my former letters I alluded to the assaults of tiny, but bloodthirsty, and far from despicable enemies, the Ticks. The young ones of the present season are just now exceedingly numerous; they congregate in great masses on the tips of leaves, and at the extremities of the stalks and blades of grass that grow beside the roads, or overhang the paths of the woods, waiting for an opportunity of selecting some more exalted animal to become their prey. On the slightest touch of any extraneous body they adhere to it, so that in walking through the woods we become almost covered with them. The utmost care is required to avoid touching the herbage; and if we sit down on a prostrate log in the forest, though only for a moment, myriads are presently crawling over our clothes. They are very minute, from the size of a small pin's head to that of a grain of sand, so that they can scarcely be brushed off when once attached. They soon insinuate themselves beneath the clothes, and seeking out some protected part of the body, especially where there is any hollow or angle, they thrust into the flesh a horny tubular proboscis, the extremity of which is armed with reflected barbs, and suck the blood of their victim at leisure. The sensation produced by the assaults of these minute ones is rather one of itching than of pain; they are too well moored to be removed by any rubbing, and too well shielded to be hurt by it; hence they riot in impunity, till, on disrobing at night, the usual search reveals some halfscore of ruthless rogues battened on gore, and swollen to ten times their legitimate bulk. Even then it is no easy matter to dislodge them; for the barbs at the tip of the rostrum resist and hold fast in the flesh when the insect is pulled, nor do they yield without considerable force, and some laceration.

I was surprised at the instant readiness with which these little parasites leave their watching-stations on the herbage, and cleave to passing animals. But, last evening, I had an opportunity of seeing how this is managed. I noticed a full-grown Tick on the extremity of a leaf, to which it held on with its hindmost pair of feet, while all the six other limbs were held out in the air, and kept waving to and fro. On my bringing the tip of my finger to it, it adhered instantly with these free feet, letting go the leaf at the same moment; and I infer that this is the approved method of proceeding with both young and old.

It is pitiable to see the poor brutes, the dogs and horses, and cattle. Unable to free themselves from their insect pests, which appear instinctively to know where they may bleed their victims in security, the poor patient creatures are obliged to endure them. Around the eyes, within and behind the ears, at the angles of the limbs, and at the base of the tail, we see the vile Ticks crowded, of all sizes, according to their various degrees of bloatedness; some dropping off in succession, when unable to carry more, and making room for empty and thirsty expectants. The poor animals well appreciate the relief which is occasionally rendered them by their human friends, and will stand patiently and quietly, while the disgusting vermin are plucked off, one by one. A day or two ago, I picked up in the high road a large Tick, that had no doubt dropped spontaneously from some beast, when sated with blood. Its natural size would have been about that of this letter [O], and scarcely thicker than paper; but it now appeared of the dimensions of a large horse-bean, both in diameter and thickness, tensely swollen, and as if ready to burst. Its body was a mere bag, filled with black clotted blood: no motion was perceptible in it, yet it was probably still alive.

It is commonly stated here, and I think it is probably correct, that these Ticks live three years. The first season they are called Seed-ticks—the minute ones mentioned above; the next year they become Yearling-ticks; and the third, Old-ticks. They are among the most disagreeable pests of the country; I dislike them even more than the Mosquitoes; though their season, to be sure, is much more brief.

I have heard that in India the residents distinguish two kinds of tiger-hunting, one of which is less agreeable than the other; viz. that in which you hunt the tiger, and that in which the tiger hunts you. And so it seems that this style of doing business, in which a rascally Tick lays wait for, and catches me, is to be put down as a non-agreeable variation of insect-hunting.

But I will now talk of superior game, and give some traits of the prowess of "a foeman worthy of our steel." One of our neighbours has been kept in a state of feverish vexation lately by the frequent depredations made in his corn-field by a Bear. Bruin is as fond of roasting-ears as the squirrels, or as the planter himself, and as his great splay feet trample down much more than he eats, the mischief which he does is commensurate. A night or two ago one of the negro boys came running to the house, stammering and spluttering—"O, mas'r, mas'r! big bear in corn-patch; I see 'un get over." All was bustle in an instant; bullets were cast—a job that has always to be done at the moment they are wanted—and our friend

Jenkins and his overseer crept out with their rifles to the field, under the guidance of Washington, the black boy. There was sufficient evidence of the truth of the report; the marks of broad paws were deep in the soft earth; the spot where the huge monster had climbed the rails was plainly shown, while the trodden-down rows of ripening corn gave proof of the diligence with which he had labored at his ruinous work. But somehow or other he had smelt a rat; perhaps the lad had involuntarily uttered the usual nigger interjection of astonishment, "Heigh!" or in his hurry to carry tidings, had given an alarm; however, the beast had made good a premature retreat, and the planter and his servants had only to follow the same course, meditating schemes of revenge.

The manner in which they hope to outwit him is curious. Bruin is a sober, sedate, methodical old gentleman; he has a determined *modus operandi* for everything, from which he will not deviate. Among other of his stereotypical habits is that of getting into a field, night after night, in the same manner, and at the same place; climbing over the very identical spot of the fence at which he mounted on the first occasion of his trying the corn. The scratches produced by his claws, and the smears from his soiled feet, make this spot sufficiently obvious. Just at this place, then, the overseer has fixed up a loaded rifle, making it point upwards at such an angle that the muzzle may face the animal's breast as he mounts the rails. A stick is attached to the trigger, and this is made fast, at right angles, to a transverse stick, which rests on two forks about breast high, a few inches from the fence, on the outside. In rising on his hind feet to put his fore paws on the rails, the Bear will press with his breast against the transverse stick, which, driving back the trigger, will discharge the contents of the rifle full into his heart. I have not yet heard of the result in this particular case, but it is an approved method of proceeding, and sanguine expectations are entertained of success.

The predilections of Bruin are not confined to corn. He is an epicure and a gourmand, and especially relishes well-fed pork. The hogs that run freely in the woods are too sharp for him, but the home-fed porkers that are confined in the yard have no means of escape, and the farmer has occasionally to lament the loss of a fat hog on which he had been looking with complacent approval, and pleasing anticipations of the pickle tub. Our shaggy friend, however, has felt a similar approval, and indulged similar anticipations; and some moonshiny night has issued from his lonely den at the roots of some ancient sycamore in the neighbouring swamp, and climbing the pig-fence, has taken the squealing pig in his arms, and borne him away in his paternal hug.

It is very seldom that a bear is met with in the woods, for his activity is chiefly nocturnal; but a highly curious rencontre is said to have taken place one day in a part of the forest not very remote from this place, which I will give you, as illustrative of the manners, both human and ursine, of these parts.

A planter had ridden out into the wood to look after some strayed cattle, carrying with him the redoubtable cow-whip, consisting of a handle three feet long, and of a lash of twisted raw hide thirty feet long, which was coiled on his right arm. Suddenly a huge bear starts up before him, from behind the gnarled roots of an old tree. The man could not resist the impulse to give the animal a lash with his whip, but, to his surprise, the bear showed a disposition to fight. It was rather an awkward predicament, but the horse was intelligent and agile, and as the rider made him face the bear, he was able, by leaping nimbly to and fro, to evade the ferocious brute, stung to madness by the repeated blows of the terrific cow-whip. At length the bear acknowledged his master, and turned tail for flight; when a thought struck the planter that he might possibly drive him home, as he would a refractory bullock. He accordingly kept close behind the animal, driving him along one of the numerous cattle-paths that thrid the forests, admonishing hint, by a severe cut with the whip, whenever he attempted to leave the track, until at length the poor creature patiently went as he was driven. A distance of six miles was thus traversed by pursuer and pursued, till the planter came within hail of his own house, when his son came out with a rifle and shot the poor persecuted bear.

This story may seem apocryphal, but it is so entirely in consonance with the habits of the people, that I see no reason for disbelieving it, though I have only hearsay-evidence for its truth. Such an attempt, under the circumstances, is quite likely to have been made by a southern planter; and when devised, the nature of the cow-whip, and the power and skill with which it is wielded in compelling semi-wild cattle to obedience, present means adequate to the emergencey.

As I sit in the cool of the evening, at the back-door of the house where I am residing, I have an opportunity of witnessing those singular evolutions of the Chimney Swallows *(Hirundo pelasgia),* which are the prelude to their nightly repose. There is a tall chimney rising from the smithy a few rods distant, round the summit of which some hundreds of swallows assemble every evening, about sunset. They come one by one from all parts, trooping to the common lodging at the same hour; and as soon as each arrives, he begins to wheel round and round in the air above the chimney-top. In a few minutes a large number are collected, which sweep round in a great circle, twittering and chirping; others continuing to arrive every moment, which immediately take their part in the circumvolution. By and by, one and another, and another, drop, as it were, into the chimney, as the circle passes over it, until they pour down in a stream, with a roaring sound, which, when heard from within the building, sounds like the sullen boom of a distant cataract. At length, when objects begin to be dim and indiscernible, all have entered and taken up their places within the shaft, where they remain for the night. In the morning, near sunrise, they emerge in a dense stream, pouring out like bees, make a few wide evolutions, and disperse on their daily occupation.

Letter XI

Aug. 15th

I was out last night 'Possum-hunting, and snatch an early hour this morning to describe to you the important affair, amusing enough, certainly, if not very profitable. For several days past, the "niggers," on bringing in the daily cart-load of water-melons for house-consumption, have been loud in complaints of the robberies committed by the "'Possums;" and though it would be perfectly competent for these sable gentlemen to impute to Mr. Possum their own delinquencies, the value of a water-melon is scarcely a sufficient inducement even for a negro to lie and thieve, seeing that he has abundantly more than he can devour in his own patch, and those, in all probability, finer and better grown than "mas'r's." The report was therefore received with all due credit, and an expedition against the 'Possums was resolved on as soon as the *vis inertiae* could be overcome.

By the aid of my persuasions this consummation was achieved last evening, and we determined on a sally.

As soon as field-work was done, and supper swallowed, preparations commenced. The overseer blew his horn to call such of the hands as were within hearing, out of whom some half-a-dozen were selected, nothing loth; for Sambo likes the wild excitement of a hunt, especially by night, as well as his betters, and enters into it with as much zeal and zest. One or two were set to saddle the horses, others to collect the dogs of the establishment, and others to search up axes for felling trees, knives for clearing away tangled briers in the woods, and a few other small implements, while another was sent into the swamp to procure a dozen pine-knots for torches. Meanwhile the overseer was busy with lead, ladle, and bullet-mould, at the smithy fire, casting ball for the rifles. These preliminaries disposed of an hour or more; there was no hurry, for it would have been useless to go out until night was well commenced, as it was desirable to allow the depredators full time to issue from their retreats, and begin their nocturnal business in the melon-patches.

About half-past nine, then, we set out, a goodly and picturesque cavalcade. There was, first, my worthy host, Major Kendrick, a stout sun-burnt fellow of six feet two, as erect as a sundial, grizzled a little with the labours of some sixty years in the back woods of Georgia, but still hale and strong, with as keen an eye for a wild-cat or a 'coon as the stalwart nephews by his side. His attire would be deemed peculiar with you, though here it is the approved thing. A Panama hat made of the leaves of the palmetto, split fine, low in the crown, and very broad in the flap; a "hunting shirt," or frock, of pink-striped gingham, open all down the front, but girded with a belt of the same; the neck, which is wide and open, is bordered with a frill, which lies upon the shoulders; loose trowsers, of no describable colour, pattern, or material; short cotton socks, and stout half-boots, of domestic manufacture. Such is the costume of our "king of men," and all the rest of us approach as near to it as we may.

But who are "the rest of us?" Why, the two strapping youths, who call the planter uncle, Zachariah and Bill, each emulous of his patron's stature and accomplishments; Jones, the overseer, a wiry fellow, originally from the far east (Connecticut, I believe), but grown a southerner by a dozen years' experience in negro-driving; and the humble individual who pens these lines, who begins at length to be known by his proper name, instead of "the stranger." We five were mounted on very capital steeds, and behind and around us marched on foot our sable ministers.

It was a lovely night. The sky, almost cloudless, had a depth of tint that was rather purple than blue; and the moon, near the full, was already approaching the zenith. A gentle breeze, warm and balmy, breathed in the summits of the trees, and wafted to us the delicate perfumes from leaf, flower, and fruit, from gum and balsam, with which the night air is commonly loaded. Bright as was the night, however, it was thought requisite to have artificial light, especially as we should have to explore some tall woods, whose gloomy recesses the moon's beams were quite insufficient to illuminate. The knots of the pitch-pine answer admirably for torches, being full of resin, and maintaining a brilliant flame for an hour or more. The glare of broad red light which these flambeaux cast on the leafy walls along which we rode, and the beautiful effect produced on the surrounding shrubs and intervening trees, when the torchbearers passed through some narrow belt of wood, or explored some little grove, was highly novel and picturesque; the flames, seen through the chequering leaves, played and twinkled, and ever and anon frightened a troop of little birds from their roost, and illuminated their plumage as they fluttered by.

At length we reached the melon-patch, and having dismounted and tied our horses to the hanging twigs of the roadside trees, we crossed the rail-fence to beat the ground on foot. It was a large field, entirely covered with melons, the long stems of which trailed over the soft earth, concealing it with the coarse foliage and the great yellow flowers of the plant; while the fruit, of all sizes, lay about in boundless profusion, from the berry just formed, to the fully matured and already rotten-ripe melon, as large as a butter-firkin. Abundant evidences were visible of the depredations of our game, for numbers of fine ripe melons lay about with large cavities scooped out of them, some showing by their freshness and cleanness that they had been only just attacked, while others were partially dried and discoloured by the burning sun. Moths of various species were collected around the wounded fruit, some of them (which I should have prized for my cabinet, if I had had time and means to capture and bring them home) inert and bloated with the juices which they had been sucking; others fluttering by scores around, or attracted by the light to dance round the torches.

The party had dispersed. I accompanied the planter to the edge of a wood at one side of the patch, while the young men took up similar stations at some distance. The object was to intercept the vermin in their retreat, as, on being alarmed from their repast, they at once make for their fastnesses in the lofty trees. A negro with his pine-knot, stood at each station, illuminating the hoary trunks of the great trees.

Meanwhile the other servants were scouring the field with the dogs, shouting and making as much noise as possible. Again the twinkling lights looked beautiful, and the sound of the negroes' sonorous voices, raised in prolonged shouts with musical cadences, and now and then a snatch of a rattling song, the favourite burden being how a " big racoon" was seen—

"——— a sittin' on a rail,"

fell very pleasantly on the ear. Occasionally the barking of the curs gave token that game was started; and, presently, the approach of the sound towards us was followed by what looked to be a white cat scampering towards the very chestnut-tree before us, closely pursued by one of the mongrel curs. My friend's fatal rifle turned the creature over as soon as seen; but the very next instant another appeared, and scrambling up the fissured trunk, made good its retreat among the branches.

In the course of an hour another was shot, one was caught and worried by the dogs, and some half-a-dozen others were just glimpsed as they scuttled past us, the light for an instant revealing their grey bodies, but too briefly to allow an aim. We heard, by the reports of our distant friends' rifles, that they had their share of success; and when we assembled at the edge of the field, half-a-dozen Opossums and a Racoon were thrown across the crupper of one of the beasts. The appearance of the latter had been curiously in accordance with the negroes' song; for one of the young men creeping quietly along the fence, had seen the furry gentleman "sittin' on a rail," and looking with outstretched neck and absorbed attention into the field, wondering, doubtless, what all the uproar was about. His senses were not so locked, however, as not to be aroused by the gentle footfall of our young friend; before he could raise his rifle, the Racoon had leaped from the fence, and scoured up an immense sycamore. It seemed a hope-less case; but young Zachariah, vexed at being done by a 'coon, continued to peer up into the tree, hoping that he might get another glance of the animal. Familiar with the habits of the wild denizens of the woods, the youth directed his patient searching gaze to the bases of the great boughs, well knowing that in the fork of one of these the wily creature would seek shelter. At last, he saw against the light of the moon, what seemed the head of the Racoon projecting from one of the greater forks, and steadily watching it, distinctly saw it move. The fatal ball instantly sped, and down came the creature, heavily plumping on the ground.

I had seen Racoons before, yet I looked at the carcase with interest. You prob-ably are aware that it is an animal about as large as a fox, to which it bears some resemblance. It seems, however, larger, from the fulness of its thick and soft fur, and is more heavy-bodied. Its grey coat, black and white face, and bushy tail, al-ternately banded with black and light grey, entitle it to admiration; while the Opossum, clothed in rough wiry hair, of a dirty greyish white hue, with a long rat-like naked tail, is anything but prepossessing.

The torches were extinguished, and we sauntered slowly home, my friend the planter amusing me by relating a favourite legend to the glory of one Major Scott, who seems in these parts to be the very "Magnus Apollo" of rifle-shooting. It was to this effect:—An old he-racoon had made himself somewhat notorious by his depredations in the poultry-yards, and by his successful stratagems to evade pun-ishment. His favourite fastness was in the topmost boughs of a very lofty syca-more, beyond rifle-reach. One day, a certain Colonel Sharp, who vaunted his skill as a rifleman rather strongly, went out expressly to bring down this same Ra-coon. The wily rogue, from his impregnable retreat, hearing footsteps, calls out,

"Who's there?" "It's I, Colonel Sharp, the smartest shot in all creation, and I'm come out for you." "Oh, ho!" says 'coon, and, laughing immoderately, begins to play all sorts of pranks, jumping on the boughs, and wagging his tail from side to side, as the unsuccessful shots followed in rapid succession. At length, other footsteps were heard; "Who now?" "It's Major Scott, a lookin' out for 'coons." "O Major! don't waste your powder, I give in; I'm a gone 'coon!" And down he came, and surrendered at discretion.

The Opossum which had been worried by the curs, was not by any means dead when we reached the house, and I had an opportunity of witnessing the curious dissimulation which has made the name of this animal proverbial. Though, if left alone for a few moments, the attention of the bystanders apparently diverted from it, it would get on its legs and begin to creep slily away; yet no sooner was an eye turned towards it, than it would crouch up, lie along motionless, with all its limbs supple, as if just dead; nor would any kicks, cuffs, or handlings avail to produce the least token of life, not the opening of an eyelid, or the moving of a foot. There it was, dead, evidently, you would say, if you had not detected it the moment before in the act of stealing off. The initiated, however, can tell a real dead 'Possum from one that is shamming, and the overseer directed my attention to the last joints of the tail. This, during life, is prehensile, used to catch and hold the twigs like a fifth hand; and even in the hypocritical state in which I saw it, the coil of the tail-tip was maintained, whereas in absolute death this would be relaxed permanently. The propriety of correct classification was impressed on me during my examination. I inadvertently spoke of it as "a singular creature;" but *creature,* or rather "critter," is much too honourable a term for such an animal, being appropriated to cattle. The overseer promptly corrected my mistake. "A 'Possum, Sir, is not a critter, but a varmint."

An hour or two's sport was the only object of the expedition, the game being all consigned to the blackies. The flesh of both Opossum and Racoon is scarcely ever eaten by the whites, and never in summer; and though the fur of the latter is of some value, it was not of sufficient importance to be retained.

Figs are now ripe. There is a fine prolific tree in our garden, and I had watched with much interest the gradual maturing of the fruit, and the putting on at length of the soft blue bloom, which is the token of ripeness; until this appears the fig is not worth eating. Somewhat impatient to taste this far-famed fruit fresh

Opossum

from the tree, I had plucked one which appeared to my inexperienced eye ripe, being plump, soft, and deep brown; but the acridity of the milky juice that oozed from the skin, and the chaffiness of the interior, rather damped my enthusiasm. "If this is your ripe fig," said I to myself, "it is but a sorry affair." But only a day or two thereafter, I perceived a great change; several of the fruits were bloomed all over with that soft, blue, powdery surface, which we are familiar with on our own plums. I gathered one, but it was too soft and tender to bear even the pressure of my fingers necessary to hold it; the skin was thin, and devoid of any acrid milk; the interior pulpy, and of the most luscious sweetness. I certainly award the palm to the fig, of all the fruits I have ever tasted.*

By the side of the narrow winding path, which I traverse every day, there is, a little way within the forest, a Chinquapin-tree *(Castanea purmila).* It is a miniature representative of the gigantic Chestnut, agreeing with it in almost every respect except in size, rarely exceeding twenty feet in height, the leaves, the fruit, and everything in proportion. The little nuts are now ripening, and about the size of a small marble. In the centre of this small tree there is a structure whose dimensions would seem to have better suited the magnitude of the towering Chestnut; an enormous nest composed of sticks, thorny twigs, briers, dried weeds, and similar trash, interwoven into a mass as big as a half-hogshead, strong and impenetrable. There is a small hole near the bottom of the structure, into which the owner and builder finds access; but it is impossible for any one else to make acquaintance with the interior except by cutting it to pieces with an axe. This is the dwelling of the Yellow Rat *(Mus Floridanus),* a little sylvan creature, quite common in this part of the State, but rarely seen, doubtless because its activity is principally nocturnal. Such nests as this are frequently found in the woods, almost always being built in the Chinquapin-tree; but as the little creature (or rather, *varmint)* does no manner of harm, the people are averse to any interference with it by destroying its nest. It lives on nuts, berries, and roots; is a pretty cleanly little thing, about the size of our English rat, but far more prepossessing, clothed in soft fur of a pale yellowish grey on the back, buff on the sides, and white on the belly.

There is another kind of Rat nearly as common, and more often seen, from its favourite resort being rather to the open field than to the woods. In old neglected pastures, and weed-covered wastes, its tracks or pathways may constantly be seen, and itself, not rarely, running through them, occasionally sitting upon its haunches to look round and reconnoitre. It is commonly known as the Wood Rat *(Arvicola hispidus),* rather a Vole than a Rat; it is not quite so large as the Yellow Rat, and not nearly so pretty, being of a dull brown above, and grey be-

---

*I have since eaten the tropical fruits of Jamaica, the mango, the pine, the guava, the sweet-sop, the custard-apple, the banana, the rose-apple, the star-apple, the naseberry, but their excellencies have not altered the opinion I have expressed above. Not one of them comes up to a perfectly ripe fig, eaten fresh from the tree.

neath. Its food is chiefly animal, and it is not reputed to do any harm, except that it robs the cotton-fields in autumn of a few stray tufts to make its nest warmer.

Just where the now dwindled stream, called Mush Creek, crosses the high road to Pleasant Hill, there are several bushes bordering the way-side, which have a very ornamental appearance. The plant is called the Burning Bush *(Euonymus angustifolius),* from its brilliant appearance both in blossom and fruit. The flowers, which were numerous in June, were yellow and red, but they have now given place to a multitude of berries, about as large as a cherry. These are of a flesh-colour, or salmon-pink, and when ripe, they open by a cross-like fissure, dividing into four lobes, and revealing four seeds within, of a brilliant scarlet hue, so that a playful imagination might fancy the bush to be on fire.

The architectural instincts of many Hymenopterous insects have always afforded matter of admiration to the students of natural history. I have recently had opportunities of making some observations of interest on some little-known species, and as the investigations have now become mature, will make known the results to you.

One of the many things that struck my attention on first coming into these parts, was to see, in most of the farm-houses, lumps of yellowish mud stuck on the walls and rafters, and particularly on the large projecting chimneys. Some of these were of irregular shape, nearly as large as one's fist, and others were cylindrical, as thick as one's thumb, and three or four inches long. The little boys (and boys in these backwoods, as I have before intimated, know a good deal about natural history) informed me that these were the nests of the Dirt-daubers; and on taking down one of the shapeless lumps which had been fixed on the wall right over my bed's head, and carefully opening it, I found within it many long-oval cells, lined with a thin coat of brittle shelly substance. These were arranged side by side in two rows, each containing the slough of a perfected insect. In a much smaller nest I found but one cell, and no *exuvia,* but six spiders all dried. The long thimble-like nests were divided into cells in a single series, by transverse partitions of mud. The children soon showed me the insects to which the nests belonged; although, as the season was spring, they were not then building. They were several species of the genus *Pelopaeus;* slender bodied wasps, resembling in form the Sand-wasps and Ichneumons of Europe.

As the summer advanced, I cultivated an acquaintance with these funny little architects, and had opportunities of watching the whole process of building; and thus of setting at rest, to my own satisfaction, the disputed point of ownership to these nests, which some entomologists have attributed to *Eumenes,* supposing the *Pelopaeus* to be parasitical.* I transcribe now from my journal.

June 30.—I watched with much interest the proceedings of a Dauber in building her mud-cells; it is a pretty species *(Pelopaeus flavipes).* She has chosen the ceiling of a cupboard in my sitting-room, where, previously to my observing her, she had made one cell, and the half of another parallel to it; the former was closed, the latter had got its contents of spiders, and only wanted closing. Such was the *status quo.* I had not seen the Dauber go in for some time, so that when she did go in, I watched her from her recommencement. She came empty, and having for some moments peeped in and examined the contents to see that all was right, she suddenly flew out at the room-door, (which, as well as the window, was almost constantly open,) and returned in about a minute with a lump of soft wet mud in her jaws, about twice as large as her head. Where she got it in so short a time I don't know; it was perfectly kneaded, and free from all lumps and grit, and was worked when laid on as freely as butter. I suspect that it was formed of dry dust, on which she had poured a drop of fluid from her mouth. She laid the substance on the open end of the unfinished cell, and spread it about with her jaws very expeditiously and skilfully, till the orifice was quite closed up. She then flew off and returned with a similar load, which she applied upon the last to make it thicker. When she was gone the third time, in order to observe her behaviour, I thrust the head of a pin through the newly-laid mortar, opening a hole into the cell. On her return, she at once perceived the hole, and deposited her lump upon it, spreading it about as before. I played her the same trick

---

*The following observations of Mr. Westwood's show how fallacious it often is to draw positive conclusions in science from mere analogy. "According to Palisot de Beauvois the insect *Pelopaeus* places in each cell *a* green caterpillar, or spider [quasi, but one] which is then closed; but according to Bonnet, the cells are revisited by the parent fly, after the grub has consumed the enclosed food, in order to give it a fresh supply, and which is repeated until it has attained its full growth. Such is the opinion given in various works; but W. Saunders in a memoir on the habits of some Indian insects (Trans. Entom. Soc. vol. i. p. 62), seems to have satisfactorily proved that these nests are of *Eumenes,* and that *Pelopaei* are parasites there. In support of this opinion I may observe, 1st, that the legs of the female *Pelopaeus* are similar, and unprovided with apparatus for the construction of such nests; and 2nd, that it is only among the bees and wasps that we find the habit of constructing nests with materials brought from a distance."—*Classif. of Insects,* ii. 206.

several times, at all of which her proceedings were the same, save that at length she seemed to become very angry, and endeavoured to catch the house-flies that were flying and crawling near. I have no doubt that she suspected them of having a hand in it. At all events, she jumped at them very snappishly, whenever they came near, and sometimes even with the load in her mouth, but I did not see that she caught one. Once, too, a large *Ichneumon* was lurking about, at whom she fiercely flew, and I think they had a short struggle. At times she would linger at a little distance, after depositing her load, apparently hoping to catch the insidious housebreaker, "in the manner," as lawyers say.

At length I broke off a large piece from the side and bottom of the old part, exposing the spiders to view; this, however, she speedily built up as before, at two or three loads, adding to the standing part all round the hole, and not at one side only. After this I did not put her industry to the task any more, but suffered her to finish her work, which she did by adding another layer or two to the end. I, however, made a hole in the first cell, which was quite hard and dry, to see if she would observe it, which she did at once, and clapped her load of mortar on it. I noticed that while working, though the wings were closed incumbently, she kept up a shrill buzz, like that of a bee when held in the fingers; her antennae, which were usually carried nearly straight, were during the plastering curled up, and continually vibrating, and moving on the surface of the work, evidently trying it by touch, which seemed to me adverse to the theory that calls the antennae "ears." In seeking her materials she was gone never more, often less, than a minute, and always brought a lump similar in appearance, which was invariably carried in the jaws, without any aid from the feet.

July 1.—The Dauber built another cell to-day, on the other side of the first, which is now therefore in the middle. I again pestered her by sticking a small tin-tack in the newly-laid mud, just where she would have to deposit the next load. When she came, she appeared quite "bothered;" she ran backward and forward, and round and round, over the cells for some time, with the mud in her jaws, as if at a loss what to do in so novel an exigency. It was a different case from the former; a hole could be stopped up, but here was an intruding substance just where she wanted to deposit; should she lay it on, the incumbrance would be more firmly imbedded; should she place it elsewhere, it would be wasted, not being needed, or perhaps be positively injurious; should she attempt to remove the evil, her mouth was occupied, and she was unwilling to lose her burden. At length, however, as the least of the evils, she seized the tack with her jaws and drew it out, dropping her mud in the effort. When she was away the next time, I bundled up a worsted thread, and pressed it on the soft work, which presented a still more serious obstacle, as she could seize only a small part of it, which would yield without coming away; however, by taking hold of several parts of it successively, and tugging at them a long time, and by walking round and round with it in her mouth, she at length got it out. These instances of sagacity and perseverance greatly pleased me. After laying on a load, she always cleans her antennae with her fore feet, and her feet with her jaws: on arriving she never alights at the nest, but always on the inside of the cupboard-front, and crawls along the ceiling to it.

August 6.—I pulled down the nest of the Yellow-footed Dauber, to which other cells had been added in succession after the last record. On examining them now, I find three perfected insects have made their exit, one has died in making its way out, two are in pupa, one black and near perfection, the other white and newly turned, and two are in larva, one large, the other very small, making eight originally in the nest. Many of the spiders remain uneaten: most of them are handsomely studded with scarlet spots on a black ground. It was in looking at these pupae, that I first was aware how a difficulty of no ordinary magnitude is got over. How do insects whose abdomen is peduncled, draw it out of the pupa skin, seeing the peduncle is so slender? I should have guessed that the skin would be ruptured, but it is not so. These Daubers have a very long and slender peduncle; but the skin of the pupa, closely adherent in every other part, is as wide around the peduncle as around the abdomen, like a loose garment stretched from the summit of the thorax to that of the abdomen. What a beautiful example of Divine foresight in creation!

July 14.—In a corner of a closet stood a little phial about an inch and a half high, which had held ink, but being uncorked, the contents had dried up. Looking at it this morning I was surprised to find it closed with a white dry substance like pipeclay; and on breaking this, was still more surprised to find the clue of the mystery. It held no less than eighteen spiders, of a few of which, however, the abdomen was wanting. The case was clear: a Dauber, to save herself the labour of building a cell, had found and made use of this substitute; a very curious instance of insect laziness, or rather, perhaps, of the economy of industry.

July 21.—I perceive that the Dauber last mentioned has returned to the phial, and having, no doubt, observed that it had been handled, has taken out every one of the spiders, which she has strewn around, and having filled the bottle with newly-caught spiders, has again sealed it up with mud. I think we may infer from this that the parent exercises a measure of watchful guardianship over her young, sealed as they are from her sight and direct interference.

Thus far my journal. The species which selected the phial I did not see, and therefore cannot identify; the Yellowfoot is the artificer of the shapeless masses first referred to; shapeless, because the cells when finished are included in an irregular heap of additional mud. At the present time the other species of *Pelopaeus* begins to be busy, fabricating its more artful thimble-shaped nests. It is difficult to convey by words an idea of its mode of working; but its general proceedings are as before, as respects bringing the mud, &c. The commencement of a cell is made by laying down the load, and working it into an oval ridge, one extremity of which is to be the apex of the thimble-cell. The next row is laid on the ridge, but so as to be higher at the apex than at any other part, and made slightly concave: when the tip is made, the work proceeds regularly by additions to the edges, which are smoothly laid on, and always in the same slanting direction that had been given at first, by raising one end of the incipient oval; so that an unfinished cell in any stage of progress appears like a cylinder cut off by a diagonal section. This is not casual, but invariable, as the ridges remaining plainly mark the precise limits of every separate load. When a little more in length is finished than suffices for a single cell the work ceases awhile; an egg is laid in the bottom (though this end is generally uppermost) and spiders are brought in. This kind usually (not always) selects a very beautiful species of *Tetragnatha,* bright green with white spots; and it is worth remarking that spiders are carried both with the jaws and feet; one of the fore-legs of the spider being grasped in the mouth, while its body is held under the body of the fly, and sustained by the anterior and middle-legs and feet, the posterior pair being extended behind as usual during flight. The accompanying engraving represents this species carrying a spider to its nest.

When the first cell is stocked, it is closed up by a transverse partition of mud, and the thimble goes on increasing in length as before; when finished one will contain three or even four cells; and then a new one is commenced adjoining

Pelopaeus and nest

to and parallel with it. In both this and the other species, I believe the inclosed grub eats only the abdomens of the spiders (which are so stung as to be helpless but not dead); as the cephalo-thorax and legs of each may generally be found afterwards in the cell.

This species of *Pelopaeus* seems to be undescribed. It is distinguished by having the first segment of the abdomen gradually thickened, and furnished on its under surface with a curious spur-like appendage.

The great profusion of insects which has struck me hitherto as so remarkable has begun to subside; many species that were common have either become scarce or have altogether disappeared, while those that have come into season are comparatively few. Still, however, in favourable spots and in fine weather, the air is still gay with these beautiful beings. The good housewives are now drying their peaches for winter store. The fruit is pared, stoned, and sliced, like apples for a tart, and the pieces are spread on cloths to dry in the sun, and then strung on threads and suspended in a dry room. The saccharine juices of the drying fruit attract many day-flying insects, and among others gorgeous butterflies congregate to suck the tempting morsels. I have taken several fine specimens lately under these circumstances.

In the garden the beds of *Mirabilis jalapa* continue in profuse blossom, and the twilight-loving Hawkmoths resort hither to rifle their tubes of the abundant nectar. Two species of large size and unusual beauty have just occurred to me. One is the Green-clouded Hawk *(Sphinx satellitia)*, a species which closely resembles the Oleander Hawk of Europe *(S. nerii)*, being variously clouded and blotched with dark green, on a pale ground, the colours blended with the beautiful softness so characteristic of this tribe of moths. As it is not figured by Abbott, it is probably a rare insect. The other species is even more beautiful, the colours having the definiteness and vividness of those which we look for in the butterflies. The ground-colour is drab or pale buff on the body and front wings, marked in a symmetrical manner with black; the hind wings are clouded with green, crimson, and black in a charming manner. This is called, by Abbott, the Painted Hawk *(Sphinx vitis)*; the caterpillar, which is varied with green, red, and white, and marked with black lines, is said to feed on the leaves of the vine and the magnolia.

In the hottest part of the day, beneath the beams of the almost vertical sun, I occasionally find running along the dusty road, or the parched paths of the wastes, insects of the genus *Mutilla.* They resemble large wasps deprived of wings, at least in the female sex, which more commonly occurs. Their prevailing colours are black and red, disposed in alternate bands; in one species *(M. coccinea)* these are peculiarly bright, the red being a vivid scarlet, and both colours having a satin-like lustre: other kinds are duller. The apterous female has a projecting sting, and is highly venomous; cattle are said sometimes to die from being stung by these insects, probably in lying down on them; they are therefore much dreaded. I have taken on one occasion the male, but I am not certain to which species it belonged, as it differed from both the females; the wings were purple like those of a *Scolia.*

Many kinds of lace-winged flies *(Neuroptera)* have occurred to me, beside the

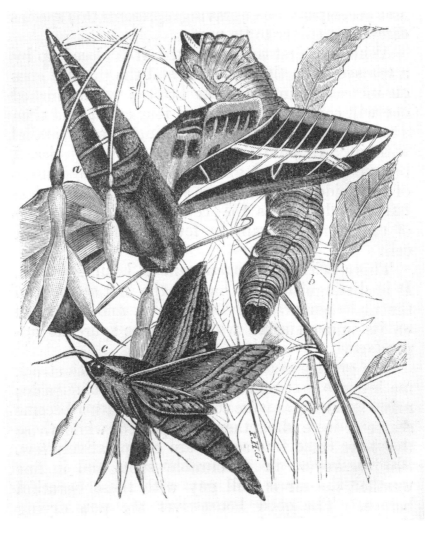

Hawkmoths
a. The Painted Hawk *(Sphinx vitis).*
b. Caterpillar of the same.
c. The Faint-lined Hawk *(Sphinx tersa).*

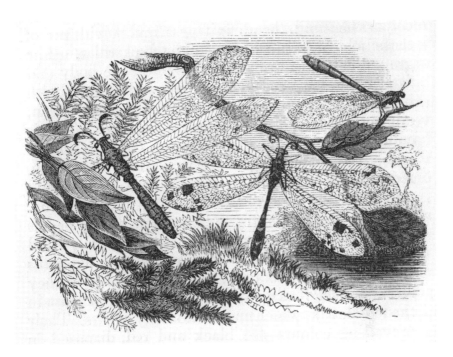

Myrmeleons

numerous Dragon-flies; such as a clear-winged Pearl-fly *(Chrysopa),* with a white body curiously spotted with black; and particularly some of the very elegant Ant-lion flies *(Myrmeleon);* one of which has the wings perfectly transparent, others are variously spotted. These insects fly slowly and feebly, strongly contrasting with the vigorous action of the Dragon-flies, to which they bear some resemblance. Their wings, indeed, are ample, but their bodies are small and slender; and powerful flight does not depend so much on the dimensions of the wings, as on the size of the muscles that work them, which are contained within the thorax. The greater Dragon-flies rest with the wings horizontally expanded, as in flight; the smaller kinds *(Agrionidae)* bring their upper surfaces together, as butterflies do; but the Myrmeleons close their wings, in repose, by bringing the inner edges into contact, the wings sloping down on each side like the roof of a house, in the position assumed by most moths; and, when resting, they usually project the abdomen upwards, above the closed wings, at an angle with the body.

The curious instincts of the larvae of these flies are well known. I have had no opportunity of verifying the received statements by observation, having met with the grub only on one occasion, viz. a day or two since. It was in the wall of an old out-house, among the clay between the logs. It ran equally well forward or backward, by little starts. I killed and offered it an ant, but it took no notice of it. I have often found that insects will not eat even their usual prey, if it be not taken by themselves, or presented in the circumstances to which they are accustomed. Perhaps they do not trust the giver:

"Timeo Danaos, et dona ferentes."

Letter XII

September 1st

The manners of these Southerners differ a good deal from those of their more calculating compatriots, the Yankees of the north and east. In many respects the diversity is to the advantage of the former; there is a bold gallant bearing, a frank free cordiality, and a generous, almost boundless hospitality, in the southern planter, which are pleasing. But the abiding thought that "the people," as being the source of law, are therefore above law, which is deep-seated throughout this land of "free institutions," is much more frequently made operative in the south than in the north. Here "every man is his own law-maker and law-breaker, judge, jury, and executioner."*

The darkest side of the southerner is his quarrelsomeness, and recklessness of human life. The terrible bowie-knife is ever ready to be drawn, and it *is* drawn and used too, on the slightest provocation. Duels are fought with this horrible weapon, in which the combatants are almost chopped to pieces; or with the no less fatal, but less shocking rifle, perhaps within pistol-distance.

Slavery, doubtless, helps to brutalize the character, by familiarizing the mind with the infliction of human suffering. If an English butcher is popularly reputed unfit to serve on a jury, an American slave-owner is not less incompetent to appreciate what is due to man. I had intended to give you some particulars of the working of "the domestic institution," for I have witnessed some of its horrors; but I will not allow my pen to trace much of this, especially as you may learn it from other sources. I am obliged to be very cautious, not only in expressing any sympathy with the slaves, but even in manifesting anything like curiosity to know their condition, for there is a very stern jealousy of a stranger's interference on these points.

*Not long ago a travelling menagerie arrived at the neighbouring village; the proprietor, in some way or other, offended an overseer, who called together a few of his companions, and rolled the caravans over, down a steep ravine. The iron cages of the beasts were scattered on every hand; fortunately they were too strong to give way, or these forests might have become stocked with lions and tigers, in addition to bears and panthers. The cries and howlings of the wild beasts are said to have been fearful.

Still, facts will ooze out: in confidential conversation I have heard things not generally known, even here, which are truly dreadful. Instruments of torture, devised with diabolical ingenuity, are said to be secretly used by planters of the highest standing, for the punishment of refractory negroes; devices which I dare not describe by letter. It is but right, however, to say, that these practices were told me with expressions of reprobation.

Floggings of fifty, or a hundred lashes, with a stout cow-hide whip, are frequent, especially at this season of cotton-picking—the most trying time of the year for the negroes. The work is severe, and the quantity demanded as the day's task often proves short when weighed at night, in which case the lash is pretty surely applied. Desertion is, therefore, more common at this season: the chance of a poor wretch's escape, through a thousand miles of hostile country, without funds, without friends, without knowledge of geography,—every white man he sees his enemy, *ipso facto,* and his colour betraying him to all,—is small indeed; yet such is the pressure of the bitter yoke, that it is constantly attempted.

It is to counteract this tendency to desertion that the patrol system has been devised. The young men of a given neighbourhood enrol themselves in a band, and scour the country by night, taking the duty in turns, to arrest every negro who is abroad without a written pass. Armed parties frequently go in pursuit of runaways, who are shot down relentlessly if they oppose, or refuse to surrender. The patrols are allowed this power, not indeed by law, but by public opinion.

The aid of trained dogs is also used in the pursuit of runaways. Bloodhounds, of high breeding and of great ferocity, are taught to follow the human trail in this manner. A negro is sent into the woods, and told to climb up into a tree; when sufficient time has been allowed him, the hound is set on the scent, and is soon at the foot of the tree, which he will not leave till the party come up and release the poor slave. If any accident prevent him from mounting the tree in time, his life will probably pay the forfeit; for these ferocious dogs not unfrequently kill their victims.

Hunger adds its sharp spur to the many goads which impel the wretched sable race to fight or flee. In proportion to the sensuousness of the negro temperament—a character which no one can deny to it, but which is certainly not likely to be lessened by that utter privation of all intellectual enjoyment to which slavery dooms him—does this iron enter into his soul. I believe more slaves run away from the want of food, than even from the terror of the lash. The ordinary allowance, for each adult, is a peck of corn-meal, and three pounds and a half of meat per week; sometimes a little molasses is added, and, in the fruit season, the orchard affords them a considerable help. But, when this is over, the allowance is very short for the support of robust men toiling in daily field-labour from morn to night.

What will be the end of American slavery? I know that many dare not entertain this question. They tremble when they look at the future. It is like a huge deadly serpent, which is kept down by incessant vigilance, and by the strain of every nerve and muscle; while the dreadful feeling is ever present, that, some day or other, it will burst the weight that binds it, and take a fearful retribution.

But what can be done? The laws of this State absolutely forbid emancipation; so that, if an Alabama planter desire to manumit one or all of his slaves, he dares not do it here. His only means of accomplishing his wish, is to take them to some other State, the laws of which are less rigid, and give them freedom there. I know of some who have done this.

Yet surely such an act is a gigantic triumph of principle, that we can scarcely overrate. Not only does it defy almost universal opinion, but it is a sacrifice of property so valuable that all other property is worthless without it. Slaves are indispensable in Alabama, while the present condition endures. A man may have a thousand acres of land, but if he have no slaves to cultivate his cotton and corn, his acres are a mere waste, for free labour is out of the question. I know of planters in this neighbourhood, who possess from one hundred to two hundred slaves, valued at from two hundred to one thousand dollars each (not including children, who are commonly sold by weight, at from seven to ten dollars per pound), —a property which may, perhaps, be worth 100,000 dollars, or about 20,000£. sterling. The greatest portion of this has come down to the present possessor by inheritance; he has not been trained to habits of personal industry, but has always looked to his slaves as the means of his livelihood. Now, to expect a man voluntarily to throw up such an estate as this—reducing himself by one act, from affluence to absolute poverty and helplessness—is to expect a miracle of disinterested benevolence, such as the world does not see once in a century.

Nor is the case much altered, on the supposition of legislative emancipation; for the men who are to make the law are the very planters in question, or their delegates: and it is vain to expect them to do that for themselves collectively, which they would not do individually.

Besides, this aspect of the matter touches only the pecuniary interest of the possessors. There is another subject which, perhaps, involves a yet grander difficulty: What is to become of the slaves, if they be emancipated? To throw two millions of persons, uneducated and uncivilized, smarting under a sense of accumulated wrongs, at once loose upon society, would be more than dangerous, it would be certain destruction.

Yet the institution is doomed. Its end approaches surely, perhaps swiftly. Its fall cannot but be ardently desired by every right-thinking mind, for it is one begun, pursued and perpetuated in iniquity and cruelty; but when it comes, it can hardly be other than a terrible convulsion. I never felt this so strongly, as since I have had personal and close observation of the elements of the strife, the parties at issue. In spite of the beauty and grandeur of the country, the lucrative remuneration which a person of education receives for his talents and time, and the rich and almost virgin field for the pursuit of natural history (no small temptation to me),—I feel slavery alone to be so enormous an evil, that I could not live here: I am already hastening to be gone.

Letter XIII

September 20th

A few evenings since I accompanied the overseer for a mile or two through a neighbouring swamp. His object was to get a little sport, in the way of hunting racoons, opossums, wild cats, or any other game that might occur; mine, rather to see the interior of the lone forest, with its strange sights and sounds, beneath the gloom of night. The result, in the matter of game, was almost *nil;* the dogs started an opossum or two, but they took to the lofty trees, and, in the darkness, no shot could be obtained. But I enjoyed the novel and somewhat exciting circumstances greatly.

The sun was barely gone from the tops of the forest-trees, when we set out through the swamp; a district studded with the low Fan-palm *(Chamaerops serrulata).* This species does not rise with a tall stipe from the ground, like the kindred Palmetto *(C. palmetto),* that grows around Mobile, but spreads its broad-folded fan-like leaves on every side, within reach of the cattle, that munch the rigid tips, and make them ragged and unsightly. A handsome tall yellow flower, the Gerardia *(G. flava),* bearing some slight resemblance to our Foxglove, except in colour, was growing here; and a still lovelier one, the Cardinal-flower *(Lobelia cardinalis),* whose fine scarlet blossoms are among the autumnal ornaments of English gardens. But, generally, flowers are scarce in these gloomy recesses; and, even of such as delight in such situations, most are now out of season.

Leaving the swamp, we crossed a belt of low underwood, so tangled with vines and briers as to be scarcely penetrable. It was not yet so dark but that we could discern the wild fruit on the trees; the clusters of the purple fox-grape, large and handsome to the eye, and somewhat sweet, but with a rank musky odour; the large scarlet haws of several species of thorn, some of which are fleshy and grateful to the taste; and two or three kinds of wild plum, of which one at least is not despicable, though others are harsh and worthless.

Again we plunged into the deep swamp, which every moment grew grander and more gloomy. The ground was damp and mouldy, but not wet, except in patches, so that, in this respect, we could walk with ease; and the trees were large, set far apart, with but little underbrush. They were principally of one kind, the Beech, a noble tree, with the same smooth, blue, pillar-like trunk as its European congener, but attaining a loftier elevation. In the deep rich soil of these swamps, it frequently exceeds a hundred feet in height, with a magnificent head of foliage. The roots spread to a great distance, and form a sort of net-work on the surface of the ground, in some measure impeding the progress, or at least making it more tortuous than the trunks seem to require.

On one of these hoary beeches, I saw an object that interested me much. A spot of bluish light appeared at a distance, resembling that of a glowworm, which, on coming to it, I found to proceed from a foliaceous lichen or fungus, growing on the bark of a tree within reach, in the form of a rosette or cockade, about as large as a shilling. The substance of this was somewhat fleshy, or rather cartilaginous, and was luminous throughout, as if penetrated with light, which was feeble, and of a pale blue tint, like that which proceeds from wood decomposing, under certain circumstances, and known as *touchwood*. I am not aware that any lichen, or, indeed, any plant, is recognised as self-luminous in a growing state; but this I examined with too much curiosity, not to be sure of what I have stated.*

Night was by this time thoroughly set in. A dim sepulchral light struggled from the sky above, just sufficient to enable us to avoid the trees, but all around was shrouded in the most pitchy darkness. Suddenly we were startled by a voice, apparently close at hand, clear, loud, and of an unearthly hollowness, "Ho! Waugh ho! Waugh ho! Waugh ho-o-o-o!" It seemed like the challenge of a sentinel, arresting our intruding footsteps; and fancy, if I had been alone, might have con-

---

*While these pages were passing through the press, I met with the following observations by Dr. Lindley, which show that the case above mentioned is not without precedent:—

"The genus *Rhizomorpha* (which, it may be observed, is a spurious genus, consisting of imperfectly developed *Sphaeriae, Polypori,* &c.) vegetates in dark mines, far from the light of day, and is remarkable for its phosphorescent properties. In the coal mines near Dresden, the species are described as giving those places the air of an enchanted castle; the roof, walls, and pillars, are entirely covered with them, their beautiful light almost dazzling the eye. The light is found to increase with the temperature of the mines.

"Several species of genuine Fungi have been observed to be phosphorescent, in various parts of the world. *Agaricus Gardneri* (Berk.), which grows on a sort of Palm, called Pintada, in Brazil, is highly luminous. Such, also, is the case with *Agaricus olearius,* in the south of Europe, as observed by Delille. Mr. Drummond has found two or more luminous species at the Swan River, and Rumphius observed the same phenomenon in Amboyna."—*Veget. Kingd.* p. 39.

strued it into the warwhoop of a Seminole, preparing to take my scalp. But my companion, to whom the sound was familiar, told me that it was the voice of an owl; and presently the wings of some bird swept noiselessly by before our faces. Jones's rifle was instantly at his shoulder, a line of fire illuminated for a moment the columnar trunks of the solemn forest fane, and a great soft-feathered creature was ruffling and choking at our feet, in the agonies of death. It was a noble bird, when I came to examine it, after our darkling excursion was over. A great round cat-like face, with feathery ears standing up three inches high, large staring, yellow, moony eyes, a body nearly as big as that of a turkey, and plumage mottled and barred all over with black, orange, and white, showed our prize to be the Great Eagle Owl *(Bubo Virginianus)*.

The crack of the rifle startled others of the same species from their moody meditations; and prolonged "Waugh hoes!" sounded forth on all sides, the notes taken up again and again successively, and repeated in the distance, as far as the ear could faintly catch the strain. I found that they called to and answered each other; and as the sounds can be readily imitated, I tried the power of my own voice, and had the satisfaction of a prompt response.

Returning by a different route homeward, we skirted the edge of a cypress swamp, a tract invested with a gloom far more savage and sombre than any through which we had passed. Nothing can be more dismal than the interior of one of these swamps, even by day, half-tepid stagnant water covering the ground, the density of the timber and the black opacity of the foliage almost shutting out the light, while the gaunt horizontal branches are hung with far-pendent ragged masses of that Spanish moss that I have before alluded to, the very type of dreariness and desolation. Such trees always remind me of an army of skeletons, giants of some remote age, still standing where they had lived, and still wearing the decaying tatters of the robes which they had worn of old.

We did not venture to explore the nocturnal horrors of these dreary glades; but as we peered into their thick darkness, the melancholy "Quah!" of the Nightheron *(Nycticorax Americanus)*, a hoarse and hollow note, boomed out from the solitude; presently followed by the sound of flapping wings, as the jealous fowl sought a retreat in the more remote recesses, still more secure from the prying intrusion of man.

Individually the Cypress *(Taxodium disticha)* is no less remarkable than in its association. It is a tree of noble stature, being occasionally seen 120 feet in height,

The Eagle Owl

and very valuable for the durability of its timber; hence it is much in request for building. The negroes collect from its bark a resin of a red hue and pleasant fragrance, which they apply to wounds with some success; perhaps the smallness of the quantities which they are able to procure enhancing its reputation. But the most singular feature in the economy of this tree is that its root usually swells into a great cone, or bee-hive shaped protuberance, several yards in circumference, from the summit of which the trunk springs. These protuberances, which are commonly known as cypress-knees, are hollow in the interior, and covered with a crimson bark like that of the exterior.

On our return we found the family yet up and abroad; though it was past the usual hour for retiring to rest, the balmy warmth of the evening had tempted them to remain at the doors, in the light of the yard-fire. It is customary here to have a sort of tripod in the yard, on which a fire is lighted at dusk, and kept up until the household have gone to bed. It is the duty of a negro boy to keep this fire constantly bright with splints of pine, so as to maintain a perpetual blaze, as the object is to illuminate the yard and its contiguous offices. It is pleasant to watch the effects of the light either transmitted through or reflected from the quivering leaves of the surrounding trees, the flame now rising brightly and playing in tongue-like flickering spires, now sinking and dying to a ruddy glow, then suddenly reviving under the watchful charge of the sable minister who plays the part of vestal virgin at this altar.

Insects often play around the fire. Beetles "wheel their drony flight" in buzzing circles round for a few turns and are gone; and moths come fluttering about, and often scorch their plumy wings. A few evenings ago I took at the light-stand a specimen of a very handsome Sphinx, the Blind Hawk *(Smerinthus excaecatus)*, the front wings of which are of a rich brown dashed and clouded with black, and the hinder pair crimson, with a large black eye-spot on each, having an azure pupil. It was an unusually large specimen, and quite uninjured, though it flew among the ashes of the fire.

But this night, after our swamp excursion, I procured in the same manner an insect of more interest though of less beauty. It was the Mole-cricket *(Gryllotalpa)*, a species allied to, but in some respects differing from a well-known European insect. Its structure and economy are so curious, so calculated to illustrate the Divine skill and wisdom in creation, that I shall describe it somewhat in detail.

The Mole-cricket is a very curious insect, a singularly faithful representative of a quadruped among insects. The fore-legs, instead of being long and slender, as usual, are short, thick, and remarkably strong; the thigh is dilated into an oval plate, with a sort of groove into which the shank folds down so close as to seem of one piece; the shank is triangular, notched at the bottom into strong teeth, curved outwards like fingers, with a hollow palm, from the midst of which the tarsi proceed; these are also sharp and tooth-like, and lie flat on the shank, the points projecting; they have but slight power of motion. This whole apparatus is so fixed, that the broad toothed palm is directed obliquely outwards, exactly like the strong forefeet of a Mole, and is used in the same manner, and for the same purpose, viz. to scrape away the earth and throw it behind in forming its burrow, which it effects with great force and rapidity. The rest of the insect is equally adapted for free motion through its self-made cavity: the whole body is long and cylindrical, without projecting points; the legs lie close to the body, except the burrowing hands; the head and thorax are peculiarly strong, hard and shelly, of a spindle form (swelling in the middle), the latter, into which the head is somewhat retractile, much resembling in shape the carapace of a lobster. The upper wings or elytra are somewhat oval, of a smoky semi-transparent brown hue, with strong veins forming an irregular network.

This insect has the faculty of producing a stridulous sound, though not of so lively a character as some others of its tribe. The mode in which this is produced is highly curious. A strong vein running from the base of the left elytron in the male insect, "is found on the underside to be regularly notched transversely like a file. When the wing-covers are closed, this oblique part of the wing-covers lies upon the upper surface of the corresponding part of the right wing-cover; and when a tremulous motion is imparted to the wing-covers, this bar rubs against the corresponding bar of the right wing-cover, and thus produces a vibration, which is communicated to the other parts of the wing-covers; which, being divided into a number of irregular spaces, have each a distinct vibration, and produce a separate sound, which unitedly forms the stridulation, or chirrup, so well known."*

This sound is confined in all cases to the male insect, the females wanting this peculiarity of structure. The true wings are capacious, triangular and fan-

*Westwood.

like, each folding up into a long slender filament, extending out behind beyond the tail. When unfurled they are found to be composed of a transparent membrane, netted with a delicate tracery, like the finest lace.

Thus, as we often find in natural history, an object which to the incurious appears ugly, and even repulsive, presents on close examination so many points of interest, so many exquisite contrivances, and even so much delicacy and beauty in its several parts and their arrangement, that our dislike changes to pleasure and admiration as we contemplate it.

To the last segment of the abdomen are joined two flexible organs tapering to a point, which so much resemble the antennae, that they have been termed caudal antennae, but I think this resemblance is only in appearance, not in structure; for I cannot perceive with a microscope any trace of those numerous joints into which the antennae are so distinctly divided. They appear to me to be mere fleshy tubes, useful probably by their sensibility to indicate to the insect the presence of any obstruction in its dark burrow when retiring backwards. Under a lens they look very like the tail of a rat, being covered with short brindled hair. Most parts of the insect are clothed with a short velvety pile, particularly close and fine on the thorax, legs, and under surface of the body. They appear to be carnivorous, and even cannibal in their propensities; a friend had several in one box, and the next morning found them reduced to two. It may be, however, that in a state of liberty this would not take place; the habits of animals in a state of confinement are not to be considered as an invariable indication of their natural manners.

They fly only by night, and then, according to Gilbert White, in curves, rising and sinking, like a woodpecker. This one was probably attracted by the light of the fire—rather an interesting circumstance, when we remember that some persons have considered the European Mole-cricket to be luminous, and to be the cause, or at least *a* cause, of the phenomenon known under the name of *Ignis fatuus.*

Letter XIV

The unhealthy season is now considered over. Fevers and agues are always preva-
lent in September, probably induced by the miasmata arising from decaying vegetation in the equinoctial rains; but they do not usually extend into this month.
The autumn has set in, with coldish nights, but we have had no sign of frost as
yet. With very few exceptions, such as the button-wood and the chestnut, whose
leaves are withered and fallen, the forest-trees are still unchanged, wearing the
green livery of summer yet.

Deer-hunting has now commenced. The Virginian Deer *(Cervus Virginianus)*
is very abundant in these woodland regions, and is now in the best condition,
the fur having put on that grizzled colouring which distinguishes it in winter,
the hair becoming tubular, whitish, soft, inelastic, and brittle. The animal is now
said to be "in the grey," as in the summer he is "in the red."

The country is particularly favourable for hunting; the forests being generally open, with varied ground, interchanging with plantations studded with
swamps where animals can find shelter, and intersected with shallow streams.
The ground which a southern hunter best likes is that which is designated by the
name of "hammocks;" undulating hills, covered with oak, hickory, and magnolia, threaded by a good number of roads and cattle-paths. Of such land there is
a good deal in this neighbourhood.

Though there are some gentlemen who keep packs of thorough-bred hounds
in this country, and follow their hunting *secundum artem,* after the fashion of
the old country, it is more usual to kill the deer by wholesale, in a sort of battue.
This kind of hunting is called "driving the deer," and is founded on the habit
which the animal has of taking the same paths through the woods day after day.
The hunters choose their stations at different points in the course of these tracts,
while the dogs are sent through the forest to rouse the game. On the alarmed
animals come, trooping along their familiar paths, and are shot down by the
fatal rifle, as they pass the respective stations of the hunters. A few days ago,
at a single hunt of this kind, as many as seventy deer were killed. It occasionally happens that the acute smell of the deer becomes cognisant of the hunter's

proximity, when they swerve from the path, and dash into some neighbouring swamp, safe from pursuit.

In open ground, and even through the forest, the deer is often pursued in a more legitimate manner, on horseback. The excited planters at such times dash boldly between the myriad trunks at full speed, and even plunge through the closer and more dangerous second growth, at the risk of limb and life; for the horizontal branches of the young trees often strike them severely, and sometimes tear the rider with violence from his horse. But this style of procedure suits the southern genius. The rifle is the only weapon employed; the deer is sometimes killed by a ball discharged from on horseback at headlong speed, the reins lying abandoned on the neck.

The warm nights of September afford another kind of deer-hunting, which is highly enjoyed by some. The animals resort, for the refreshment of a cool bathe, and for relief from the persecutions of the clouds of musquitoes, to the rivers and pools, where they stand for hours in water up to the neck. Two men go together in a canoe, in the bows of which is set up a short staff, with an upright board on the top. On the front side of this board is a shelf, on which is placed a lantern. The light casts a broad glare on all before, while the board throws the boat and the hunters into deep shadow. One man in the stern paddles the canoe very softly and slowly along, while his comrade lies in the fore part, keeping a sharp look-out ahead, the muzzle of his rifle just projecting in front of the board, so that the light may fall on the sight-pea. The deer allow the boat to approach within fifteen paces, as they stand gazing on the light in utter amazement, and are shot down without fail. The carcasses are then hauled on board, and the canoe pursues her way.

The Virginian Deer has all the elegance and grace of our own Fallow Deer, to which it bears a general resemblance in size and figure. A young lady in a family which I was visiting not long ago had a half-grown fawn, which was indeed a beautiful and engaging pet. Kindness had rendered it tame and confiding, at least towards its gentle mistress. It was allowed the range of a large field, and would often come to the house and prance about the lawn. I could not help admiring the beauty of the animal, and the grace of every motion. It would approach me if I stood quite still, stretching out its pretty head and taper neck towards my hand; but it was so extremely timid, that at the slightest stir its whole body and every limb would start, and on the least motion it would bound away,

Deer-shooting by Night

then stop, and turn and look again. When standing still it would be continually starting in this way, and when it trotted or walked, it lifted its little feet so high, and bent its slender limbs as if motion itself were a pleasure. It would occasionally stand a few moments, with one fore-leg bent up, the hoof nearly touching the belly. Its long and graceful ears were almost ever in motion, now directed forwards, now backwards, now erect, to catch the slightest sound. The large swimming black eye reminded me of the descriptions of that of the gazelle, which I should think can scarcely be superior in beauty and softness. It usually carried its neck upright, and there was a fairy lightness and elegance in its whole appearance which made it the prettiest of pets.

The Wild Hog occasionally varies the hunter's amusement and affords good sport. I have before alluded to these sylvan swine, runaways from domestication, of course, or the offspring of such, but yet absolutely wild in habits, possessing all the acuteness of senses, all the perfection of resources, that distinguish a savage animal.

They are generally of a brindled foxy colour, or black; as long as they are unmarked they are free game, and are hunted in the usual manner with avidity. The pork of the wild hog has little fat, but there is a peculiar game flavour, which is altogether lacking in the flesh of a denizen of the sty. A tame hog would have scarcely a minute's lease of life if put to his speed before a pack of hounds, but these wild ones manage to lead the dogs a gallant chase and even to baffle them.

One Christmas-day, a party of some twenty horsemen, with sixteen or eighteen couple of hounds, met at a known cover to try for a fox. For a time they beat the bush, a capital jungle, but found no trail. At length one dog gave tongue in the covert, and a good run of half an hour followed, without a fault, though not a glimpse of Reynard had yet been seen. One of the party then gave the view halloo, shouting, "A black fox! A black fox!" Another invisible run for nearly an hour longer, up beside a "branch," or rivulet, brought the company to the thicket near the spring-head, whence issued a long grunt. On the coming up of the hounds, out bolted a black pig, making off with unabated speed for another thicket. A shout of laughter and acclamation hailed the development of the game, and all agreed that the gallant swine should be spared to run again. The reluctant hounds were accordingly whipped off.

As I pass through the oak woods on my morning walk to the school, I frequently see the lairs of the forest swine. These consist of fallen leaves, brought together into heaps as large as the diameter of a waggon-wheel, and nearly a yard high, and in these cool mornings I often see them reeking with steam, the luxurious rogues having upstarted but a moment before, probably disturbed by the sound of my approaching footsteps. The people tell me, what indeed I should certainly infer from the appearance of the smoking beds, that the boar and sow sleep side by side in these cosy nests, and surely none could be devised, in the circumstances, softer, drier, or warmer.

A neighbouring overseer, an enthusiastic old sun-dried backwoodsman, talks of feral cattle existing in some of the more inaccessible swamps between these parts and the Florida border. He has been engaged in parties to hunt them, shooting the cows for their beef; the bulls are fierce and dangerous assailants. I give this only on his authority, for the planters hereabout know little concerning wild cattle, but I saw a plantation-cow the other day slaughtered with the same characteristic weapon, the rifle. She was a savage animal, the dread of the household, and the winter's stock of beef being about to be salted down, her fate was decided on. The planter took his rifle, and entered the field; the cow turned and stood at bay beneath a tree, tossing her head and lowering defiance. The deadly bullet sped, and entered the very centre of the forehead, just beneath the bony ridge that supports the horns. For a few seconds she stood motionless; not a muscle stirred; the head still presented the lowering threatening attitude in which it had received the shot; at length the huge body leaned against the tree, and sank heavily upon the earth.

But I turn from the exploits of these mighty hunters to detail my own successes in the pursuit of minuter game. The insect season has been waning for some time. Since August, butterflies have been comparatively few, both as to the number of species and of individuals. Yet their abundance up to that time may be inferred from the fact, that on the morning of the 25th of August I counted twenty different species abroad. The following thirteen I saw during about half an hour that I spent in the garden, soon after sun-rise:—

Papilio Philenor.	Grapta interrogationis.
” Calchas.	Cynthia Huntera.
Argynnis columbina.	Hipparchia Sosybius.
” vanillae.	Eudamus Tityrus.
Colias Nicippe.	Hesperia Orcus?
” Eubule.	Pamphila Otho?
Pamphila ———?	

In the course of a ride in the forenoon the seven following were observed, in addition to those already enumerated:—

Papilio Troilus.	Limenitis Ursula.
Melitaea Tharos.	Hipparchia Andromacha.
Colias Delia.	Thecla Comyntas.
Eudamus Rathylius.	

Other species were active on the days that preceded and that followed this.

The insects most worthy of observation at this season are those Orthoptera, almost peculiar to autumn, the Walking Leaves and the Spectres. Of the former, belonging to the genus *Mantis,* we have two or three species of large size. They bear a resemblance to a cockroach, but have the thorax greatly elongated, so as to be equal in length to the whole body besides; the wings and their covers are, however, more delicate than in the *Blatta,* and the whole insect is more slender. They are predatory and fierce, and are furnished in an extraordinary manner with weapons for the warfare they wage upon other insects. The fore-legs are of great length and stoutness. The tibia is set with sharp spines or teeth, and one long curved one at the extremity. The femur is armed with similar spines along its edge. The insect stations itself on a leaf or twig, with its fore parts elevated, and its armed limbs stretched widely apart. On the passing of any fly, the warrior makes a cut at it, as if with a drawn sword, and with so true an aim as frequently to seize the prey, the tibia folding back upon the femur, and the spines interlocking. With these the Mantis can grasp very hard, so as to drive the spines through the skin of the human hand, while the flying insects on which it preys are pierced and cut through by the merciless blow, and are immediately handed to the mouth, to be munched into mince-meat by the horny jaws. The tarsi, in the act of making the stroke, are doubled back out of the way. The voracity of these creatures was shown by one which I kept confined for a few days in a box. During that time he ate off a great part of one of his own fore-legs, leaving only the haunch and a small piece of the thigh.

The Spectres, Walking Rods, or Devil's Walking-sticks, as they are variously called *(Phasma),* are curious for their almost linear slenderness and great length. One species, which was given me the other day, is about five inches long, exclusive of the antennae and limbs, and as thick as a goose-quill. It was when alive of a lavender-grey hue, marbled all over with a faint netted pattern. The legs are long, and set far apart, so that it crawls with great length of stride, and with rapidity, though awkwardly. The insect, when touched or annoyed, turns up the tail over its back, in a threatening attitude, which has given it a reputation for being highly venomous—an altogether erroneous notion.

This specimen was a female, and laid several eggs while I had it. These were about as large as sweet-peas, oval, somewhat flattened, partly black and partly whitish, with a curious arched dome, made of transparent net-work, thrown over one extremity, which is flat, with a kind of rim. This little vaulted chamber looks like the lantern of a light-house.

Another species, about half as long as this, and no thicker than whipcord, of a

Mantis

pale green hue *(Bacteria linearis),* when touched, jumps headlong, like the *Phryganeae,* and stretching out its two fore-legs parallel to the antennae, and close to these organs, remains motionless, trusting, doubtless, to its exact similitude to a slender green twig broken off for eluding the observation of its enemies. It can, however, run pretty fast, when it chooses to take to its heels.

Lately I had occasion to allude to the Great Eagle Owl, a giant among birds; I have just met with one of the same tribe, no bigger than a thrush, yet in all respects as truly an owl as the other, a cat-faced, long-eared, moon-eyed, soft-plumaged, splashed and speckled night-walker. It was the little Mottled Owl *(Strix naevia)*. I met with him in this way. Going into an old deserted house, I saw, on one of the beams, by the wall, this little type of wisdom, which, frightened by my intrusion, flew from side to side, alighting generally at every turn. I wished to secure it for my collection, and went out for a stick to knock it down. I did not succeed in this, however; but in its alarm, it failed to alight as it flew against the side of the house, and fluttered to the ground, whence it could not easily rise. I now gave it several blows, but, being reluctant to give it pain, they were not sufficient to disable it, though they excited its pugnacity; for during the infliction, it uttered several times a cry like the caterwauling of a cat, and repeatedly snapped its bill; it showed fight, too, by turning round and snapping at my fingers when I attempted to touch it. I seized it by one wing, and brought it into the school, from whence it flew out at the window, but soon alighting in a corner of the fence, I easily secured it. Its feeble helplessness by daylight was very remarkable; by night it would doubtless have shot out of the ruined house on the first alarm, and sailed away on smooth and easy wing, far beyond reach.* This species, though common in the north, is quite a rarity in these southern regions.

*Wilson, writing of what appears to be this same species in an immature condition, thus graphically alludes to its difference of habit by day and by night. "Those who have seen this bird only in the day, can form but an imperfect idea of its activity, and even sprightliness, in its proper season of exercise. Throughout the day it was all stillness and gravity; its eyelids half shut, its neck contracted, and its head shrunk seemingly into its body; but scarcely was the sun set, and twilight began to approach, when its eyes became full and sparkling, like two living globes of fire; it crouched on its perch, reconnoitred every object around with looks of eager fierceness; alighted and fed, stood on the meat with clenched talons, while it tore it in morsels with its bill, flew round the room with the silence of thought, and perching, moaned out its melancholy notes, with many living gesticulations, not at all accordant with the pitiful tone of its ditty, which reminded one of the shivering moanings of a half-frozen puppy."—*The Red Owl.*

Letter XV

The grand occupation of autumn is cotton picking. It commenced in early fields more than a month ago, is now far advanced, and by the end of this month will be pretty nearly over. I have already spoken of the beauty of the cotton-plant when in full blossom; scarcely less beautiful is the appearance of a field of cotton at this season, when the produce is ripe. The fine dark-green foliage is relieved by the bunches of downy cotton of the purest white, bearing a curious resemblance to a meadow on which a light shower of snow has just fallen.

The pods open chiefly during the night. If one is opened by force, the cotton-fibres are found to be so closely packed into a hard dirty-white mass, as scarcely to be recognised, and no manipulation will make them assume a downy appearance. When the capsules, which are three, or occasionally four-celled, burst naturally, the cotton springs out, and swells to four or five times the bulk of the pod, assuming the most beautiful softness, and the most delicate whiteness, and forming three oval bunches of snowy down, each about as large as a hen's egg. As soon as the sun has exhaled the dew, these are fit for picking; and the night's opening should be picked if possible on the next day, or it will be lost.

In the evening the negroes,—men, women, and children,—bring in the produce of their picking, in large deep baskets, to the gin-house, when the overseer weighs each one's lot. As every negro has an allotted task, differing according to the ability of the individual, it is a matter of anxiety to see whether this is accomplished or not; if it falls short, the whip may pretty certainly be expected, especially if the overseer is a rigorous disciplinarian. The cries of the poor wretches proceeding nightly from the gin-house, "Oh! Mas'r! Pray, Mas'r!" the low plaintive tones of the men, and the shriller wails of the women and children, are very painful to hear.

The cotton has now to undergo a very interesting process. In the picking, the workpeople pull out the whole bunch from the pod, and drop it into the basket. If we examine one of these bunches, we shall see that it consists of several oval seeds densely clothed with fine long white hairs, which are the cotton. In the variety chiefly grown here, the seeds are black, but are covered with a very short underclothing of green silky down, among the bases of the white fibres. The latter adhere to the seed with considerable force, but must of course be removed before they are fit for the manufacturer. This separation of the fibre from the seed is accomplished by an effective and ingenious machine, the cotton-gin.

The following description will give you an idea of this valuable machine, and of its operation.

The hopper is a long box with one side perpendicular and the other diagonal: the latter is of iron bars about an inch wide, and set with interstices about one-eighth of an inch apart, and the angle at the bottom is not closed, but allows a narrow admission into a box below. Behind the slope of the hopper are two cylinders running the whole length, and revolving in the frame-work of the machine. One cylinder is of solid wood, and carries some fifty or more circular saws of sheet iron, a foot in diameter, so fixed that the teeth enter a little way into the hopper, between the sloping bars.

The cotton is thrown into the hopper from above, and the wheel which communicates motion to the cylinders is set going by means of mules. The teeth of the saws now catch hold of the fibres, and drag them through the interstices, but as these are too narrow to allow the seeds to pass, the fibres are separated, and the naked seeds fall down through the crevice at the bottom. The teeth of the saws come forth loaded with the cotton fibre, which are taken off by the action of the second cylinder. This is a hollow drum, the surface of which is covered with brushes, and being made to revolve with a greater rapidity than the saws, and in the opposite direction, the cotton is brushed off, and falls in downy lightness and purity into a receiver below. With such a machine as this, one man will clear three hundred pounds of cotton in a day. The seeds are thrown in heaps, that fermentation may destroy the germinating principle, and are then used as manure.

The cotton is packed into bales for exportation by the aid of powerful screws. The bale is put within a strong frame, around which the open mouth is firmly fastened. When the bag is so full that you think not another handful can be received, a pile of cotton nearly equal in height to the whole length of the bale is laid on the top, and by the force of the jack-screw is gradually pressed down into the bale.

Mules are a good deal used for farm purposes here, and good he-asses are imported expressly for breeding them. I have noticed a very curious circumstance connected with these animals, viz. that in a great number, perhaps in nine out of every ten, *the legs are banded with transverse dark stripes,* more or less distinctly. If I remember aright, Mr. Bell, in his "British Quadrupeds," mentions a mule so marked, as an instance of the power of imagination in the dam, she having borne her first colt to a zebra, while the one with banded legs was a younger birth with an ass for its sire. But the extensive familiarity with mules which their abundance here has given me, induces me to suspect that in this case the assigned cause may have had no real connexion with the result. The tendency to a banded arrangement of colours is one of the marks by which the genus *Asinus* is distinguished from *Equus,* in which the disposition is rather to spots.

One of the children lately found on a leaf of dog-wood a most singular caterpillar. It is about an inch in length, somewhat fivesided, the back flat, truncate at each end; the head invisible when at rest, being drawn into the body, so that I had to turn it over a great many times before I could distinguish head from tail, which at last I did only by catching sight of the six little white feet; for it has no prolegs, but the whole underpart except near the head is soft and fleshy, and clings with its whole surface to the ground, moving with a sort of undulation in crawling like the belly of a slug, except that it is dry, and not slimy. The middle of the body is velvety green, bordered with white, and having on the centre of the back a white ring surrounding a brown centre: each end of the body is of the same reddish-brown hue. It has four fleshy horns, one at each corner of the green on the back, which are studded with sharp hairs radiating in every direction; outside these, at both ends, are shorter horns similarly armed; and a row of similar armed projections, but of lighter colour, defends each side. When the hand touches these spines, a sting is felt exactly like that of a nettle, but of greater smart, which continues for about an hour. By this sting the boys discovered it; but on my being told of it, I disbelieved it, till I was convinced by actual experiment, repeated more than once. It crawls slowly. I subsequently obtained another of these larvae, on the leaves of a sassafras bush; it is doubtless that of some butterfly or moth, but I did not succeed in rearing either individual.

The same urticating property is possessed by the caterpillar of the Corn Emperor *(Saturnia Io).* This is of far superior size, being longer than my little finger, and as thick; its ground colour is very pale bluish green, with a white band bounded by crimson lines running down each side, in which are the spiracles; between the prolegs are on each segment a pair of red, triangular network spots. Every segment has six tubercles, which sting on the slightest touch, like a nettle, causing a little red tumour, with considerable pain: those segments which do not bear the prolegs, have eight bundles of spines; these spines are of a yellower green than the body.

Madame Merian (if I recollect rightly, for I have not here any means of reference), has mentioned a caterpillar of Surinam which has the same power of stinging. These, however, are the only cases in which it has ever fallen under my own observation.

Let me mention to you some particulars of the history of yet another caterpillar, a still greater oddity in its way. Early in the month of September I found upon an apple-tree many singular looking spindle-shaped cases or cocoons, made of a strong tough silk of a dirty white hue. The extremities were tapered to a point; the length was from one and a half to two inches; the upper end terminated in a silken band, fastened tightly round a twig, from which the case was suspended. The surface was thickly studded with pieces of twigs, from one-third to two-thirds of an inch long, attached longitudinally, but somewhat slightly: these were most numerous in the upper part. I made an incision in the silk, and found within a smooth plump caterpillar, dull reddish-brown, tapering at the extremities, the head and first three segments horny and polished, white with black spots. I threw the cases into a box, and the next day examined one or two more, and found that some contained pupae. In a large cocoon there was a dark brown pupa, much elongated, with no vestige of wings in the usual place, the head, legs, and antennae very small (for all these members can be traced in a Lepidopterous pupa, as in the imago); in another was a pupa much smaller, which had wings of middling size, and short thick antennae. I had reason to think that this cocoon was used by the caterpillar as a shelter or defence, while projecting the three polished segments of its body to eat in the manner of *Phryganea,* for on suddenly opening the box I saw one draw his head within the cocoon at the lower end, vanishing just as I looked at him. This induced me, by making a hole near the top of the cocoon and touching the larva behind, to drive him clean out, as I have done a *Phryganea,* at the lower end, which is tubular and open. But soon after I found by actual observation that the manners of the larva had the supposed resemblance to the *Trichoptera,* for at night I saw that the caterpillar crawled about the leaves, dragging the tent after him as far as it would allow, the first three segments being projected. I could not but admire the circumstance, that this resemblance between insects of very different orders was made still more complete by the bits of stick which were stuck about the case so profusely, and of which I could not discover the use. I at first thought they might have been the living twigs to which the web was first fastened, as a stay until it attained form, and that they had afterwards been cut off by the caterpillar, to free the case when finished: but if so, there would surely have been but two or three, instead of a dozen or two. Perhaps they were intended to make it more rough looking and less observable. Those cases which I had cut partly open were soon accurately closed nearly as tight and strong as ever, by an internal coat of silk over the incision.

On the evening of the 5th of October I was surprised at seeing in my box a little moth, which was fluttering his wings so swiftly as to render them almost invisible. On his becoming still, I observed that the wings were almost totally destitute of scales, and consequently transparent: the posterior pair very minute. On the posterior wings there was a very narrow band on the inner margin, which was clothed with black scales, and a few very sparingly scattered on an undefined stripe that ran down the anterior wings. The head, thorax, and abdomen, which were somewhat robust, were thickly clothed with black down; the antennae doubly pectinate, curled, and very short. The moth measured half an inch in length and an inch in spread of wing. It flew but a very few inches at a time, but constantly (or nearly so) vibrated its wings. When these organs were not in motion they were deflexed, and the abdomen was turned up. It was a male, and had proceeded from one of the smaller cases, at the mouth of which the pupa skin was left protruding about two-thirds of its length. Another pupa had just begun to make its head visible from the mouth of another cocoon. I then opened some of the larger female cocoons, but in most of them the pupae were filled with a soft satiny dust, of a buff-brown colour. In one cocoon I found the female evolved from the pupa; the exuviae of which were likewise filled with this downy dust. The perfected female had little of the form of a moth, but appeared like a transparent bag of soft eggs; the anterior parts were dark brown, and the limbs were very minute, flabby and almost undistinguishable, looking nearly decomposed. No wings were to be seen, and there was not a vestige of down upon the body, except two or three tufts near the tail, which resembled that left in the pupa-skin. I should have supposed that it was dead, but that at intervals there were certain motions which indicated the possession of vitality. "Take it for all in all," larva, pupa, and imago, this was the most singular moth that ever it was my fortune to make acquaintance with. I have ascertained that it is the *Thyridopteryx ephemeraeformis* of Stephens.

Letter XVI

November 1st

My communications now become fewer and more remote, for the aspects of nature are less varied than in summer; this is the period of old age and death with many plants and animals; and where life endures, its vigour is devoted rather to the perfecting of that which has already appeared than to the production of new forms. Seeds, not flowers, are characteristic of autumn; yet a few of the latter linger yet, and many of the former are sufficiently interesting to beguile the time and enchain the attention of the naturalist.

My daily walk still presents many objects of interest. Let me describe it to you, for it is not in the same district as that in which I asked your company some months ago, my lodgings now lying in quite another direction from the school. We first descend a hill by a narrow rocky path through some bowery underwood, much matted and tangled with briars *(Smilax)* and vines, and creeping plants of many species. The foliage of the slender shrubs, as brightly green as if it were July, hangs overhead, and nearly meets across the narrow pathway, and here morning after morning is my eye delighted with a constant succession of glorious blossoms of a large *Ipomaea,* closely like the *Convolvulus major* of English gardens, but of twice the diameter, and of the most lovely light purple hue. The plant grows along the sides of this lane in profusion, and the twining shoots depend gracefully down on either hand, bearing the noble trumpet-like flowers. Like the well-known favourite I have just compared it to, our sylvan beauty is emphatically a morning flower. The elegant words of the poet apply pre-eminently to it:—

"The morning flowers display their sweets,
    And gay their silken leaves unfold,
As careless of the noon-tide heats;
    As fearless of the evening cold.

"Nipp'd by the wind's unkindly blast,
    Scorch'd by the sun's directer ray,
The momentary glories waste,
    The short-lived beauties die away."

For "the sun is no sooner risen with a burning heat," than our lovely Ipomaea shrivels up, "and the grace of the fashion of it perisheth." May I learn the sacred lesson which its fleeting glory is fain to teach!

In these thickets a plant called Poke *(Phytolacca decandria)* holds a prominent place, being conspicuous for its long racemes, sometimes nearly a foot in length, of glossy black berries, set on crimson footstalks; the stem and the nerves of the leaves are of the same crimson hue, greatly enhancing the beauty of the plant. It is very common in the corners of rail-fences, and by roadsides, as well as in bushy wastes. The berries are full of a rich purple juice, which leaves a fine permanent stain; this hue is said to be communicated to the viscera of birds that feed on the berries.*

Even more conspicuously beautiful than this, is the Dogwood *(Cornus florida),* which is now in fruit. It is said to be handsome when in flower, being covered with blossoms, each consisting of an involucre of four large white heart-shaped bracts, so abundantly that the effect is said to be like that of the apple-tree in bloom. This, however, I have not seen, for it flowers in April, even before the leaves appear. Its aspect now is fine, for the umbrella-like heads of the low trees are covered with berries of a vivid scarlet, oval in form, polished, and united like those of the honeysuckle. Their luscious appearance tempts the taste, but they are found to be nauseously bitter.

After emerging from this verdant bridle-path, my way leads through a grove of Persimon-trees *(Diospyros Virginiana).* Here the appetite is regaled, for they are loaded with fruit, which has been sweetened and mellowed by frosty nights. The tree grows to a large size for a fruit-tree, sometimes reaching to fifty feet in height, with a spreading head; the fruit is somewhat like a greengage plum in size and form, but is rounder, and reddish yellow; its pulp contains from one to eight

*"The fruit called Poke-berries is a favourite repast with the Robin, after they are mellowed by the frost. The juice of the berries is of a beautiful crimson, and they are eaten in such quantities by these birds, that their whole stomachs are strongly tinged with the same red colour. A paragraph appeared in the public papers, intimating, that from the great quantities of these berries which the robins had fed on, they had become unwholesome, and even dangerous food; and that several persons had suffered by eating of them. The strange appearance of the bowels of the bird seemed to corroborate this account. The demand for, and use of them, ceased almost instantly; and motives of self-preservation produced at once what all the pleadings of humanity could not effect."—*Wilson's Amer. Ornith.*

semi-oval dark brown stones. It is so hard and harsh as to be quite uneatable till the skin is shrivelled by the frost, when it becomes soft, sweet, and very agreeable; to my taste much superior to any plum. The Opossum is very fond of a ripe persimon; its flesh, through feeding on this and other fruits, becomes very good at this season, and is brought to table, though rejected in summer.

Now we get into the lofty woods; swampy, but not very wet soil, where the most prominent trees are several species of oaks, as the Chestnut Oak, *(Quercus palustris)*, the Black-jack *(Q. ferruginea)*, and the Scarlet Oak *(Q. coccinea)*. The first of these is a magnificent tree for its lofty structure and finely formed head of foliage, as well as for the large size of its leaves and acorns. The last is conspicuous by the brilliant scarlet hue of its leaves at this season, whereby it materially assists in contributing to the bright and various colours which the forest is beginning to assume.

But there are nobler trees than Oaks in this swamp. There are the Magnolias, or Laurels, as they are called here, two species of which at least are common, if not a third. These are the Big Laurel *(M. grandiflora)*, and the Umbrella Laurel *(M. tripetala)*, and perhaps the Cucumber-tree *(M. cordata)*. The first of these is among our largest forest-trees, straight as a ship's mast, with a fine pyramidal head of massy foliage, whose evergreen verdure maintains its colour and its gloss undimmed by the storms of autumn and the frost of winter. The fleshy conical fruits, four inches in length, are now ripening their numerous cells, from which project pulpy red seeds, depending by long filaments.

The Umbrella-tree is so called from its leaves, which are of extraordinary appearance; they are eighteen or twenty inches long, and six or eight broad; and being often disposed in a radiating manner at the end of a stout shoot, they expand a surface of three feet in diameter. The tree itself does not aspire to the magnitude of its sister, being scarcely more than a shrub. Its large conical fruit is of a dull rose-colour. The Magnolias, in their smooth grey bark and pillar-like outline of the trunk, bear a resemblance to the beech,—that queen of the forests.

The character of the timber changes presently, and we see scarcely anything but coniferous trees. The earth, where it can be discerned, is covered with a dense coat of needle-like pine-leaves, brittle and brown, the accumulation of many years (their resinous character resisting decomposition), intermixed with sheets and shreds of the scaly bark. The Long-leafed and the Pitch Pine *(Pinus palus-*

tris and *P. rigida)* are the monarchs here, exercising a joint dominion, which admits of no other rival. Both these are towering trees, the latter the more branchy, with a deeply furrowed trunk; the former with a scaly peeling bark, great exudations of turpentine, and slender leaves a foot long, disposed in brushes, the bases being enclosed in a papery sheath. The turpentine on many of these trees runs down in great masses, congealing as it descends, while fresh streams flowing down over the old, and congealing in turn, form immense accumulations. If fire is applied to these exudations they catch at once, and burn vividly until the tree is destroyed.

I saw a Long-leafed Pine fired in this manner one day, and a fine sight it was. The light was applied to the flowing resin, which was in a flame in a moment, the fire running upward with increasing rapidity, till in a brief time the whole of one side of the tree to a height of fifty feet was in a blaze; the forked flickering tongues of flame catching and licking with greedy fierceness as if they demanded more aliment for their insatiable throats.

After an hour or two, the turpentine that lay in the bark and that had accumulated on the exterior was devoured by the fire, and the wood being too hard to be readily penetrated, the flame had gradually gone out, leaving a blackened stick with a glowing point here and there. But now came the grandest part of the spectacle. The interior of the trunk was decayed, and the fire had found its way through some broken branch into the hollow, where, speedily consuming the half-rotten wood of the centre, it made its way to the summit, from which a volume of flame fiercely shot for many yards a perpendicular pyre. It was a tall chimney in a blaze; the interior, seen through openings here and there (I mean, after some hours had elapsed), was like a furnace, while the roaring of the flame from the top was like the surging of the sea upon the shore.

The planter at whose house I lodge being lately in want of some tar, manufactured it in the following manner. A number of the boughs and knots of these two species of Pine were gathered from the swamp, and built up into a stack in the yard. A few grooves had been first made in the hard ground of the site, all converging into one principal channel, which led off to one side. Here a hole was dug to receive a tub, with a spout of bark from the channel projecting over it. Earth was now heaped over the stack, leaving only a few orifices for air, and the pile was lighted. The tar, which is nothing but resin smoked and partly burned, soon began to trickle, and increased to a stream, which lasted until the whole wood was consumed.

But to proceed with our walk, which we have nearly finished. The nature of the foliage, and its scantiness in these pine swamps, admits of much more light than in the forests generally; and hence the ground is much overrun with herbage. All through the autumn, several species of *Oenothera* have opened their beautiful blossoms to the evening air, courting the softened rays of the moon and stars rather than of the sun. One sort in particular, the large-flowered Evening-primrose *(Oe. grandiflora),* with its fine blossoms of brilliant yellow, as wide as a tea-cup, is well worthy of admiration. Some species of Willow-herb *(Epi-lobium)* discharges its feathery down here, which is borne by the breeze into our eyes, nose, and mouth, and hangs about in ragged slovenly bunches. But most characteristic is the plant called the Golden-rod *(Solidago),* which covers many acres with tall coarse herbage, and spikes of small but close-set yellow blossom. Many autumnal insects, as the *Hymenoptera* and *Diptera,* and some moths, flutter around these spikes of blossom, which else would present few attractions.

Hence we emerge into the high road, bounded on both sides by the hardwood forest, where the oaks and hickories, the sycamore and the tulip-tree, the chestnut and the sweet-gum, cast a greenwood shade, varied, however, now with gorgeous tints, like the rays that stream through the painted window of some old cathedral, by the dying foliage. Beneath these trees the eye of an entomologist is often caught by droppings which indicate caterpillars of large size feeding on the leaves above; and thus I have been guided to the discovery of some fine species: while, not uncommonly, we discern far up in the trees the great cocoons of some of the Emperor Moths *(Saturnia, Ceratocampa,* &c.) suspended from the twigs by a narrow ribbon of strong silk, and rocking in the breeze. The cocoon of the Swallow-tailed Emperor *(S. luna),* for instance, is affixed to the liquidambar or sweet-gum; that of the Corn Emperor *(S. Io)* to the oak, and that of the great Yellow Elephant Moth *(C. imperatoria)* to the sycamore. The caterpillars of some of these moths are of magnificent dimensions, and often richly coloured. A few weeks ago one of my little lads came to tell me of one which he had just found, and which he described as unusually gigantic—too big, in fact, to be touched. On my coming to the spot, the prize was *non inven-*

tus, having crawled away. On my asking the lad why he had not put the caterpillar into a collecting canister which he had, he exclaimed with unfeigned astonishment, "Law, sir! he would'nt *begin* to go in!" meaning, not to ascribe any reluctance on the part of the insect to the change of residence, but that the orifice of the box was not wide enough to receive even the smallest extremity of its body.

Letter XVII

December 1st

How slight a thing will touch the chords of sympathy! The smallest object, the faintest note, will sometimes awaken association with some distant scene or by-gone time, and conjure up in a moment, all unexpected, a magic circle, which unlocks all the secret springs of the soul, and excites emotions and affections that had slept for months, or perhaps years! The unlooked-for sight of a little bird lately had such an effect upon me. It was an unpretending little thing, a sort of sparrow, called the Snow-bird *(Fringilla nivalis),* of no great beauty in plumage, being of a dark slate-colour above, and white below, and with nothing but a feeble chirp for a song. But it had been in Canada one of the most familiar of our birds, hopping about every way-side, and sitting upon every fence; and the first time I saw it in these distant southern regions, it seemed like an old friend come to tell me of old familiar faces, and to converse with me of old familiar scenes. I almost felt disappointed that it did not seem as glad to see me as I was to welcome it; but it hopped away at my approach, and sat on the fence-rail preening its feathers, without a suspicion of my sentimental emotions.

The same pleasure was renewed, in less degree, by the recognition of other feathered favourites, which I had known in the north, and which in their autumnal migration have lately appeared among us. I lately heard the sweet warble of the Song Sparrow *(F. melodia),* always heard with delight, but peculiarly welcome at this season, when our groves are almost mute, or at least destitute of song. The Yellow-bird *(Carduelis tristis)* begins to occur in restless flocks, flitting from weed to weed, with alternate openings and closings of the wings, twittering all the way, very much like our English goldfinch. None of them are now dressed in the gay livery of bright yellow and deep black, in which they ornament the Canadian pastures, but they have all put on their sober winter attire of russet olive, in which they might well be mistaken for a family of hen canaries, escaped from their cage.

Besides these, which are all of the Finch tribe, many of the soft-billed birds, which feed on insects, are now hopping about our woods. Such are the Maryland Yellow-throat *(Sylvia trichas),* the Yellow-backed Warbler *(S. pusilla),* the Prairie

Warbler *(S. minuta)*, and others of this delicate and lovely genus; and some of the Thrushes, as the Wood Thrush *(Turdus melodus)*, the Red Thrush *(T. rufus)*, the Gold-crowned Thrush, *(T. aurocapillus)*, and the Red-breasted Thrush, *(T. migratorius)*, which in Newfoundland we used to call the Blackbird, and in Canada the Robin. Species of these families, and perhaps even these particular species, have haunted our southern woods all through the summer, but we have lately received such large accessions of numbers from the north, driven by the inclemency of early winter to our milder skies, that we seem repeopled. Many of these, however, are only transient sojourners; they pass through our district on their way still farther south, spreading themselves, indeed, as they go, and continually dropping stationary colonies, until the most adventurous reach the sunny isles of the West Indies, and the ever verdant forests of Mexico, and Central America.

The youths here sometimes take a number of the smaller birds by a process similar to that which in some parts of England is called bat-fowling. I was present a few nights ago at the operation, which seemed to me a poor cowardly mode of destroying inoffensive and feeble creatures, with neither sport nor profit to recommend it. A naturalist might indeed obtain a few specimens by this means, in a better condition than such as are shot, inasmuch as they are generally killed without laceration.

Three or four lads proceeded to some thickets soon after night had set in; one of them carrying a lighted pine-knot, another a stout staff, and the rest slender branches of the trees, stripped of their leaves. The torch being elevated at some little distance from a thick bush, the lad with the staff began to thresh the bush, while the others stationed themselves so as to intercept, and whip down with their twigs the frightened birds, that, awakened from their roost, scudded out towards the light. A good many were struck down dead, mostly of one species, the Towhe Bunting *(Fringilla erythrophthalma)*. It is a prettily marked little bird, which I have not seen in the north, though sufficiently abundant here; its plumage is black above, with white bands on the wings; the sides are chestnut red, and the under parts white. The iris of the eye, which is red, imparts a peculiar aspect to its physiognomy. Its note resembles the word "towhé," whence its common name. This little bird is considered a delicacy; and several are spitted together and roasted like larks with us. This, in fact, constituted the inducement, but though pine-knots here do not cost much, I was tempted to exclaim, *"Le jeu ne vaut pas la chandelle."*

Letter XVIII

December 20th

We have nothing like winter yet. The weather resembles what you have in Canada in September; the trees have lost their gay autumnal tints, and have put on a sober russet hue, but in general they still wear their foliage. The seedlings are still fresh and green, and, in the swamps, the magnolias, the water-oak, the holly, and the palmetto are as verdant as in summer. Herbs and weeds still fill the angles of the fences, and the fields of autumn-sown rye are clothed in a flush of tender green, like that of a meadow in June. Some few flowers still linger, and on sunny days butterflies and other insects flutter in the beam.

In the course of a ride to Selma, a little town a few miles distant, I had the pleasure of seeing a flock of Parrots *(Psittacus Carolinensis)*. The bird is not at all common in these parts, and indeed it was the first occasion on which I had ever seen one of this beautiful tribe in a state of wild nature. There were eighty or a hundred in one compact flock, and as they swept past me, screaming as they went, I fancied that they looked like an immense shawl of green satin, on which an irregular pattern was worked in scarlet and gold and azure. The sun's rays were brilliantly reflected from the gorgeous surface, which rapidly sped past, like a splendid vision.

Wilson tells us that the Carolina Parrot feeds greedily on the seeds of the cocklebur, and that its rarity or abundance in any locality is partly dependent on the presence of this plant. If this be so, the beautiful parroquet ought to be common, for there is no lack of the vile weed in question, as the poor horses and cattle find to their cost, for their legs and sides are sometimes almost covered with the tenacious burs, especially after they have spent the night in neglected pastures. The curiously hooked bristles which grow on the exterior of these seed-vessels constitute one of those beautiful provisions which we find for the dispersion of seeds to a distance from their place of birth: they catch hold of the hair of animals, adhering on the slightest touch, and maintain their grasp with a tenacity which almost defies removal.

I had heard with some incredulity that the Beaver inhabits the Alabama river, in the clay banks of which it is said to form its habitation. This is described as a simple burrow, with none of the architectural instinct displayed in its construction that marks the celebrated dams of the northern builders. I had supposed that the Beaver did not extend its range nearly so far south as this region; but all doubt was removed by specimens having been recently brought to me, taken in the immediate neighbourhood. Being on the point of returning to England, I wished to purchase all I could procure, knowing the value of beaver fur in the market; but when I came to examine the skins, the almost total absence of the under-coat of woolly down that constitutes the real worth of the fur, told me that, however interesting in a scientific view the specimens might be, and were, as illustrating the geographical distribution of animals, and also as exemplifying the influence of climate upon their covering, beaver fur from Alabama, even collected in winter, is in a pecuniary sense valueless.

That noble bird, the Turkey, is now in high condition, and is abundant in our woods, where I frequently hear the gobblers. The "pen," which in a former letter I described as a device for outwitting them, is now brought into full requisition, and many are caught in this manner. Other modes are likewise practised, such as the following:—As a flock of turkeys is known to be very regular in habit, coming day after day to the same spot, at the same hour, the fowler who has surprised them feeding has nothing to do but to mark the place, and to build up a "blind," or screen of logs, bushes, and branches of trees. To this he resorts before day, and hides himself with his dog, whom he has trained to lie as quiet as himself. Soon after it is light, the fowls come to their familiar spot, when the hunter, waiting till he gets several in a line, fires, and does great execution. The dog at the same moment dashes in the midst of the flock, which rises on the wing, and takes to the nearest tree; here the birds sit gazing on the dog, with absorbed attention, unobservant of the sportsman, who thus picks them down at his leisure.

On dry frosty mornings, the sportsman goes into the woods about nine or ten o'clock, and creeps silently to and fro till he hears the well-known sound of the birds scratching,—a sound recognisable at a great distance. He then glides cautiously towards the place, and if he can succeed in approaching within range before he is discovered by the turkeys, gets a shot or two among them.

The probabilities of success are much heightened by the use of the contrivance called the "yelper." This is a pipe, made of reed,—or, better still, of the thigh-bone of a turkey; by blowing through which the human breath is modulated so as to offer the closest imitation of the yelping cry of the hen-turkey. The hunter hides himself in a screen or thicket till he hears indications of the presence of the fowls; he now blows his pipe, which they answer; he suffers five minutes to elapse in silence, then "yelps" again. He needs the utmost wariness, patience, and knowledge of the birds' habits; sometimes the flock silently approach the call, without answering, and prematurely discover the delusion; at other times they respond without approaching, as if suspecting treachery. The young males of the season are incautious; but old birds are wary, suspicious, and acute-sensed; and to outwit these requires great practice and knowledge.

The chase of the Deer is now over; it lasts from the middle of September to the end of November, when it gives place to fox-hunting, and with this the planters merrily wind up the year. Ours is the Grey Fox *(Canis Virginianus),* which replaces in these regions the Red Fox *(C. fulvus)* of the north,—a handsome species, with fur of an iron-grey hue, becoming whitish on the belly, and red on the cheeks, sides, and legs: his brush, which is ample, is rufous grey, with a black line running down the middle, and a black tip.

Reynard has all the art and cunning that characterise the subtle brotherhood elsewhere; and many an ingenious shift has he to baffle the hounds and secure a whole skin. A common trick with him is to run up the trunk of some sloping tree in the forest, and leap off as far as possible, to break the scent. Sometimes he will run along the top rail of the fence for a hundred yards or more, and creep round with a circuit to his former track, when the dogs are past.

The report which was given me a day or two since (I am not myself a hunter) of what was considered a good run, may serve as a fair sample of the sport—if I do not spoil the effect by my untechnical mode of describing it. The trail was found in a thicket, and the hounds being set on it, pursued it through the cotton and stubble-fields (the crops of the former being now all gathered), till they roused Reynard in a marshy thicket. The dogs were now open-mouthed; the fox doubles, and away in full sight across a pasture field and waste-ground for half a mile to some tangled wood. The horsemen dash on through this, with characteristic impetuosity, and presently break out into the tall forest. The "varmint" is discovered stealing along by a fence; at length, hard pressed, he runs up a tree, and turns at bay, with snarl, and snap, and bared teeth. His hour seemed come, but it was determined to give him another chance; the hounds were accordingly called off; and, after another half-hour's run, he was killed in a thicket, and I have the honour of possessing his brush.

Letter XIX

I ate my Christmas dinner on board the steamer, on my voyage down the Alabama river, partaking of a turkey that would be considered something remarkable in Leadenhall Market. It weighed eighteen pounds when trussed for the spit; and if we allow for the feathers and quills, the head, the viscera and the feet, this sturdy gobbler could not have been much less than five-and-twenty pounds,—a tolerable weight for a bird!

The voyage from the upper country occupied two days and one night,—about the same period as my ascending passage in the spring, notwithstanding the force of the current, which, when the river is straitened by the beetling cliffs of some narrow gorge, is powerful and rapid. But considerable delay was caused by our stoppages to take in cargo—for we were laden, at length, almost to the very water's edge, with cotton. Down rushed the bales along the slippery planks in quick succession, as soon as the steamer came beneath the slide—an interesting spectacle, from the impetus which they acquired in the descent, especially in the more precipitous stations. I looked with pleasure on the magnificent scenery of the heights; I had seen the celebrated gorges of the Hudson, to which these of the Alabama bear much resemblance. There is something very romantic in sailing, or rather shooting, along between lofty precipices of rock, crowned with woods at the summit. One such strait we passed through just at sunrise; the glassy water, our vessel, and everything near, still involved in deepest shadow; the grey, discoloured limestone towering up on each side; while the trees, and just a streak on the topmost edge of one cliff, were bathed in golden light from the newly risen sun.

To-morrow, if all be well, I expect to sail for England, the dear home to which, in all my wanderings, my heart ever turns. I have, in fact, said adieu to the land, having taken my place on board a large cotton ship, which is now in the bay, some fifteen or twenty miles from the city.

I have been amused by observing the crew stowing the cargo. After what I said of the way in which the cotton is screwed into the bales, you would suppose that these were incapable of further compression. But it is not so. When the

Shipping Cotton on the Alabama River

stowed bales in the hold are in contact with the upper deck, another layer has to be forced in. This is effected, bale by bale, by powerful jack-screws, worked by four men. When you see the end of the bale set against a crevice, into which you could scarcely push a thin board, you think it impossible that it can ever get in; and, indeed, the operation is very slow, but the screw is continually turned, and the bale does gradually insinuate itself.

The men keep the most perfect time by means of their songs. These ditties, though nearly meaningless, have much music in them, and as all join in the perpetually recurring chorus, a rough harmony is produced, by no means un-pleasing. I think the leader improvises the words, of which the following is a specimen; he singing one line alone, and the whole then giving the chorus, which is repeated without change at every line, till the general chorus concludes the stanza:—

> "I think I hear the black cock say,
>   Fire the ringo, fire away!
> They shot so hard, I could not stay;
>   Fire the ringo! fire away!
> So I spread my wings, and flew away;
>   Fire the ringo! &c.
> I took my flight and ran away;
>   Fire, &c.
> All the way to Canadáy;
>   Fire, &c.
> To Canaday, to Canaday,
>   Fire, &c.
> All the way to Canaday.
>   Ringo! ringo! blaze away!
>   Fire the ringo! fire away!"

Sometimes the poet varied the subject by substituting political for zoological allusions. The victory over the British at New Orleans—that favourite theme with all Americans—was chosen. Thus:—

> "Gin'ral Jackson gain'd the day;
>   Fire the ringo, &c.
> At New Orleans he won the day;
>   Fire the ringo, fire away!"

But I have done. The pilot waits for this letter. The low shore of Mobile Point is hardly visible from the cabin windows; the breeze comes fresh and cool off the land; the green water is curling and frothing under the rudder. Adieu!

Appendix

Taxonomic Lists of the Plants and Animals Mentioned by P. H. Gosse in *Letters from Alabama* (1859)

GARY R. MULLEN

The following six tables provide taxonomic lists of 392 of the 408 plants and animals mentioned by Gosse in *Letters from Alabama* (1859). They are grouped in six categories for the convenience of the reader, depending on one's particular interest: plants (189), insects (94), marine fishes (14), reptiles and amphibians (15), birds (59), and mammals (21). The figures in parentheses indicate the number of taxa represented in each table. Included are the scientific and common names, precisely as Gosse spelled them, together with the scientific and common names of the respective taxa as they are known today, and the family to which each belongs. In the case of the insects, the respective order is also provided. The names and dates following the currently accepted scientific names indicate the author of the original published description of the species and the year in which it was published. All entries are listed alphabetically by order (in the case of insects), family, and genus (as Gosse referred to it). In some cases Gosse only mentioned a species by its common name. In these cases the entries are placed after the entries with scientific names within the respective family.

Because of difference in the format used by taxonomists in their respective specialties (e.g., botany, entomology, ornithology) to indicate scientific names of species, there are a few unavoidable inconsistencies in the following tables (e.g., in the case of plants, the author names are abbreviated rather than spelled out; and additional author name[s] are included for some species). Recognizing these different notations among taxonomists and official lists by various scientific societies, the format here generally follows that adopted by the Integrated Taxonomic Information System (ITIS) as it appears in their database (www.itis.gov). Likewise, there are differences among taxonomists in the spelling of common names. In some groups, the common name is spelled all in lowercase letters; in others, only the first letter of the name is capitalized, or the first letter of each word is capitalized. For the purpose of consistency, only the first letter of the currently recognized common names is capitalized in the tables that follow. Although there are often multiple common and colloquial names by which each species is known, in most cases only the generally accepted English name, according to ITIS, is included in the tables.

An additional sixteen plants and animals that Gosse mentions in his narrative are not included in the tables. Most of these are members of various groups of marine and terrestrial invertebrates, including corals, mollusks, isopods, and arachnids (mites, ticks, spiders, and pseudoscorpions).

The lead author assumes full responsibility for any errors or inaccuracies in the taxonomic tables that follow.

Plants

Family	Gosse's Scientific and Common Names	Current Scientific and Common Names
	Coniferae	Gosse's general term for *Pinus* Pines
Anonaceae	*Anona palustris* Swamp Papaw	*Asimina parviflora* (Michx.) Dunal Smallflower pawpaw or *Asimina triloba* (L.) Dunal Pawpaw
Aquifoliaceae	holly	*Ilex* species Holly
Arecaceae	*Chaemerops palmetto* Fan-palm, Palmetto	*Sabal palmetto* (Walt. Lodd. ex Schult. & Schult. f. Cabbage palm, Cabbage palmetto
	Chamaerops serrulata Fan-palm	*Serenoa repens* (W. Bartram) Small Saw palmetto
Asclepiadaceae	*Asclepias*	*Asclepias* L. Milkweed
	Asclepias parviflora Swallow-wort	*Asclepias perennis* Walt. Aquatic milkweed
	Asclepias tuberosa Butterfly weed, Swallow-wort	*Asclepias tuberosa* L. Butterfly milkweed, Butterflyweed
Asparagaceae	*Yucca aloifolia* Adam's needle	*Yucca aloifolia* L. Aloe yucca
	Yucca Filamentosa Bear's Grass	*Yucca filamentosa* L. Adam's needle
Asteraceae	*Helianthus scaber*	*Helianthus* species (identification uncertain) Sunflower
	Solidago Golden-rod	*Solidago* L. Goldenrod
	Zinnia	*Zinnia* L. Zinnia
	Zinnia multiflora	*Zinnia peruviana* (L.) L. Peruvian zinnia
Balsaminaceae	cocklebur	*Xanthium strumarium* L Rough cockleburr

Family	Gosse's Scientific and Common Names	Current Scientific and Common Names
	balsam	*Impatiens capensis* Meerb. Spotted touch-me-not
Bignoniaceae	*Bignonia* Cross Vine	*Bignonia capreolata* L. Cross vine
	Bignonia radicans Trumpet-flower, trumpet flower	*Campsis radicans* (L.) Seem. ex Bureau Trumpet creeper
	Catalpa syringaefolia Catalpa	*Catalpa bignonioides* Walt. Southern catalpa
Bromeliaceae	*Tillandsia usneoides* Spanish moss	*Tillandsia usneoides* (L.) L. Spanish moss
Cactaceae	*Opuntia* P. Mill Prickly-pear, Prickly pear	*Opuntia* P. Mill. Prickly pear
Campanulaceae	*Lobelia cardinalis* Cardinal-flower	*Lobelia cardinalis* L. Cardinal flower
Cannaceae	*Canna angustifolia* Indian Shot	*Canna indica* L. Indian shot
Caprifoliaceae	*Caprifolium sempervirens* Scarlet Woodbine, Sweet-brier, Trumpet Honeysuckle	*Lonicera sempervirens* L. Trumpet honeysuckle
	honeysuckle	*Lonicera* L. Honeysuckle
Celastraceae	*Euonymus angustifolius* Burning Bush	*Euonymus atropurpurea* Jacq. Eastern wahoo
Commelinaceae	*Commelina erecta* Comfrey	*Commelina erecta* L. Erect dayflower
Convolvulaceae	*Convolvulus major* "of English gardens"	Probably *Ipomoea purpurea* (L.) Roth Common morning-glory
	Ipomoea	*Ipomoea* L. Morning-glory
	Ipomaea coccinea Scarlet Cypress-vine	*Ipomoea coccinea* L. Scarlet morning-glory
	Ipomaea Quamoclit Crimson Cypress-vine	*Ipomoea quamoclit* L. Cypressvine

Family	Gosse's Scientific and Common Names	Current Scientific and Common Names
Cornaceae	*Cornus* dogwood	*Cornus* L. Dogwoods
	Cornus florida Dogwood	*Cornus florida* L. Flowering dogwood
Cucurbitaceae	*Cucumis anguria* Prickly Cucumber	*Cucumis anguria* L. West Indian gherkin
	Cucumis melo Musk-melon, Queen Anne's Pocket Melon	*Cucumis melo* L. Cantaloupe
	Cucurbita citrullus Water-melon, water-melon	*Citrullus lanatus* (Thunb.) Matsum. & Nakai Watermelon
	Cucurbita lagenaria Gourd, Calabash	*Lagenaria siceraria* (Molina) Standl. Bottle gourd
	Cucurbita ovifera? Smell Lemon	*Cucurbita pepo* L. var. *ovifera* (L.) Harz Field pumpkin
Cupressaceae	*Taxodium disticha* Cypress	*Taxodium distichum* (L.) L. C. Rich. Bald cypress
	Thuja occidentalis	*Thuja occidentalis* L. Eastern white cedar, Arborvitae
Droseraceae	*Dionaea muscipula* Venus's Fly-trap	*Dionaea muscipula* Ellis Venus flytrap, apparently transplanted from Carolinas
Ebenaceae	*Diospyros Virginiana* Persimon-tree	*Diospyros virginiana* L. Persimmon
Ericaceae	*Andromeda arborea* Sorrel-tree	*Oxydendrum arboreum* (L.) DC. Sourwood
	Vaccinium stamineum Green-wooded Whortleberry	*Vaccinium stamineum* L. Deerberry
Fabaceae	*Cassia occidentalis* Florida Coffee	*Senna occidentalis* (L.) Link Coffee senna
	Erythrina herbacea Coral-tree	*Erythrina herbacea* L. Eastern coralbean

Family	Gosse's Scientific and Common Names	Current Scientific and Common Names
	Gleditschia triacanthos Honey Locust, honey locust, Three-thorned Locust	*Gleditsia triacanthos* L. Honeylocust
	Glycine frutescens Virgin's Bower	*Wisteria frutescens* (L.) Poir. American wisteria
	Mimosa ———	*Albizia julibrissin* Durazz. Mimosa, Silk tree
	Schrankia uncinata Sensitive Brier	*Mimosa microphylla* Dryand. Littleleaf sensitive-briar
	Vexillaria mariana Banner-pea	*Clitoria mariana* L. Butterfly-pea
	Vexillaria Virginiana Banner-pea	*Centrosema virginianum* (L.) Benth. Spurred butterfly pea
	horse-bean	*Vicia faba* L. Broad-bean
	sweet pea	*Lathyrus* species Sweet pea
Fagaceae	*Castanea Americana* Chestnut	*Castanea dentata* (Marsh.) Borkh. American chestnut
	Castanea pumila Chinquapin-tree *Quercus coccinea* Scarlet Oak	*Castanea pumila* (L.) P. Mill. Allegeny chinkapin *Quercus coccinea* Muenchh. Scarlet oak
	Quercus ferruginea Black-jack	*Quercus marilandica* Muenchh. Blackjack oak
	Quercus palustris Chestnut oak	*Quercus palustris* Muenchh. Pin oak; possibly *Q. coccinea* Scarlet oak
	Willow-oaks	*Quercus phellos* L. Willow oak
Grossulariaceae	gooseberry	*Ribes* L. Currants and Gooseberries
Hamamelidaceae	*Liquidambar styraciflua* Sweet Gum	*Liquidambar styraciflua* L. Sweetgum

Family	Gosse's Scientific and Common Names	Current Scientific and Common Names
Hydrangeaceae	*Hydrangea quercifolia* Oak-leafed Hydrangea	*Hydrangea quercifolia* Bartr. Oakleaf hydrangea
Lamiaceae	*Marrubium vulgare* Hore-hound	*Marrubium vulgare* L. Horehound
Lauraceae	*Laurus benzoin* Spice-wood	*Lindera benzoin* (L.) Blume Northern spicebush; possibly the rarer *Lindera melissifolia* (Walt.) Blume Southern spicebush
	Laurus sassafras Sassafras, Sassafras-tree	*Sassafras albidum* (Nutt.) Nees Sassafras
Loganiaceae	*Spigelia Marylandica* Indian Pink	*Spigelia marilandica* (L.) L. Indianpink
Magnoliaceae	*Liriodendron tulipiferum* Tulip-tree, Poplar, Whitewood	*Liriodendron tulipifera* L. Tuliptree, Tulip poplar
	Magnolia cordata Cucumber-tree	*Magnolia acuminata* (L.) L. Cucumber-tree
	Magnolia grandiflora Big Laurel	*Magnolia grandiflora* L. Southern magnolia
	Magnolia tripetala Umbrella Laurel, Umbrella-tree	*Magnolia tripetala* (L.) Umbrella magnolia, Umbrella-tree
	laurels, magnolias	*Magnolia* L. Laurels and Magnolias
Malvaceae	*Gossypium herbaceum* cotton, Cotton Plant	*Gossypium hirsutum* L. Upland cotton
	Hollyhock	*Alcea rosea* L. Hollyhock
	Hibiscus	*Hibiscus* L. Rosemallow
Meliaceae	*Melia azedarach* pride of China	*Melia azedarach* L. Chinaberry
Moraceae	Figs	*Ficus* L. Fig

Family	Gosse's Scientific and Common Names	Current Scientific and Common Names
Musaceae	*Musa* plantain	*Musa* L. Banana, observed in the Bahamas
Nyctaginaceae	*Mirabilis jalapa* Four o'Clock, Marvel of Peru	*Mirabilis jalapa* L. Common four o'clock
Nyssaceae	*Nyssa sylvatica* Black Gum, Sour Gum, Sour Gum-tree	*Nyssa sylvatica* Marsh. Black gum, Black tupelo
Oleaceae	ash	*Fraxinus* species: *F. americana* White ash; *F. pennsylvanica* Green ash; *F. caroliniana* Carolina ash
	Lilac	*Syringa* L. Lilac
Onagraceae	*Epilobium* Willow-herb	*Epilobium* L. Willow weed
	Oenothera	*Oenothera* L. Evening primrose
	Oenothera fruticosa Tree primrose	*Oenothera fruticosa* L. Narrowleaf evening-primrose
	Oenothera grandiflora Evening-primrose	*Oenothera grandiflora* L'Hér. ex Ait. Largeflower evening-primrose
Orobanchaceae	*Gerardia flava*	*Aureolaria flava* (L.) Farw. Smooth yellow false foxglove
Oxalidaceae	Oxalis	*Oxalis* L. Oxalis
Papaveraceae	*Argemone Mexicana* Horned Poppy	*Argemone mexicana* L. Mexican pricklypoppy, Yellow pricklypoppy
	scarlet poppy	*Papaver rhoeas* L. Corn Poppy
Passifloraceae	*Passiflora caerulea* Passion-flower	*Passiflora caerulea* L. Blue passion flower

Family	Gosse's Scientific and Common Names	Current Scientific and Common Names
	Passiflora incarnata Passion flower	*Passiflora incarnata* L. Purple passionflower
Phytolaccaceae	*Phytolacca decandria* Poke, Poke-berry	*Phytolacca americana* L. American pokeweed, Poke, Pokeberry
Pinaceae	*Pinus palustris* Long-leafed pine, Long-leafed Pine, long-leafed pine	*Pinus palustris* P. Mill. Longleaf pine
	Pinus rigida Pitch Pine, pitch-pine	*Pinus rigida* P. Mill. Pitch pine; more likely *P. elliotti* Engelm Slash pine
Plantaginaceae	Foxglove	*Digitalis* L. Foxglove
Platanaceae	*Platanus occidentalis* Button-wood	*Platanus occidentalis* L. American sycamore
Poaceae	*Andropogon nutans*	*Sorghastrum nutans* (L.) Nash Yellow indian grass
	Cynodon dactylon Crowfoot-grass, Crowfoot Grass	*Cynodon dactylon* (L.) Pers. Bermudagrass
	Miega macrosperma	*Arundinaria gigantea* (Walt.) Muhl. ssp. *macrosperma* (Michx.) McClure Giant cane
	Zea mays bread corn, Indian Corn, maize	*Zea mays* L. Corn
	rye	*Secale cereale* L. Cultivated rye
Ranunculaceae	*Clematis* Virgin's Bower	*Clematis virginiana* L. Virgin's bower
	Delphinium azureum Larkspur	*Delphinium carolinianum* Walt. ssp. *Carolinianum* Carolina larkspur
	Delphinium staphisagria Larkspur	Probably *Consolida ajacis* (L.) Schur Rocket larkspur

Family	Gosse's Scientific and Common Names	Current Scientific and Common Names
Rosaceae	*Cerasus Virginiana* "of the north"	*Prunus serotina* Ehrh. Black cherry
	Crataegus Thorn	*Crataegus* L. Hawthorns
	Fragaria Virginiana strawberry	*Fragaria virginiana* Duchesne Thickleaved wild strawberry
	Rubus idoeus raspberry	*Rubus idaeus* L. American red raspberry, presumably cultivated
	apple-tree	*Malus pumila* P. Mill. Cultivated apple
	green-gage plum	*Prunus domestica* L. European plum
	haws	*Crataegus* species Hawthorn
	peaches	*Prunus persica* (L.) Batsch Common peach
	wild plum	*Prunus* species Plum; at least 10 native plums in Alabama
Rubiaceae	Mocha berry	*Coffea arabica* L. Arabian coffee, native to Yemen and Ethiopa
Rutaceae	lemon tree	*Citrus×limon* (L.) Burm. f. Lemon
Scrophulariaceae	*Verbascum nigrum* Mullein	*Verbascum thapsus* L. Common mullein
Smilacaceae	*Smilax* "briars"	*Smilax* L. Greenbriars
Ulmaceae	*Ulmus alata* Elm, Wahoo	*Ulmus alata* Michx. Winged elm
Urticaceae	English elm	*Ulmus procera* Salisb. English elm
	nettle	*Urtica dioica* L. Stinging nettle
Vitaceae	purple fox-grape	*Vitis* L. Grapes, Fox grapes

Insects

Order	Family	Gosse's Scientific and Common Names	Current Scientific and Common Names
Blattodea	Blattidae	*Blatta*	Gosse's general term for cockroaches
Coleoptera	Carabidae	*Carabi*	Carabidae Ground beetles
	Cerambycidae	*Cerambyx* Prioni	Long-horned beetle (unidentified species) Subfamily Prioninae Long-horned beetles
		Longicornes	Cerambycidae Long-horned beetles
		Prionus coriareus	*Prionus coriarius* (Linnaeus, 1758) Tanner or Sawyer—Europe
		Prionus imbricornis	*Prionus imbricornis* (Linnaeus, 1767) Tilehorned prionus
		Tetraopes tornator	*Tetraopes texanus* Horn, 1878 Milkweed beetle
	Cicindelidae	*Cicindela(e)*	Cicindelidae Tiger beetles
	Coccinellidae	*Coccinella borealis*	*Epilachna borealis* (Fabricius, 1775) Squash beetle
		Coccinelladae Lady-birds	Coccinellidae Ladybird beetles
	Dynastidae	*Dynastes Tityrus*	*Dynastes tityus* (Linnaeus, 1763) Eastern Hercules beetle
		Orcytes Maimom	*Strategus antaeus* (Drury, 1773) Ox beetle
	Dytiscidae	*Dyticidae* water-beetles	*Dytiscidae* Predaceous diving beetles

Order	Family	Gosse's Scientific and Common Names	Current Scientific and Common Names
	Elateridae	*Alaus oculatus* Click Beetle, Ocellated Clickbeetle	*Alaus oculatus* (Linnaeus, 1758) Eyed click beetle
	Geotrupidae	 Common Dorr of England	*Geotrupes stercorarius* (Linnaeus, 1758) Dorr, Clock, Dung beetle
	Lucanidae	*Lucanidae*	Lucanidae Stag beetles
		Lucanus	*Lucanus* Stag beetles
		Lucanus cervus Stag Beetle, Stag-beetle	*Lucanus cervus* (Linnaeus, 1758) Stag beetle—Europe
		Lucanus dama Deer-beetle	*Lucanus capreolus* (Linnaeus, 1764) Stag beetle
		Lucanus Elaphus Elk-beetle	*Lucanus elaphus* Fabricius, 1775 Giant stag beetle
	Passalidae	*Passalus cornutus*	*Odontotaenius disjunctus* (Illiger, 1800) Horned passalus
	Scarabaeidae	*Cetonia*	Scarabaeidae, Subfamily Cetoniinae
		Cetonia aurata Rose Chafer	*Cetonia aurata* (Linnaeus, 1758) Rose chafer
		Coprobius volvens Pill Chafer, "black"	*Canthon pilularius* (Linnaeus, 1773) Tumblebug
		Gymnetis nitida Chafer	*Cotinis nitida* (Linnaeus, 1758) Green June bug

Order	Family	Gosse's Scientific and Common Names	Current Scientific and Common Names
		Lamellicornes	Lamellicornes Scarab beetles
		Phanaeus carnifex Ball Chafer	*Phanaeus vindex* MacLeay, 1819 Rainbow scarab
		Scarabaeus Lamellicorn beetle	*Scarabaeus* L.; Linnaeus used *Scarabaeus* for all scarab beetles
		Trichius delta	*Trigonopeltastes delta* (Forster, 1771) Delta flower scarab
Dermaptera	Forficulidae	*Forficula* ———? Earwig	Gosse's general term for earwigs
Diptera	Asilidae	*Asilus Polyphemus* "Bee-catcher"	Undetermined species Robber fly
	Bombyliidae	*Bombylius* ———? Bee-fly	Undetermined species Bee fly
	Muscidae	*Musca*	Gosse's general term for *Musca domestica* (Linnaeus, 1758) and other muscoid flies House fly and related species
	Mydidae	*Mydas clavatus*	*Mydas clavatus* (Drury, 1773) Mydas fly
	Ptychopteridae	*Bittacomorpha crassipes* Star Crane-fly	*Bittacomorpha clavipes* (Fabricius, 1781) Phantom crane fly
	Syrphidae	*Milesia ornata*	*Milesia virginiensis* (Drury, 1773) Yellowjacket hover fly
Ephemeroptera	Ephemeridae	*Ephemera*	Referring to *Ephemera* and related genera of Mayflies
Hemiptera	Aphididae	*Aphides* Plant-lice	Aphidae Aphids

Order	Family	Gosse's Scientific and Common Names	Current Scientific and Common Names
	Cicadidae	*Cicadae*	*Tibicen auletus* (Germar, 1834) Northern dusk-singing cicada and *Neocicada heiroglyphica* (Say, 1830) Heiroglyphic cicada
	Notonectidae	*Notonecta* Boat-fly	Notonectidae Backswimmers
	Pentatomidae	*Pentatoma* plant bugs	*Euthyrhunchus floridanus* (Linnaeus, 1767) Florida predatory stink bug
	Reduviidae	*Emesa filum* Hair Spectre	Subfamily Emesinae Thread-legged bugs
	Reduviidae	*Hammatocerus Purcis*? Chequered Bug	*Triatoma sanguisuga* (LeConte, 1856) Kissing bug
Hymenoptera	Apidae	*Apis mellifica*	*Apis mellifera* Linnaeus, 1758 Honey bee
		Xylocopa	*Xylocopa virginica* (Linnaeus, 1771) Carpenter bee
		Xylocopa violacea Violet bee	*Xylocopa violacea* (Linnaeus, 1758) Carpenter bee—Europe
	Ichneumonidae	*Ichneumon*	Gosse's general term for Ichneumon wasps
	Mutillidae	*Mutilla*	*Dasymutilla* and *Pseudomethocha* species Velvet ants
		Mutilla coccinea	*Dasymutilla occidentalis* (Linnaeus, 1758) Eastern velvet ant, Cow killer
	Scoliidae	*Scolia*	*Scolia* or related genus Scoliid wasps
		Scolia quadrimaculata	*Campsomeris quadrimaculata* (Fabricius, 1775) Scoliid wasp

Order	Family	Gosse's Scientific and Common Names	Current Scientific and Common Names
	Sphecidae	*Pelopaeus*	*Sceliphron* Mud daubers
		Pelopaeus	*Trypoxylon clavatum* Say, 1837 Organ-pipe mud dauber
		Pelopaeus flavipes Yellow-footed Dauber	*Sceliphron caementarium* (Drury, 1773) Black-and-yellow mud dauber
	Vespidae	*Eumenes*	*Eumenes* species Potter wasps
		Polistes	*Polistes* (undetermined species) Paper wasps
Lepidoptera	Bombycidae	*Bombycidae* "moths"	Bombycidae Lappet moths, Silkworm moths
	Cossidae	*Cossus*	*Prionoxystus robiniae* (Peck, 1818) Carpenterworm
	Erebidae	*Callimorpha Lecontei*	*Haploa colona* (Hübner, [1803]) Colona moth
		Deiopeia bella Pinkwing, Pink-wing Moth	*Utetheisa bella* (Linnaeus, 1758) Ornate bella moth
	Geometridae	*Geometrae*	Gosse's general term for Geometers, Inchworms, Loopers, Measuringworms
	Hepialidae	*Hepialidae* Ghost Moths	Hepialidae Ghost moths, Swifts
	Hesperiidae	*Eudamus Bathylius*	*Thorybes bathyllus* (J. E. Smith, 1797) Southern cloudywing
		Eudamus Tityrus White-spotted Skipper	*Epargyreus clarus* (Cramer, 1775) Silver-spotted skipper

Order	Family	Gosse's Scientific and Common Names	Current Scientific and Common Names
		Hesperia Catullus	*Pholisora catullus* (Fabricius, 1793)
		Sooty Skipper	Common sootywing
		Hesperia malvae	*Pyrgus centaureae* (Rambur, 1842)
			Grizzled Skipper—Europe
		Hesperia Orcus	*Pyrgus oileus* (Linnaeus, 1767)
			Tropical checkered-skipper
		Hesperia Phylaeus	*Hylephila phyleus,* male (Drury, 1773)
		Banded Skipper	Fiery skipper
		Hesperia Proto	*Muschampia proto* (Ochsenheimer, 1808)
			Sage skipper—Europe
		Hesperia species	*Pyrgus communis* (Grote, 1872)
			Common checkered-skipper
		Hesperiadae Skippers	Hesperiidae Skippers
		Pamphila Otho?	*Wallengrenia otho* (J. E. Smith, 1797)
			Southern broken-dash
		Pamphila ——?	Skipper (Undetermined species)
	Lycaenidae	*Lycaenadae*	Lycaenidae Blues, Coppers, and Hairstreaks
		Polyommati butterflies; no name given	Subfamily Polyommatinae Blues
		Polyommatus argiolus	*Celastrina ladon* (Cramer, 1780) Spring azure; *Celastrina argiolus* (Linnaeus, 1758)—Eurasia
		Polyommatus pseudargiolus	*Celastrina argiolus* (Linnaeus, 1758)
		Pale Azure	Spring azure—Eurasia

Order	Family	Gosse's Scientific and Common Names	Current Scientific and Common Names
		Thecla Hairstreaks	*Satyrium* Hairstreaks
		Thecla Comyntas	*Everes comyntas* (Godart, 1824), synonym *Cupido comyntas* Eastern tailed-blue
		Thecla falacer Hairstreak	*Satyrium calanus* (Hübner, 1809) Banded hairstreak
		Thecla favoninus	*Satyrium favonius* (J. E. Smith, 1797) Southern oak hairstreak
		Thecla hyperici	*Strymon melinus* (Hübner, 1818) Gray hairstreak
		Thecla Mopsus Coral Hairstreak	*Satyrium titus* (Fabricius, 1793) Coral hairstreak
		Thecla Paeas Red-striped Hairstreak	*Calycopis cecrops* (Fabricius, 1793) Red-banded Hairstreak
	Noctuidae	*Amphipyra pyramidea*	*Amphipyra pyramidoides* Guenée, 1852 Copper Underwing Moth
		Catocala Crimson Underwings	*Catocala* Underwing moths
		Catocala Epione Purple Underwing	*Catocala epione* (Drury, 1773) Epione underwing
		Catocala Ilia	*Catocala ilia* (Cramer, 1775) Ilia underwing
	Nymphalidae	*Argynnis columbina* Variegated Fritillary	*Euptoieta claudia* (Cramer, 1775) Variegated fritillary
		Argynnis vanillae Vanilla Fritillary	*Agraulis vanillae* (Linnaeus, 1758) Gulf fritillary

Order	Family	Gosse's Scientific and Common Names	Current Scientific and Common Names
		Cynthia cardui	*Vanessa cardui* (Linnaeus, 1758)
		Painted Lady	Painted lady
		Cynthia Huntera	*Vanessa virginiensis* (Drury, 1773)
		Painted Beauty	American lady
		Danais Archippus	*Danaus plexippus* (Linnaeus, 1758)
		Archippus	Monarch
		Grapta Caureum	*Polygonia interrogationis* (Fabricius, 1798)
		Violet-tip Butterfly	Question mark; *Polygonia c-aureum* (Linnaeus) Asian comma—Asia
		Grapta interrogationis	*Polygonia interrogationis* (Fabricius, 1798)
			Question mark
		Hipparchia ———?	*Cercyonis pegala* (Fabricius, 1775)
		Pale-clouded Ringlet	Common wood-nymph
		Hipparchia Alope	*Cercyonis pegala* (Fabricius, 1775)
		Blue-eyed Ringlet	Common wood-nymph
		Hipparchia Andromacha	*Lethe portlandia* (Fabricius, 1781)
		Pearly-eye, Pearly Eye	Southern pearly-eye
		Hipparchia areloata	*Neomympha areolatus* (J. E. Smith, 1797)
		Red-lined Ringlet	Georgia satyr
		Hipparchia Eurythris	*Megisto cymela* (Cramer, 1777)
		Dusky Argus	Little wood-satyr
		Hipparchia gemma	*Cyllopsis gemma* (Hübner, 1809)
		Silver-spotted Ringlet	Gemmed satyr

Order	Family	Gosse's Scientific and Common Names	Current Scientific and Common Names
		Hipparchia Sosybius Blind Argus	*Hermeuptychia sosybius* (Fabricius, 1793) Carolina satyr
		Hipparchia(e) Meadow-butterflies	Subfamily Satyrinae Satyrs
		Libythea motya Snout Butterfly	*Libytheana carinenta* (Cramer, 1777) American Snout
		Limenitis Arthemis Banded Purple "of the north"	*Limenitis arthemis arthemis* (Drury, 1773) White Admiral
		Limenitis Ursula Red-spotted Purple	*Limenitis arthemis astyanax* (Fabricius, 1775) Red-spotted purple
		Melitaea Tharos Pearl Crescent Fritillary	*Phyciodes tharos* (Drury, 1773) Pearl crescent
		Satyrus Jurtina English Meadow Brown	*Maniola jurtina* (Linnaeus, 1758) Meadow brown—Europe
		Vanessa atalanta Admiral, Red Admiral	*Vanessa atalanta* (Linnaeus, 1758) Red admiral
		Vanessa orithya	*Junonia coenia* Hübner, 1822 Common buckeye
	Papilionidae	*Papilio Ajax* Zebra Swallow-tail, Zebra Swallowtail	*Eurytides marcellus* (Cramer, 1777) Zebra swallowtail
		Papilio Asterius black swallowtail butterfly	*Papilio polyxenes* Fabricius, 1775 Black swallowtail
		Papilio Calchas Arched Swallowtail	*Papilio palamedes* Drury, 1773 Palamedes swallowtail

Order	Family	Gosse's Scientific and Common Names	Current Scientific and Common Names
		Papilio Glaucus	*Papilio glaucus* Linnaeus, 1758
		Black Emperor Swallow-tail	Eastern tiger swallowtail, black form
		Papilio Philenor Boisd.	*Battus philenor* (Linnaeus, 1771)
		Blue Swallowtail	Pipevine swallowtail
		Papilio Thoas	*Papilio cresphontes* Cramer, 1777
		Yellow Emperor Swallowtail	Giant swallowtail
		Papilio Troilus Green-clouded Swallowtail, Green Clouded Swallowtail	*Papilio troilus* Linnaeus, 1758 Spicebush swallowtail
		Papilio Turnus	*Papilio glaucus* Linnaeus, 1758
		Tiger Swallow-tail, Tiger Swallow-tail Butterfly	Eastern tiger swallowtail, yellow form
	Pieridae	*Colias*	Colias Sulphur and Yellow butterflies
		Colias Caesonia Black-based Yellow	*Zerene cesonia* (Stoll, 1790) Dogface
		Colias Delia	*Eurema lisa* (Boisduval and Le Conte, 1830) Little yellow
		Colias Diara Black-banded Yellow	*Eurema daira* (Godart, 1819) Barred yellow
		Colias Eubule, Boisd.	*Phoebis sennae* (Linnaeus, 1758) Cloudless sulphur
		Colias Nicippe Black-bordered Yellow	*Eureme nicippe* (Cramer) Sleepy orange
		Delia	*Eurema lisa* (Boisduval and LeConte, 1830) Little yellow

Order	Family	Gosse's Scientific and Common Names	Current Scientific and Common Names
		Pontia(e)	*Pontia,* a Eurasian genus, probably *Pieris rapae* (Linnaeus, 1758) Cabbage butterfly
		Xanthidia Delia Black-edged Sulphur	*Eurema lisa* (Boisduval and LeConte, 1830) Little yellow
		Xanthidia Tucunda Black-banded Sulphur	*Eurema daira* (Godart, 1819) Barred yellow
	Psychidae	*Thyridopteryx Ephemerae-formis*	*Thyridopteryx ephemerae-formis* (Haworth, 1803) Evergreen bagworm moth
	Saturniidae	*Ceratocampa* Emperor Moths	Subfamily Ceratocampinae; *Ceratocampa,* invalid genus Royal Moths
		Ceratocampa imperatoria Yellow Elephant Moth	*Eacles imperialis* (Drury, 1773) Imperial moth
		Ceratocampa imperialis Great Plane-tree Moth	*Eacles imperialis* (Drury, 1773) Imperial moth
		Saturnia Emperor Moths	Subfamily Saturniinae *Saturnia,* invalid genus Silkmoths
		Saturnia Io Corn Emperor	*Automeris io* (Fabricius, 1775) Io moth
		Saturnia luna Green Emperor, Swallow-tailed Emperor	*Actias luna* (Linnaeus, 1758) Luna moth
	Sesiidae	*Aegeria exitiosa* Peach Hawk-moth	*Synanthedon exitiosa* (Say, 1823) Peachtree borer moth
	Sphingidae	*Macroglossa stellarum* Humming-bird Hawk-moth	Probably *Amphion floridensis* B. P. Clark, 1920 Nessus sphinx moth; Possibly *Proserpinus gaurae* (J. E. Smith, 1797) Proud sphinx moth

Order	Family	Gosse's Scientific and Common Names	Current Scientific and Common Names
		Sesia Pelasgus	*Hemaris thysbe* (Fabricius, 1775)
		Humble-bee Hawkmoth	Hummingbird clearwing moth
		Smerinthus excaecatus	*Paonias excaecatus* (J. E. Smith, 1797)
		Blind Hawk	Blind-eyed sphinx moth
		Sphingidae	Sphingidae hawk moths, sphinx moths
		Sphinx Carolina	*Manduca sexta* (Linnaeus, 1763)
		Tobacco Hawk-moth	Carolina sphinx moth, Tobacco hornworm
		Sphinx nerii	*Erinnyis oenotrus* (Cramer, 1782)
		Oleander Hawk	Oleander sphinx moth
		Sphinx pampinatrix	*Darapsa myron* (Cramer, 1780)
		Hawk-moth	Virginia creeper sphinx moth
		Sphinx satellitia	*Eumorpha pandorus* (Hübner, 1821)
		Green-clouded Hawk	Pandorus sphinx moth
		Sphinx tersa	*Xylophanes tersa* (Linnaeus, 1771)
		Faint-lined Hawk	Tersa sphinx moth
		Sphinx vitis	*Eumorpha vitis* (Linnacus, 1758)
		Painted Hawk	Vine sphinx moth
Mantodea	Mantidae	*Mantis*	Gosse's general term for mantids; specifically describes *Stagmomantis carolina* (Johannson, 1763)
		Walking Leaves	Carolina mantis
Neuroptera	Chrysopidae	*Chrysopa*	*Abachrysa eureka* (Banks, 1931)
		Pearl-fly	Green lacewing

Order	Family	Gosse's Scientific and Common Names	Current Scientific and Common Names
	Myrmeleonidae	*Myrmeleon*	*Myrmeleon* and *Brachynemurus* species; *Dendroleon obsoletus* (Say, 1839)
		Ant-lion flies	Antlions
Odonata	Aeshnidae	*Aeshna*	*Aeshna* Fabricius, 1775
		Dragon-fly	Darners
	Calopterygidae	*Agrion*	*Calopteryx*
			Broad-winged damselflies
		Agrion Virginica	*Calopteryx maculata* (Beauvois, 1805)
		Emerald Virgin Dragon-fly	Ebony jewelwing
		Agrionidae	Calopterygidae
		Smaller Dragon-flies	Broad-winged damselflies
	Libellulidae	*Libellula*	*Libellula* or related genus
			Skimmers
		Libellula ——?	Unidentified species of *Libellula* or related genus
			Skimmers
		Libellula Berenice	*Erythrodiplax* species; *Erythrodiplax berenice* (Drury, 1773)
			Seaside Dragonlet—Europe
Orthoptera	Gryllotalpidae	*Gryllotalpa*	*Neocurtilla hexadactyla* (Perty, 1832)
		Mole-cricket	Northern mole cricket
	Romaleidae	*Romalea microptera*	*Romalea microptera* (Beauvois, 1817)
		Locust	Eastern lubber grasshopper
	Tettigoniidae	*Gryllus*	Gosse was referring to katydids (Tettigoniidae); Linnaeus included all mantids, grasshoppers, crickets, and katydids as *Gryllus*
		Pterophylla concava	*Pterophylla camellifolia* (Fabricius, 1775)
		Katedid	Common true katydid

Order	Family	Gosse's Scientific and Common Names	Current Scientific and Common Names
Phasmatodea	Diapheromeridae	*Bacteria linearis*	*Diapheromera femorata* (Say, 1824)
		Walking Rods	Northern walkingstick
		Phasma	*Megaphasma denticrus* (Stål, 1875)
		Spectres, Walking Rods, Devil's Walking-sticks	Giant walkingstick
Trichoptera	Phryganeidae	*Phryganea, Phyrganeae*	Gosse's general term for case-making larvae of some of the larger caddisflies, including the family Phryganeidae
Zygentoma	Lepismatidae	*Lepisma*	*Lepisma saccharina* Linnaeus, 1758
			Silverfish

Marine Fishes

Family	Gosse's Scientific and Common Names	Current Scientific and Common Names
Carangidae	purple-banded pilot	*Naucrates ductor* (Linnaeus, 1758) Pilotfish
Carcharhinidae	sharks	Sharks, undetermined species
Coryphaenidae	dolphin, coryphene	*Coryphaena hippurus* Linnaeus, 1758 Dolphin, Mahi-mahi
Echeneidae	remora	Probably *Echeneis naucrates* (Linnaeus, 1758) Sharksucker
Exocoetidae	flying-fish	Flying fishes, undetermined species
Haemulidae	hog-fish	*Haemulon plumierii* (Lacepède, 1801) White grunt
Ictaluridae	*Silurus catus* cat-fish	*Ariopsis felis* (Linnaeus, 1766) Hardhead catfish, or *Bagre marinus* (Mitchill, 1815) Gafftopsail catfish
Kyphosidae	spotted rudder-fish	*Kyphosus sectatrix* (Linnaeus, 1758) Bermuda chub, or *Kyphosus incisor* (Cuvier, in Cuvier and Valenciennes, 1831) Yellow chub
Labridae	*Labrus* wrasses	Any of 6 or more possible genera of labrids, undetermined species Wrasses
Lutjanidae	yellow-tail ("misnomer")	*Lutjanus synagris* (Linnaeus, 1758) Lane snapper
	market fish	Probably *Lutjanus analis* (Cuvier, in Cuvier and Valenciennes, 1828) Mutton snapper; Possibly *Lutjanus campechanus* (Poey, 1860) Red snapper
Scombridae	king-fish	*Scomberomorus cavalla* (Cuvier, 1829) King mackerel

Family	Gosse's Scientific and Common Names	Current Scientific and Common Names
Serranidae	groper	Possibly *Mycteroperca microlepis* (Goode and Bean, 1879) Gag grouper or
	"mouth and throat . . . brilliant vermillion"	*Mycteroperca venenosa* (Linnaeus, 1758) Yellowfin grouper; "brilliant vermillion" mouth and throat, problematic
Sparidae	*Sparus*	Probably *Sparus* (Linnaeus, 1758), undetermined species
	sea-breams	Porgies

Reptiles and Amphibians

Family	Gosse's Scientific and Common Names	Current Scientific and Common Names
Bufonidae	*Bufo musicus* Toad	*Anaxyrus terrestris* (Bonnaterre, 1789) Southern toad
Cheloniidae	*Chelonia mydas*	*Chelonia mydas* (Linnaeus, 1758) Green sea turtle
Chelydridae	*Chelydra serpentina* Snapping Turtle, Alligator Tortoise	*Macrochelys temminckii* (Troost in Harlan, 1835) Alligator snapping turtle
Colubridae	*Coluber coccineus*, SAY Scarlet Viper, Blunt-tailed Moccasin Snake	*Cemophora coccinea* (Blumenbach, 1788) Scarlet snake
	Coluber porcatus, Bosc. Copper-belly	Probably *Nerodia erythrogaster* (Forster in Bossu, 1771) Plain-bellied water snake
Elapidae	*Vipera fulvia*, HARLAN Scarlet Viper, Blunt-tailed Moccasin Snake	*Cemophora coccinea* (Blumenbach, 1788) Scarlet snake
Emydidae	*Emys* Mud-turtles, Terrapins, water-tortoise; *Emys* at the time was used for any chicken, map, or pond turtle	Most likely *Chrysemys* Painted turtles; *Pseudemys* Cooters, Red-bellied turtles; *Trachemys* Sliders
Phrynosomatidae	*Agama undulata* Scorpion	*Sceloporus undulatus* (Bosc and Daudin in Sonnini and Latreille, 1801) Eastern fence lizard
	Agama undulata Scorpion; "tail . . . of a blue colour"	*Plestiodon* species (genus for all skinks with bright blue tails)
Polychrotidae	*Anolis bullaris*	*Anolis carolinensis* (Voigt, 1832) Green anole

Family	Gosse's Scientific and Common Names	Current Scientific and Common Names
Ranidae	*Rana clamata?*	*Pseudacris crucifer* (Wied-Neuwied, 1838) Spring peeper or *Anaxyrus quercicus* (Holbrook, 1840) Oak toad
Teiidae	*Tachydromus sexlineatus* Fast-runner	*Aspidoscelis sexlineata* (Linnaeus, 1766) Six-lined racerunner
Trionychidae	*Trionyx ferox* Soft-back, "Tortoise"	Most likely *Apalone spinifera* (Lesueur, 1827) Spiny softshell; possibly *Apalone mutica* (Lesueur, 1827) Smooth softshell
Viperidae	*Crotalus* Rattlesnake	*Crotalus,* genus that includes all Rattlesnakes
	Crotalus durissus Rattlesnake	*Crotalus horridus* Linnaeus, 1758 Timber rattlesnake

Birds

Family	Gosse's Scientific and Common Names	Current Scientific and Common Names
Accipitridae	*Elanus furcatus* Swallow-tailed Kite	*Elanoides forficatus* (Linnaeus, 1758) American swallow-tailed kite
	Falco borealis Red-tailed Hawk	*Buteo jamaicensis* (Gmelin, 1788) Red-tailed hawk
	Ictinia Mississippiensis Mississippi Kite	*Ictinia mississippiensis* (A. Wilson, 1811) Mississippi kite
Alcedinidae	*Alcedo alcyon* Kingfisher, belted kingfisher	*Megaceryle alcyon* (Linnaeus, 1758) Belted kingfisher
Anatidae	*Anas moschata* Muscovy duck	*Cairina moschata* (Linnaeus, 1758) Muscovy duck
	Anas sponsa wood-duck	*Aix sponsa* (Linnaeus, 1758) Wood duck
Apodidae	*Hirundo pelasgia* Chimney Swallow	*Chaetura pelagica* (Linnaeus, 1758) Chimney swift
Ardeidae	*Ardea caerulea* blue heron, Blue Heron	*Ardea herodias* Linnaeus, 1758 Great blue heron
	Ardea candidissima white crane?	*Egretta thula* (Molina, 1782) Snowy egret
	Nycticorax Americanus Night-heron	Probably *Nyctanassa violacea* (Linnaeus, 1758) Yellow-crowned night heron
	qua-bird, night-heron	*Nycticorax nycticorax* (Linnaeus, 1758) Black-crowned night heron
Caprimulgidae	*Caprimulgus Americanus* Night-hawk	*Chordeiles minor* (J. R. Forster, 1771) Common nighthawk
	Caprimulgus Carolinensis Chuck-will's-widow	*Caprimulgus carolinensis* Gmelin, 1789 Chuck-will's-widow
	Caprimulgus Europaeus Night-jar	*Caprimulgus europaeus* Linnaeus, 1758 European nightjar
Cardinalidae	*Fringilla cardinalis* Cardinal Grosbeak	*Cardinalis cardinalis* (Linnaeus, 1758) Northern cardinal

Family	Gosse's Scientific and Common Names	Current Scientific and Common Names
	Fringilla cyanea Indigo bird	*Passerina cyanea* (Linnaeus, 1766) Indigo bunting
Cathartidae	*Cathartes aura* Turkey Buzzard, Turkey Vulture	*Cathartes aura* (Linnaeus, 1758) Turkey vulture
Columbidae	*Columba Carolinensis* Turtle-dove	*Zenaida macroura* (Linnaeus, 1758) Mourning dove
Emberizidae	*Fringilla erythrophthalma* Towhe Bunting	*Pipilo erythrophthalmus* (Linnaeus, 1758) Rufous-sided towhee
	Fringilla melodia Song Sparrow	*Melospiza melodia* (A. Wilson, 1810) Song sparrow
	Fringilla nivalis Snow-bird	*Junco hyemalis* (Linnaeus, 1758) Dark-eyed junco
Fringillidae	*Carduelis tristis* Yellow-bird	*Carduelis tristis* (Linnaeus, 1758) American goldfinch
Hydrobatidae	petrels	*Oceanites oceanicus* (Kuhl, 1820) Wilson's storm petrel
Icteridae	*Quiscalus versicolor* Purple Grakle	*Quiscalus quiscula* (Linnaeus, 1758) Common grackle
	Sturnus predatorius red-winged starling	*Agelaius phoeniceus* (Linnaeus, 1766) Red-winged blackbird
Numididae	Guinea-fowls	*Numida meleagris* (Linnaeus, 1758) Helmeted guineafowl
Odontophoridae	*Ortyx Virginiana* Quail	*Colinus virginianus* (Linnaeus, 1758) Northern bobwhite
Parulidae	*Muscicapa ruticilla* American redstart	*Setophaga ruticilla* (Linnaeus, 1758) American redstart
	Sylvia pusilla Yellow-backed Warbler	*Parula americana* (Linnaeus, 1758) Northern parula
	Sylvia trichas Maryland Yellow-throat	*Geothlypis trichas* (Linnaeus, 1766) Common yellowthroat
	Sylviae	*Sylvia*—Old World genus Unidentified warbler

Family	Gosse's Scientific and Common Names	Current Scientific and Common Names
Pelecanidae	*Pelecanus fuscus* pelican	*Pelecanus occidentalis* Linnaeus, 1766 Brown pelican
Phasianidae	*Meleagris gallopavo* Turkey	*Meleagris gallopavo* Linnaeus, 1758 Wild turkey
Picidae	*Picus auratus* Gold-winged Woodpecker	*Colaptes auratus* (Linnaeus, 1758) Northern flicker
	Picus Carolinus Red-bellied Woodpecker	*Melanerpes carolinus* (Linnaeus, 1758) Red-bellied woodpecker
	Picus erythrocephalus Red-headed Woodpecker	*Melanerpes erythrocephalus* (Linnaeus, 1758) Red-headed woodpecker
	Picus pileatus Pileated Woodpecker	*Dryocopus pileatus* (Linnaeus, 1758) Pileated woodpecker
	Picus principalis Ivory-billed Woodpecker	*Campephilus principalis* (Linnaeus, 1758) Ivory-billed woodpecker
	Picus varius Yellow-bellied Woodpecker	*Sphyrapicus varius* (Linnaeus, 1766) Yellow-bellied sapsucker
Psittacidae	*Psittacus Carolinensis* Parrot	*Conuropsis carolinensis* (Linnaeus, 1758) Carolina parakeet
Scolopacidae	*Scolopax semipalmata* willet	*Tringa semipalmata* (Gmelin, 1789) Willet
Strigidae	*Bubo Virginianus* Great Eagle Owl	*Bubo virginianus* (Gmelin, 1788) Great horned owl
	Strix naevia Mottled Owl	*Megascops asio* (Linnaeus, 1758) Eastern screech owl
	Strix nebulosa Barred Owl	*Strix varia* Barton, 1799 Barred owl
Thraupidae	*Tanagra aestiva* Summer Red-bird	*Piranga rubra* (Linnaeus, 1758) Summer tanager
	Tanagra rubra Scarlet Tanager	*Piranga olivacea* (Gmelin, 1789) Scarlet tanager
Trochilidae	*Trochilus colubris* Ruby-throat Humming-bird	*Archilochus colubris* (Linnaeus, 1758) Ruby-throated hummingbird

Family	Gosse's Scientific and Common Names	Current Scientific and Common Names
Troglodytidae	*Troglodytes Ludovicianus* Carolina Wren	*Thryothorus ludovicianus* (Latham, 1790) Carolina wren
Turdidae	*Sylvia sialis* Blue-bird	*Sialia sialis* (Linnaeus, 1758) Eastern bluebird
	Turdus aurocapillus Gold-crowned Thrush	*Seiurus aurocapilla* (Linnaeus, 1766) Ovenbird
	Turdus melodus Wood Thrush	*Hylocichla mustelina* (J. F. Gmelin, 1789) Wood thrush
	Turdus migratorius Red-breasted Thrush	*Turdus migratorius* Linnaeus, 1766 American robin
	Turdus polyglottus Mocking-bird	*Mimus polyglottos* (Linnaeus, 1758) Northern mockingbird
	Turdus rufus Brown Thrush, French Mocking Bird, Red Thrush	*Toxostoma rufum* (Linnaeus, 1758) Brown thrasher
	Turdus solitaries hermit thrush	*Catharus guttatus* (Pallas, 1811) Hermit thrush
Tyrannidae	*Muscicapa(e)* Fly-catchers	Referring to Tyrannidae *Muscapa,*—Old World genus Tyrant flycatchers
	Musicapa tyrannus king-bird	*Tyrannus tyrannus* (Linnaeus, 1758) Eastern kingbird

Mammals

Family	Gosse's Scientific and Common Names	Current Scientific and Common Names
Bovidae	feral cattle	*Bos taurus* Linnaeus, 1758 Domestic cattle
Canidae	*Canis fulvus* Red Fox	*Vulpes vulpes* (Linnaeus, 1758) Red fox
	Canis Virginianus Grey Fox	*Urocyon cinereoargenteus* (Schreber, 1775) Gray fox
Castoridae	beaver	*Castor canadensis* Kuhl, 1820 Beaver
Cervidae	*Cervus Virginianus* Virginian Deer	*Odocoileus virginianus* (Zimmermann, 1780) White-tailed deer
	Fallow deer	*Dama dama* (Linnaeus, 1758) Fallow deer
Cricetidae	*Arvicola hispidus* Wood Rat	*Sigmodon hispidus* Say and Ord, 1825 Hispid cotton rat
	Mus Floridanus Yellow Rat	*Neotoma floridana* (Ord, 1818) Eastern woodrat
Delphinidae	*Delphinus delphis* dolphin	*Delphinus delphis* Linnaeus, 1758 Short-beaked common dolphin; more likely *Tursiops truncates* (Montagu, 1821) Bottle-nosed dolphin
Equidae	*Asinus* zebras	*Equus asinus* Linnaeus, 1758 Ass
	Equus horses	*Equus caballus* Linnaeus, 1758 Horses
	mules	Offspring of a male ass (*Equus asinus* Linnaeus, 1758) and female horse (*Equus caballus* Linnaeus, 1758)
Felidae	wild cats	Presumably *Lynx rufus* (Schreber, 1777) Bobcat
Leporidae	*Lepus Americanus* Hare, Rabbit	Probably *Sylvilagus aquaticus* (Bachman, 1837) Swamp rabbit

Family	Gosse's Scientific and Common Names	Current Scientific and Common Names
Muridae	English rat	*Rattus norvegicus* (Berkenhout, 1769) Norway rat
Procyonidae	racoon	*Procyon lotor* (Linnaeus, 1758) Raccoon
Sciuridae	*Sciurus capistratus* Fox Squirrel, Fox-squirrel	*Sciurus niger* Linnaeus, 1758 Eastern fox squirrel
	Sciurus Carolinensis Carolina Squirrel	*Sciurus carolinensis* Gmelin, 1788 Eastern gray squirrel
Suidae	black pig, forest swine, wild hog	*Sus scrofa* Linnaeus, 1758 Wild boar
Talpidae	Mole	*Talpa europaea* Linnaeus, 1758 European mole
Ursidae	bear	*Ursus americanus* Pallus, 1780 American black bear
Vespertilionidae	*Lasiurus rufus*	*Lasiurus borealis* (Müller, 1776) Eastern red bat

INDEX

The letter *f* following a page number denotes a figure, and the letter *t* following a page number denotes a table.

Coprobius volvens, 138, 167, 246t
Coral Hairstreak, 126, 251t
corallines, 40
corals, 39; corallines, 40; madrepores, 40
Coral-tree, 78, 239t
Corn, 47, 118, 197, 243t; bears, damage to,
    174–75; bread-corn, 119, 243t; broom-
    corn, 119; corn-field, 114, 174; corn-meal,
    196–97; hominy, 56; Indian bread, 57;
    Indian corn, 56–57, 86, 118, 243t; maize,
    118, 160, 164, 243t; parching over fire,
    114–15; roasting ears, 114–15, 118, 174;
    seed-corn, 86; squirrels cause damage to,
    114. *See also* squirrel
Corn Emperor, 164, 165, 216–17, 224, 255t
Corn Poppy, 242t
Cornaceae, 239t
Cornus, 164, 216, 221, 239t
Cornus florida, 221
Coryphaenidae, 259t
coryphene, 33–34, 259t
Cossidae, 249t
Cossus, 121, 125, 249t
Cotinis nitida, 246t
cotton, 1, 4, 44, 47, 118, 160–61, 214–15, 241t;
    bales, 215, 231; basket, 214; cultivation of,
    53, 120, 160–61; gin, 215; loading, on Ala-
    bama River, 49, 231–32, 232f; picking, 196,
    214–15; seed, 160–61, 214–15; slide, 49, 231;
    smoking wild bees with, 147–48; steamer,
    laden with bales, 231. *See also* cotton-gin;
    gin-house; manure; mules; slaves
Cotton Plant. *See* cotton
cotton-gin, 215, 232. *See also* cotton; gin-house
cow. *See* cattle; manure
Cow killer, 238t
cow-hide whip, 196. *See also* cow-whip; whip
Cowper, William, 129
cow-whip, 176
crabs, 33
cranes, blue and white, 39
Crataegus, 78, 244t
cray-fish, 45
creationism, 12

Cricetidae, 267t
crickets, 257t
Crimson Cypress-vine, 129, 238t
Crimson Underwings, 164, 251t
Cross Vine, 104, 238t
Crotalus, 170–71, 262t
Crotalus durissus, 170, 262t
Crotalus horridus, 262t
Crowfoot-grass, 120, 160–61, 243t
crows, 29
crupper, 181
Cuckoo, England, 66
Cucumber-tree, 222, 241t
Cucumis anguria, 159, 239t
Cucumis melo, 157, 239t
Cucurbita citrullus, 98, 157–58, 178–79, 239t
Cucurbita lagenaria, 157, 239t
Cucurbita ovifera?, 158–59, 239t
Cucurbita pepo, 239t
Cultivated rye, 243t
Cupido comyntas, 251t
Cupressaceae, 239t
Currants, 240t
curs, 180. *See also* dogs
custard-apple, 184n
Cyllopsis gemma, 252t
Cynodon dactylon, 120, 160–61, 243t
Cynthia cardui, 80, 252t
Cynthia Huntera, 79–80, 210, 252t
Cypress, 201, 203, 239t
cypress-knees, 203
cypress swamp, 201
Cypressvine, 129, 238t

Dallas County, Alabama, 3, 4
Dama dama, 267t
Danais Archippus, 79, 151, 152–53, 252t
Danaus plexippus, 252t
Darapsa Myron, 256t
Dark-eyed junco, 264t
Darners, 257t
Darwin, Charles, 6, 12, 14, 15
Dasymutilla, 248t
Dasymutilla occidentalis, 248t

Dauber, 185–90, 249t
Deer: hunting of, 206–7, 208f, 230; semi-
    tame fawn, 207–8. See also *Cervus Vir-
    ginianus*; Fallow deer; Virginian Deer
Deer-beetle, 167, 246t
Deerberry, 239t
Deiopeia bella, 80f, 167, 249t
Delaware, 29
Delaware River, 28–29
Delia, 169n
Delille, 200n
Delphinidae, 267t
Delphinium azureum, 78, 243t
Delphinium carolinianum, 243t
Delphinium staphisagria, 78, 243t
Delphinus delphis, 42, 267t
Delta flower scarab, 247t
Dendroleon obsoletus, 257t
Dermaptera, 247t
Devil's Walking-sticks, 211, 258t. See also
    Phasma
Diapheromera femorata, 258t
Diapheromeridae, 258t
Digitalis, 243t
Dionaea muscipula, 155–56, 239t
Diospyros Virginiana, 221–22, 239t
Diptera, 224, 247t. *See also* flies
Dirt-daubers, 185–90, 249t
diseases, 206. *See also* medication
Dogface, 254t
dogs, 199, 206; curs, 180; and deer hunting,
    206–7; and fox hunting, 230; and Opos-
    sum hunting, 178, 180; and ticks, 173–74;
    and Turkey hunting, 229. *See also* hounds;
    slavery; wild hog
dogwood, 164, 216, 221, 239t
dolphin (fish), 42, 259t
dolphin (mammal), 34, 267t
Domestic cattle, 267t
dorr, 246t
Downy woodpecker, 86
Dragon-fly, 90, 126, 190; as diet of Mississippi
    Kite, 172–73; hawking, 90, 172; mites,
    166. *See also* specific species

Droseraceae, 239t
Drummond, James, 200n
Dryocopus pileatus, 265t
ducks, 134. *See also* specific species
duels, 195
Dung beetle, 246t
Dusky Argus, 63f, 64, 252t
Dynastes Tityrus, 139, 245t
Dynastidae, 245t
Dyticidae, 90, 245t
Dytiscidae, 245t

Eacles imperialis, 255t
Eagle Owl, 202f
Earwig, 111, 247t
Eastern bluebird, 266t
Eastern coralbean, 239t
Eastern fence lizard, 261t
Eastern fox squirrel, 268t
Eastern gray squirrel, 268t
Eastern Hercules beetle, 245t
Eastern kingbird, 266t
Eastern lubber grasshopper, 257t
Eastern red bat, 268t
Eastern screech owl, 265t
Eastern tailed-blue, 251t
Eastern tiger swallowtail: black form, 254t;
    yellow form, 254t
Eastern velvet ant, 248t
Eastern wahoo, 238t
Eastern white cedar, 239t
Eastern woodrat, 267t
Ebenaceae, 239t
Ebony jewelwing, 257t
Echeneidae, 259t
Echeneis naucrates, 259t
Egretta thula, 263t
Elanoides forficatus, 263t
Elanus furcatus, 171–72, 263t
Elapidae, 261t
Elateridae, 246t
Elk-beetle, 167, 246t
Elm, 159, 244t
emancipation, 197. *See also* slavery

Giant cane, 243t

Giant stag beetle, 246t

Giant swallowtail, 254t

Giant walkingstick, 258t

gingham, 179

gin-house, 214

Gleditschia triacanthos, 159, 240t

glow-worm, 200. *See also* luminous

Glycine frutescens, 84, 129, 240t

gnat, 126, 127

Goat-moth, 121–22

gobbler. *See* Turkey

Gold-crowned Thrush, 227, 264t

Golden-rod, 224, 237t

Gold-winged Woodpecker, 82–83, 265t

Gooseberry, 157, 240t

Gosse, Edmund, 5

Gosse, Jennifer, 5

Gosse, Philip Henry, ii: Alabama River, voyage down, 231–33; awed by country, 198; bird collection of, 213; bird-seeking expedition of, 87; Cahawba, horse ride to, 95–97; *The Canadian Naturalist,* 6–7, 9, 12; as clerk for Garland & Sons, 2; daily routine of, 156; difficulty sleeping, 151; *Entomologia Alabamensis,* 5, 12, 14; on field knowledge of boys, 100; on forests, 106–8; insect collecting, 210; journal of, 4, 5, 122–23, 162, 186, 189; and King's Landing, 49–54; lodging, 156, 220; Mobile, arrival in, 1, 2–3, 6, 42; Mobile, departure from, 5, 231, 233; painting insects and flowers, 156; Opossum hunting, 178–82; Selma, visit to, 228; slavery, views on, 195–98; and Southern dialect and idioms, 100–101; as a stranger, 7, 179, 195; walks of, 56–70, 209, 220, 224

Gosse, Thomas, 1

Gossypium herbaceum, 160–61, 214–15. *See also* cotton

Gourd, 157, 239t

Grapes, 244t

Grapsus pictus, 40

Grapta Caureum, 66, 252t

Grapta interrogationis, 210, 252t

grasses: and cotton, 119–20; general scarcity, 119–20. *See also* Crowfoot-grass; *Cynodon dactylon*; oats; rye; wheat

Grasshopper, 150, 257t. *See also* Locusts

Gray hairstreak, 251t

Great blue heron, 263t

Great Eagle Owl, 201, 202f, 213, 265t

Great horned owl, 265t

Great Plane-tree Moth, 142–43, 255t

Green anole, 12, 261t

Green Anolis, 77f

Green ash, 242t

Green Emperor, 163–64, 165f, 255t

Green June bug, 246t

Green lacewing, 256t

Green sea turtle, 261t

green turtles, 36

Greenbriars, 244t

Green-clouded Hawk, 191, 256t

Green-clouded Swallowtail, 79, 127, 210, 254t

green-gage plum, 221, 244t

greenwood shade, 224

Green-wooded Whortleberry, 110, 239t

Grey Fox, 230, 267t

Grizzled Skipper, 250t

groper, 38, 260t

Grossulariaceae, 240t

Ground beetles, 245t

grubbing hoe. *See* agriculture

Gryllotalpa, 203–5, 257t

Gryllotalpidae, 257t

Gryllus, 149, 150, 257t. *See also* Katedid; *Pterophylla concava*

guava, 184n

Guinea-fowl, 69–70, 264t

Gulf fritillary, 251t

Gulf of Mexico, 35, 41–42

Gulf Stream, 32

Gulf-weed, yellow, 32

gum, box for capturing bee swarm, 147–49,

gum (tree), 179

Gymnetis nitida, 162, 246t

Kite, 172–73; in Florida Keys, 39; true, 167. *See also* Grasshopper

Loganiaceae, 241t

Logcock, 88. *See also* Ivory-billed Woodpecker; Pileated Woodpecker

London, 5, 6, 44, 158

long rifle, 115–17. *See also* hunting; rifle

long-horned beetles, 245t

Longicorn beetles, 141

Longicornes, 140. *See also* beetles; specific species

Longleaf pine, 243t

Long-leafed pine, 124, 147, 222–23, 243t

Lonicera, 238t

Lonicera sempervirens, 238t

Loopers, 249t

Lower Canada, 2

Lucanidae, 246t

Lucanidae, 84, 246t

Lucanus, 167, 246t

Lucanus capreolus, 246t

Lucanus cervus, 83, 139, 167, 246t

Lucanus dama, 167, 246t

Lucanus Elaphus, 167, 246t

luminous: animals, 200, 205; fungus, 194n, 200; *Ignis fatuus,* 205; lichen, 200; plants, 200

Luna moth, 255t

Lutjanidae, 259t

Lutjanus analis, 259t

Lutjanus campechanus, 259t

Lutjanus synagris, 259t

Lycaenadae, 125, 250t

Lycaenidae, 250–51t

Lynx rufus, 267t

Macrochelys temminckii, 261t

Macroglossa stellatarum, 111, 255t

madrepores, 40

Magnolia acuminate, 241t

Magnolia cordata, 222, 241t

Magnolia grandiflora, 222, 241t

Magnolia tripetala, 222, 241t

Magnoliaceae, 241t

magnolias, 44, 191, 206, 222, 228, 241t

Maine, 158

maize, 118, 160, 164, 243t

Malus pumila, 244t

Malvaceae, 241t

Manduca sexta, 256t

mango, 184n

Maniola jurtina, 253t

Mantes, 111

Mantidae, 256t

Mantids, 256t, 257t

Mantis, 211, 212f, 256t

Mantodea, 256t

manure: cotton seed, fermented, 215

maple, 159

Marrubium vulgare, 60, 241t

marsh, 144; and fox hunting, 230

Marvel of Peru, 69–70, 191, 242t

Maryland Yellow-throat, 226–27, 264t

Mayflies, 247t

Meadow brown, 253t

Meadow-butterflies, 61, 63, 253t

Measuringworms, 249t

medication: cutaneous affectations and rheumatism, 124

Medusae, 36. *See also* Portuguese man-of-war

Megaceryle alcyon, 263t

Megaphasma denticrus, 258t

Megascops asio, 265t

Megisto cymela, 252t

Melanerpes carolinus, 265t

Melanerpes erythrocephalus, 265t

Meleagris gallopavo, 64, 264t. *See also,* Turkey

Melia azedarach, 43, 134, 241t

Meliaceae, 241t

Melitaea Tharos, 66, 210, 253t

melons, 157–59, 180; melon field, 159; melon-patch, 158, 178, 179. *See also* specific melons

Melospiza melodia, 264t

menagerie, travelling, 195n

Merian, Maria Sibylla, 217
metamorphosis, 152–53. *See* Lepidoptera
Methodist Society, Selma, 5
Mexican pricklypoppy, 242t
Mexico, 217
miasmata, 206
microscope, 205
Miega macrosperma, 118, 243t
Milesia ornata, 143, 247t
Milesia virginiensis, 247t
Milkweed, 237t
Milkweed beetle, 245t
Milkweed Butterfly, 237t
Mimosa, 240t
Mimosa ———, 105, 240t
Mimosa microphylla, 240t
Mimus polyglottos, 266t
Minerva, 152
Mirabilis jalapa, 69–70, 191, 242t
Mississippi Kite, 172–73, 263t
mites, 166
Mobile, 167, 231; Gosse's description and
    impressions of, 43–44; Gosse's trip up
    Alabama River from, 46–49; Prickly-pear
    on shore, 95; steamboat travel and com-
    munication from, 96
Mobile Bay, 44, 231
Mobile Point, 233
Mocha berry, 169, 244t
Mocking-bird, 58, 70, 266t
molasses, 197
Mole, 204, 268t
Mole-cricket, 203–5, 257t
Mollusks, marine, 33, 36, 39–40
Monarch (butterfly), 252t
moon, 179, 181, 224
Moraceae, 241t
morning-glory, 238t
mosquitoes. *See* mosquitoes
moss, 91
moths, 80, 142, 224, 249t; damage to melons
    by, 180; fire, attracted to, 203; pinned fe-
    males depositing eggs, 166; torch light,

attracted to, 180; tribes, 152. *See also* cater-
    pillar, cocoon
Mottled Owl, 213, 265t
Mourning dove, 264t
Mud daubers, 249t
Mud-turtles, 91, 93, 261t
mules, 160, 215–16, 267t
Mullein, 153, 244t
Muridae, 268t
Mus Floridanus, 184, 267t
Musa, 35, 242t
Musaceae, 242t
Musca, 35, 126, 247t
Musca domestica, 247t
Muscae, 39
Muschampia proto, 250t
Musicapa ruticilla, 41, 264t
Musicapa tyrannus, 39, 266t
Muscicapae, 154, 266t
Muscidae, 247t
Muscovy duck, 134, 263t
Mush Creek, 52, 90, 185; en route to Cahawba,
    95; flooding, 95; swampy bank, 142
Musk-melon, 157, 239t
musquitoes, 128; attacking deer, 207; clouds
    of, 207
Mutilla, 191, 248t
Mutilla coccinea, 191, 248t
Mutillidae, 248t
Mutton snapper, 259t
Mycteroperca microlepis, 260t
Mycteroperca venenosa, 260t
Mydas clavatus, 125–26, 247t
Mydas fly, 247t
Mydidae, 247t
Myrmeleon, 193f, 257t
Myrmeleonidae, 257t

Narrowleaf evening-primrose, 242t
naseberry, 184n
Naucrates doctor, 259t
naturalist, 220, 227
negro, 115, 147, 196; and bear in corn-field,

stars, 224

steamboat: on Alabama River 43, 96, 231; on Cahawba River, 96; cotton as cargo of, 46, 231, 232; pilot, 233

steamer. *See* cotton; steamboat

Stephens, P. A., 219

Stinging nettle, 244t

storms, autumn, 222

Strategus antaeus, 245t

strawberry, 53, 244t

streams, 206. *See also* rivers

stridulation. *See* insects, sound of

Strigidae, 265t

Strix naevia, 213, 265t

Strix nebulosa, 68, 265t

Strix varia, 265t

Strymon melinus, 251t

Sturnus predatorius, 39, 264t

Suidae, 268t

Sulphur butterfly, 254t

Summer Red-bird, 50, 265t

Summer tanager, 265t

Sunflower, 237t

supper, 70, 72

Surinam. *See* caterpillar

Sus scrofa, 268t

swallow, 34, 172

Swallow-tailed Emperor, 224, 255t

Swallow-tailed Kite, 171–72, 263t

swallowtails, 60. *See also* specific *Papilio* species

Swallow-wort, 78–79, 151, 237t

swamp, 90–94, 92f, 142, 159, 172, 176, 178, 203, 206, 207, 222, 228; Carolina Squirrel, 114; cypress, 201; deep, 134, 144, 199; flora, 199–200; night hunting in, 199, 200–201; three- or four-acre site, 90–91; pine , 172, 224; turtles, 91–94

Swamp Papaw, 60, 237t

Swamp rabbit, 267t

Swan River, 200n

Sweet Gum, 143, 159–60, 224, 240t

sweet pea, 155, 240t

Sweet-brier, 129, 238t. *See also* brier

sweetgum, 240t

sweet-sop, 184n

Swifts, 249t

sycamore, 91, 142–44, 175, 181, 224; American, 243t; shade, 134. *See also* Buttonwood; *Platanus occidentalis;* swamp

Sylvia, 264t

Sylvia minuta, 226–27

Sylvia pusilla, 226, 264t

Sylvia sialis, 154, 266t

Sylvia trichas, 226–27, 264t

Sylviae, 35, 264t

Sylvilagus aquaticus, 267t

Synanthedon exitiosa, 255t

Syringa, 242t

Syrphidae, 247t

Tachydromus sexlineatus, 58, 262t

Tait, Charles, 2

tallow-candle, 31

Talpa europaea, 268t

Talpidae, 268t

Tanagra aestiva, 50, 265t

Tanagra rubra, 51, 265t

tar, 223–24

Task, The, book vi, 112n, 129

Taxodium disticha, 201, 203, 239t

Taxodium distichum, 239t

tea, 57, 72

Teiidae, 262t

Tellina, 39–40

Terrapins, 91, 93, 261t. *See also* turtles

Tersa sphinx moth, 256t

Tetragnatha, 189. *See also* spider

Tetraopes texanus, 245t

Tetraopes tornator, 84, 245t

Tettigoniidae, 257t

Thecla, 124–25, 251t

Thecla Comyntas, 211, 251t

Thecla favoninus, 169n, 251t

Thecla hyperici, 169n, 251t

Thecla Mopsus, 126, 251t

Thecla Poeas, 61f, 142, 251t

thickets, 221

Willow-herb, 224, 242t
willow-oak, 124, 240t
Wilson, Alexander, 28–29, 88, 98–99, 143; Carolina Parrot, 228; Mottled Owl, 213n; Red Owl, 213n
Wilson's storm petrel, 264t
Winged elm, 244t
Wisteria frutescens, 240t
woffles, 57
Wood Rat, 184, 267t
Wood Thrush, 227, 266t
wood-duck, 48–49, 263t
wood-louse. See *Oniscus*
Woodpeckers, 86, 135–36, 205. *See also* specific *Picus* species
woods, 178, 206, 229; backwoods, 185; and bears, 176; and hogs, 175; lofty, 222; ticks, abundance in, 173. *See also* forest
wood-yards. *See* Alabama River
Worcester, England, 1
wounds: cypress resin for, 203; Sassafras root for, 124
wrasses, 39, 259t

Xanthidia Delia, 169, 255t
Xanthidia Tucunda, 169, 255t
Xanthium strumarium, 237t
Xylocopa, 100–101, 123, 248t
Xylocopa virginica, 248t
Xylocopa violacea, 123, 248t
Xylophanes tersa, 256t

Yankees, 195
yard, 203; dry and sandy, 136; hogs, 175; ornamentals and other plantings, 136–

37; trees, 134–36; yard-fire, 203. *See also* wood-yards
Yellow butterfly, 254t
Yellow chub, 259t
Yellow Elephant Moth, 224–25, 255t
Yellow Emperor Swallowtail, 141, 254t
Yellow indian grass, 243t
Yellow pricklypoppy, 242t
Yellow Rat, 184, 267t
Yellow-backed Warbler, 226, 264t
Yellow-bellied sapsucker, 265t
Yellow-bellied woodpecker, 136, 265t
Yellow-bird, 226, 264t
Yellow-crowned night heron, 263t
Yellowfin grouper, 260t
Yellow-footed Dauber, 186–88, 249t
yellow-hammer, 83. *See also* Gold-winged Woodpecker
Yellowjacket hover fly, 247t
yellow-tail, 38, 259t
"yelper." *See* Turkey
Yucca aloifolia, 43, 161, 237t
Yucca filamentosa, 161–62, 237t

Zachariah (nephew of Major Kendrick), 179, 181
Zea mays, 57, 86, 118, 243t
Zebra Swallow-tail, 60, 61f, 253t
zebras, 215–16, 267t
Zenaida macroura, 264t
Zerene cesonia, 254t
Zinnia, 169, 237t
Zinnia multiflora, 155, 237t
Zinnia peruviana, 237t
Zygentoma, 258t